Introducing Microsoft® LINQ

D0318439

Paolo Pialorsi
Marco Russo

PUBLISHED BY
Microsoft Press
A Division of Microsoft Corporation
One Microsoft Way
Redmond, Washington 98052-6399

Library of Congress Control Number: 2007924645

Printed and bound in the United States of America.

1 2 3 4 5 6 7 8 9   QWT   2 1 0 9 8 7

Distributed in Canada by H.B. Fenn and Company Ltd.

A CIP catalogue record for this book is available from the British Library.

Microsoft Press books are available through booksellers and distributors worldwide. For further information about international editions, contact your local Microsoft Corporation office or contact Microsoft Press International directly at fax (425) 936-7329. Visit our Web site at www.microsoft.com/mspress. Send comments to mspinput@microsoft.com.

Acquisitions Editor: Ben Ryan
Developmental Editor: Devon Musgrave
Project Editor: Valerie Woolley
Editorial and Production: John Pierce and Interactive Composition Corporation

Body Part No. X13-68390

Table of Contents

What do you think of this book?
We want to hear from you!

Microsoft is interested in hearing your feedback about this publication so we can continually improve our books and learning resources for you. To participate in a brief online survey, please visit: *www.microsoft.com/learning/booksurvey/*

Appendix: ADO.NET Entity Framework

What do you think of this book?
We want to hear from you!

Microsoft is interested in hearing your feedback about this publication so we can continually improve our books and learning resources for you. To participate in a brief online survey, please visit: *www.microsoft.com/learning/booksurvey/*

Dedication

To Elena and Riccardo, who waited for me too many times.

Marco

To Paola, who makes me live.

Paolo

Acknowledgments

A book is the result of the work of many people. Unfortunately, only the authors have their names on the cover and this section is only a partial compensation for the help of other individuals.

First, we want to thank Luca Bolognese for his efforts in giving us resources and contacts that helped us to write a book on beta software while it was in the middle of a release cycle. We also want to thank all the people from Microsoft who answered our questions along the way—in particular, Mads Torgersen, Amanda Silver, Erick Thompson, and Luke Hoban. Moreover, Charlie Calvert deserves special mention for his precious help at a critical moment for us.

If you understand what we wrote, we do not deserve all the credit. We had the good fortune to have some great people at Microsoft Press edit our drafts: John Pierce and Roger LeBlanc. John has followed this project since we first had the idea for it; he helped us to stay on track, answered all our questions, remained tolerant of our delays, and improved a lot of our drafts. Roger has been so accurate and patient in his editing work that we really do not have words to explain the exceptional value of his work.

Many people had the patience to read our drafts and suggest improvements and corrections. Big thanks to Teo Lachev, Alberto Ferrari, Roberto Brunetti, and Sergio Murru for their reviews.

Finally, we would like to thank Francesco Balena and Giovanni Librando, who supported us many months ago when we decided to try writing an English book.

Introduction

This is an introductory book about Language Integrated Query (LINQ). The goal is to give you a comprehensive overview of this new and powerful technology by using clear and real examples that help you to discover the capabilities of LINQ.

To start playing with LINQ, you need the new version of Microsoft Visual Studio code named "Orcas." You will find links to the latest bits on the MSDN Web site (*http://msdn.microsoft.com*).

The information covered in this book is based on beta versions of LINQ. Some features might be changed, removed, or added between now and the final release of the product. Such actions could invalidate some of the examples shown in this book. Nevertheless, we tried to focus on concepts and content not tied to specific syntax rules or build versions to make this book useful during the full product development life cycle. We are providing a Web site (*http://www.introducinglinq.com/*) where we will maintain a change list, a revision history, any corrections, and a blog about what is going on with the LINQ Project and this book.

About This Book

This book is divided into six chapters and one complementary appendix. Chapter 1, "LINQ Introduction," is a brief overview of the product features and highlights, written to give you a preview of the technology from a 10,000-foot perspective. If you are not a developer or if you are not yet deeply interested in LINQ details, read this chapter to learn what LINQ is and what you can do with it, temporarily ignoring detailed "how to" instructions and best practices. If you want to go deeper into LINQ architecture, syntax, and implementations, read Chapter 4, "LINQ Syntax Fundamentals." Chapter 5, "LINQ to ADO.NET," is the chapter you should read if you are interested in querying relational data. And read Chapter 6, "LINQ to XML," if you need to deal with angle brackets.

All of these chapters are mainly based on the C# 3.0 language, but whenever we considered it useful, we also included Microsoft Visual Basic 9.0 examples. To help you understand new features and syntax innovations of the next version of the Microsoft .NET Framework, we also covered the next versions of the C# and Visual Basic languages. If you are partial to C#, please refer to Chapter 2, "C# Language Features." If you are a Visual Basic developer, Chapter 3, "Visual Basic 9.0 Language Features," is for you, but we suggest that you also read Chapter 2. Many of the code samples in this book leverage new C# 3.0 features, and a comprehensive knowledge of that syntax is necessary to better understand LINQ. Likewise, a C# developer can take advantage of Chapter 3 to figure out when to use which language.

The appendix focuses on ADO.NET Entity Framework and provides details of the architecture and main features of the next version of ADO.NET. It gives you key information about the new entity modeling framework, which is also available and useful in LINQ through LINQ to Entities.

All sample code shown in this book is available for downloading from the book Web site (*http://www.introducinglinq.com/*). Every numbered listing has a corresponding excerpt in code samples; inline code is shown in text only as a reference and might not be present in source code files. Many examples involving relational databases are based on the well-known Northwind sample database to provide a common environment for everyone.

System Requirements

The following system requirements are needed to work with LINQ

- Supported Operating Systems: Windows Server 2003, Windows Vista, Windows XP.
- Microsoft Visual Studio code name "Orcas" March 2007 CTP or later

Support for This Book

Every effort has been made to ensure the accuracy of this book. As corrections or changes are collected, they will be added to a Microsoft Knowledge Base article. Microsoft Press provides support for books and companion content at the following Web site:

http://www.microsoft.com/learning/support/books/

If you have comments, questions, or ideas regarding the book, or questions that are not answered by visiting the site just mentioned, please send them to Microsoft Press via e-mail to

mspinput@microsoft.com

Or via postal mail to

Microsoft Press

Attn: Introducing Microsoft LINQ Editor

One Microsoft Way

Redmond, WA 98052-6399

Please note that Microsoft software product support is not offered through the above addresses.

Chapter 1
LINQ Introduction

By surfing the Web, you can find several descriptions of Language Integrated Query (LINQ), such as these:

- LINQ is a uniform programming model for any kind of data. LINQ enables you to query and manipulate data with a consistent model that is independent from data sources.

- LINQ is just another tool for embedding SQL queries into code.

- LINQ is yet another data abstraction layer.

All of these descriptions are somewhat correct, but they each focus on just a single aspect. LINQ can do a lot more than just embed SQL queries, it is much easier to use than a "uniform programming model," and it is far from being just another set of rules for modeling data.

LINQ is a methodology that simplifies and unifies the implementation of any kind of data access. LINQ does not force you to use a specific architecture; it facilitates the implementation of several existing architectures for accessing data. As with every tool, it can be used in both good and in bad ways. To get the most out of LINQ, you will have to master it.

Today, data managed by a program can belong to different data domains: an array, an object graph, an XML document, a database, a text file, a registry key, an e-mail message, Simple Object Access Protocol (SOAP) message content, a Microsoft Office Excel file.... The list is long.

Each data domain has its own specific access model. When you have to query a database, you typically use SQL. You navigate XML data with Document Object Model (DOM) or XQuery. You iterate an array and build algorithms to navigate an object graph. You use specific application programming interfaces (APIs) to access other data domains, such as an Office Excel file, an e-mail message, or the Microsoft Windows registry. In the end, you have different programming models to access different data sources.

The unification of data access techniques into a single comprehensive model has been tried in many ways. For example, there are Open Database Connectivity (ODBC) providers that allow

1

you to query an Excel file as you would a Windows Management Instrumentation (WMI) repository. However, with this approach you use an SQL-like language to access data represented through a relational model. Sometimes data is naturally represented more effectively in a hierarchical or graphical model instead of a relational one. Moreover, if the data model is not tied to the language, you probably have to manage different type systems. All these differences create an "impedance mismatch" between data and code. LINQ tries to solve these issues, offering a uniform way to access and manage data without forcing the adoption of a "one size fits all" model. LINQ leverages commonalities between the *operations* in these data models instead of flattening the different *structures* between them.

In this chapter, we will provide a comprehensive introduction to LINQ, and in the rest of the book, you can deepen your knowledge of each aspect of this new and powerful technology.

What Is LINQ?

LINQ is a programming model that introduces queries as a first-class concept into any Microsoft .NET language. However, complete support for LINQ requires some extensions in the language used. These extensions boost productivity, thereby providing a shorter, meaningful, and expressive syntax to manipulate data.

Following is a simple LINQ query for a typical software solution that returns the names of customers in Italy:

```
var query =
    from   c in Customers
    where  c.Country == "Italy"
    select c.CompanyName;
```

Do not worry about syntax and keywords (such as *var*) for now. The result of this query is a list of strings. You can enumerate these values with a *foreach* loop in C#:

```
foreach ( string name in query ) {
    Console.WriteLine( name );
}
```

Both the *query* definition and the *foreach* loop just shown are regular C# 3.0 statements. At this point, you might wonder what we are querying. What is *Customers*? Is this query a new form of embedded SQL? Not at all. The same query (and the following *foreach* code) can be applied to an SQL database, to a *DataSet*, to an array of objects in memory, or to many other kinds of data. *Customers* could be a collection of objects:

```
Customer[] Customers;
```

Customers could be a *DataTable* in a *DataSet*:

```
DataSet ds = GetDataSet();
DataTable Customers = ds.Tables["Customers"];
```

Customers could be an entity class that describes a physical table in a relational database:

```
DataContext db = new DataContext( ConnectionString );
Table<Customer> Customers = db.GetTable<Customer>();
```

Finally, *Customers* could be an entity class that describes a conceptual model and is mapped to a relational database:

```
NorthwindModel dataModel = new NorthwindModel();
ObjectQuery<Customer> Customers = dataModel.Customers;
```

As you will see, the SQL-like syntax used in LINQ is called a *query expression*. Languages that implement embedded SQL define only a simplified syntax to put SQL statements into a different language, but these statements are not integrated into the language's native syntax and type system. For example, you cannot call a function written using the host language in the middle of an SQL statement, although this is possible in LINQ. Moreover, LINQ is not limited to querying databases, as embedded SQL is.

How LINQ Works

Assuming that you understood the concept of having syntax to integrate queries into a language, you may want to see how this works. When you write the following code:

```
Customer[] Customers = GetCustomers();
var query =
    from   c in Customers
    where  c.Country == "Italy"
    select c;
```

the compiler generates this code:

```
Customer[] Customers = GetCustomers();
IEnumerable<Customer> query =
      Customers
        .Where( c => c.Country == "Italy" );
```

From now on, we will skip the *Customers* declaration for the sake of brevity. When the query becomes longer, as you see here:

```
var query =
    from   c in Customers
    where  c.Country == "Italy"
    orderby c.Name
    select  new { c.Name, c.City };
```

the generated code is longer too:

```
var query =
      Customers
        .Where( c => c.Country == "Italy" );
        .OrderBy( c => c.Name )
        .Select( c => new { c.Name, c.City } );
```

As you can see, the code apparently calls instance members on the object returned from the previous call. You will see that this apparent behavior is regulated by the *extension methods* feature of the host language (C# in this case). The implementation of the *Where*, *OrderBy*, and *Select* methods—called by the sample query—depends on the type of *Customers* and on namespaces specified in previous *using* statements. Extension methods are a fundamental syntax feature that is used by LINQ to operate with different data domains using the same syntax.

> **More Info**   An extension method appears to extend a class (the class of *Customers* in our examples), but in reality an external method receives the instance of the class that seems to be extended as the first argument. The *var* keyword used to declare *query* infers the variable type declaration from the initial assignment, which in this case will return an *IEnumerable<T>* type. Further descriptions of these and other language extensions are contained in Chapter 2, "C# Language Features," and Chapter 3, "Visual Basic 9.0 Language Features."

Another important concept is the timing of operations over data. In general, a LINQ query is not really executed until there is access to the query result, because it describes a set of operations that will be performed when necessary. The access to a query result does the real work. This can be illustrated in the case of a *foreach* loop:

```
var query = from c in Customers ...
foreach ( string name in query ) ...
```

There are also methods that iterate a LINQ query result, producing a persistent copy of data in memory. For example, the *ToList* method produces a typed *List<T>* collection:

```
var query = from c in Customers ...
List<Customer> customers = query.ToList();
```

When the LINQ query operates on data that is on a relational database (such as Microsoft SQL Server), the LINQ query generates an equivalent SQL statement instead of operating with in-memory copies of data tables. The query execution on the database is delayed until the first access to the query result. Therefore, if in the last two examples *Customers* was a *Table<Customer>* type (a physical table in a relational database) or an *ObjectQuery<Customer>* type (a conceptual entity mapped to a relational database), the equivalent SQL query would not be sent to the database until the *foreach* loop was executed or the *ToList* method was called. The LINQ query can be manipulated and composed in different ways until that time.

Relational Model vs. Hierarchical/Graph Model

At first sight, LINQ might appear to be just another SQL dialect. This similarity has its roots in the way a LINQ query can describe a relationship between entities such as an SQL *join*:

```
var query =
    from    c in Customers
    join    o in Orders
            on c.CustomerID equals o.CustomerID
    select new { c.CustomerID, c.CompanyName, o.OrderID };
```

This is similar to the regular way of querying data in a relational model. However, LINQ is not limited to a single data domain like the relational model is. In a hierarchical model, suppose that each customer has its own set of orders, and each order has its own list of products. In LINQ, we can get the list of products ordered by each customer in this way:

```
var query =
    from   c in Customers
    from   o in c.Orders
    select new { c.Name, o.Quantity, o.Product.ProductName };
```

The previous query contains no joins. The relationship between *Customers* and *Orders* is expressed by the second *from* clause, which uses *c.Orders* to say "get all *Orders* of the *c Customer*." The relationship between *Orders* and *Products* is expressed by the *Product* member of the *Order* instance. The result projects the product name for each order row using *o.Product.ProductName*.

Hierarchical relationships are expressed in type definitions through references to other objects. To support the previous query, we would have classes similar to those in Listing 1-1.

Listing 1-1   Type declarations with simple relationships

```
public class Customer {
    public string Name;
    public string City;
    public Order[] Orders;
}
public struct Order {
    public int Quantity;
    public Product Product;
}
public class Product {
    public int IdProduct;
    public decimal Price;
    public string ProductName;
}
```

However, chances are that we want to use the same *Product* instance for many different *Orders* of the same product. We probably also want to filter *Orders* or *Products* without accessing them through *Customer*. A common scenario is the one shown in Listing 1-2.

Listing 1-2   Type declarations with two-way relationships

```
public class Customer {
    public string Name;
    public string City;
    public Order[] Orders;
}
public struct Order {
    public int Quantity;
    public Product Product;
    public Customer Customer;
```

```
    }
    public class Product {
        public int IdProduct;
        public decimal Price;
        public string ProductName;
        public Order[] Orders;
    }
```

By having an array of all products declared as follows:

```
Product[] products;
```

we can query the graph of objects, asking for the list of orders for the single product with an ID equal to 3:

```
var query =
    from   p in products
    where  p.IdProduct == 3
    from   o in p.Orders
    select o;
```

With the same query language, we are querying different data models. When you do not have a relationship defined between the entities used in the query, you can always rely on sub-queries and joins that are available in LINQ syntax just as in an SQL language. However, when your data model already defines entity relationships, you can leverage them, avoiding replication (with possible mistakes) of the same information in many places.

If you have entity relationships in your data model, you can still use explicit relationships in a LINQ query—for example, when you want to force some condition, or when you simply want to relate entities that do not have native relationships. For example, imagine that you want to find customers and suppliers who live in the same city. Your data model might not provide an explicit relationship between these attributes, but you can always write the following:

```
var query =
    from   c in Customers
    join   s in Suppliers
           on c.City equals s.City
    select new { c.City, c.Name, SupplierName = s.Name };
```

And something like the following will be returned:

```
City=Torino      Name=Marco     SupplierName=Trucker
City=Dallas      Name=James     SupplierName=FastDelivery
City=Dallas      Name=James     SupplierName=Horizon
City=Seattle     Name=Frank     SupplierName=WayFaster
```

If you have experience using SQL queries, you probably assume that a query result is always a "rectangular" table, one that repeats the data of some columns many times in a join like the previous one. However, often a query contains several entities with one or more one-to-many relationships. With LINQ, you can write queries that return a hierarchy or graph of objects like the following one:

```
var query =
    from   c in Customers
    join   s in Suppliers
           on c.City equals s.City
           into customerSuppliers
    select new { c.City, c.Name, customerSuppliers };
```

The last query returns a row for each customer, each containing a list of suppliers available in the same city as the customer. This result can be queried again, just as any other object graph with LINQ. Here is how the *hierarchized* results might appear:

```
City=Torino     Name=Marco        customerSuppliers=...
   customerSuppliers: Name=Trucker        City=Torino
City=Dallas     Name=James        customerSuppliers=...
   customerSuppliers: Name=FastDelivery   City=Dallas
   customerSuppliers: Name=Horizon        City=Dallas
City=Seattle    Name=Frank        customerSuppliers=...
   customerSuppliers: Name=WayFaster      City=Seattle
```

If you want to get a list of customers and provide each customer with the list of products he ordered at least one time and the list of suppliers in the same city, you can write a query like this:

```
var query =
    from   c in Customers
    select new {
        c.City,
        c.Name,
        Products = (from   o in c.Orders
                    select new { o.Product.IdProduct,
                                 o.Product.Price }).Distinct(),
        CustomerSuppliers = from   s in Suppliers
                            where  s.City == c.City
                            select s };
```

You can take a look at the result for a couple of customers to understand how data is returned from the previous single LINQ query:

```
City=Torino     Name=Marco        Products=...     CustomerSuppliers=...
   Products: IdProduct=1   Price=10
   Products: IdProduct=3   Price=30
   CustomerSuppliers: Name=Trucker        City=Torino
City=Dallas     Name=James        Products=...     CustomerSuppliers=...
   Products: IdProduct=3   Price=30
   CustomerSuppliers: Name=FastDelivery   City=Dallas
   CustomerSuppliers: Name=Horizon        City=Dallas
```

This type of result would be hard to obtain with one or more SQL queries, because it would require an analysis of query results to build the desired objects graph. LINQ offers an easy way to move your data from one model to another and different ways to get the same results.

LINQ requires you to describe your data in terms of entities that are also types in the language. When you build a LINQ query, it is always a set of operations on instances of some classes. These objects might be the real container of data, or they might be a simple description (in terms of metadata) of the external entity you are going to manipulate. A query can be sent to a database through an SQL command only if it is applied to a set of types that map tables and relationships contained in the database. After you have defined entity classes, you can use both approaches we described (joins and entity relationship navigation). The conversion of all these operations in SQL commands is the responsibility of the LINQ engine.

> **Note**   You can create entity classes by using code-generation tools such as SQLMetal or the LINQ to SQL Designer in Microsoft Visual Studio.

In Listing 1-3, you can see an example of a *Product* class that maps a relational table named Products, with five columns that correspond to public data members.

Listing 1-3   Class declaration mapped on a database table

```
[Table("Products")]
public class Product {
    [Column(IsPrimaryKey=true)] public int IdProduct;
    [Column(Name="UnitPrice")] public decimal Price;
    [Column()] public string ProductName;
    [Column()] public bool Taxable;
    [Column()] public decimal Tax;
}
```

When you work on entities that describe external data (such as database tables), you can create instances of these kinds of classes and manipulate in-memory objects just as if data from all tables were loaded in memory. These changes are submitted to the database through SQL commands when you call the *SubmitChanges* method, as you can see in Listing 1-4.

Listing 1-4   Database update calling the *SubmitChanges* method

```
var taxableProducts =
    from   p in db.Products
    where  p.Taxable == true
    select p;
foreach( Product product in taxableProducts ) {
    RecalculateTaxes( product );
}
db.SubmitChanges();
```

The *Product* class in the preceding example represents a row in the Products table of an external database. When *SubmitChanges* is called, all changed objects generate an SQL command to update the corresponding rows in the table.

More Info   Class entities that match tables and relationships in the database are further described in Chapter 5, "LINQ to ADO.NET."

XML Manipulation

LINQ has a different set of classes and extensions to support the manipulation of XML data. We will create some examples using the following scenario. Imagine that your customers are able to send orders using XML files like the ORDERS.XML file shown in Listing 1-5.

Listing 1-5   A fragment of an XML file of orders

```xml
<?xml version="1.0" encoding="utf-8" ?>
<orders xmlns="http://schemas.devleap.com/Orders">
    <order idCustomer="ALFKI" idProduct="1" quantity="10" price="20.59"/>
    <order idCustomer="ANATR" idProduct="5" quantity="20" price="12.99"/>
    <order idCustomer="KOENE" idProduct="7" quantity="15" price="35.50"/>
</orders>
```

Using standard Microsoft .NET 2.0 *System.Xml* classes, you can load the file using a DOM approach or you can parse its contents using an *XmlReader* implementation. Regardless of the solution you choose, you must always consider nodes, node types, XML namespaces, and whatever else is related to the XML world. Many developers do not like working with XML because it requires the knowledge of another domain of data structures and uses syntax of its own.

If you need to extract all the products ordered with their quantities, you can parse the orders file using an *XmlReader* to accomplish this, as shown in Listing 1-6.

Listing 1-6   Reading the XML file of orders using an *XmlReader*

```csharp
String nsUri = "http://schemas.devleap.com/Orders";
XmlReader xmlOrders = XmlReader.Create( "Orders.xml" );

List<Order> orders = new List<Order>();
Order order = null;
while (xmlOrders.Read()) {
    switch (xmlOrders.NodeType) {
        case XmlNodeType.Element:
            if ((xmlOrders.Name == "order") &&
            (xmlOrders.NamespaceURI == nsUri)) {
                order = new Order();
                order.CustomerID = xmlOrders.GetAttribute( "idCustomer" );
                order.Product = new Product();
                order.Product.IdProduct =
                    Int32.Parse( xmlOrders.GetAttribute( "idProduct" ) );
                order.Product.Price =
                    Decimal.Parse( xmlOrders.GetAttribute( "price" ) );
```

```
                      order.Quantity =
                          Int32.Parse( xmlOrders.GetAttribute( "quantity" ) );
                      orders.Add( order );
                  }
                  break;
          }
      }
}
```

You could also use an XQuery like the following one to select nodes:

```
for $order in document("Orders.xml")/orders/order
return $order
```

However, XQuery also requires learning another language and syntax. Moreover, the result of
the previous XQuery sample should be converted into a set of *Order* instances to be used
within our code. Finally, for many developers it is not very intuitive. As we have already said,
LINQ provides a query engine suitable for any kind of source, even an XML document. By
using LINQ queries, you can achieve the same result with less effort and with unified programming language syntax. Listing 1-7 shows a LINQ to XML query made over the orders file.

Listing 1-7   Reading the XML file using LINQ to XML

```
XDocument xmlOrders = XDocument.Load( "Orders.xml" );

XNamespace ns = "http://schemas.devleap.com/Orders";
var orders = from o in xmlOrders.Root.Elements( ns + "order" )
             select new Order {
                       CustomerID = (String)o.Attribute( "idCustomer" ),
                       Product = new Product {
                           IdProduct = (Int32)o.Attribute("idProduct"),
                           Price = (Decimal)o.Attribute("price") },
                       Quantity = (Int32)o.Attribute("quantity")
                 };
```

Using the new Microsoft Visual Basic 9.0 syntax, you can reference XML nodes in your code
by using an XPath-like syntax, as shown in Listing 1-8.

Listing 1-8   Reading the XML file using LINQ to XML and Visual Basic 9.0 syntax

```
Imports <xmlns:o="http://schemas.devleap.com/Orders">
' ...

Dim xmlOrders As XDocument = XDocument.Load("Orders.xml")
Dim orders = _
    From o In xmlOrders.<o:orders>.<o:order> _
    Select New Order With {
        .CustomerID = o.@idCustomer, _
        .Product = New Product With {
            .IdProduct = o.@idProduct,
            .Price = o.@price}, _
        .Quantity = o.@quantity}
```

The result of these LINQ to XML queries could be used to transparently load a list of *Order* entities into a customer *Orders* property, using LINQ to SQL to submit the changes into the physical database layer:

```
customer.Orders.AddRange(
    From o In xmlOrders.<o:orders>.<o:order> _
    Where o.@idCustomer = customer.CustomerID _
    Select New Order With {
        .CustomerID = o.@idCustomer, _
        .Product = New Product With {
            .IdProduct = o.@idProduct,
            .Price = o.@price}, _
        .Quantity = o.@quantity})
```

If you need to generate an ORDERS.XML file starting from your customer's orders, you can at least leverage Visual Basic 9.0 XML literals to define the output's XML structure. This is shown in Listing 1-9.

Listing 1-9   Creating the XML of orders using Visual Basic 9.0 XML literals

```
Dim xmlOrders = <o:orders>
    <%= From o In orders _
        Select <o:order idCustomer=<%= o.CustomerID %>
                        idProduct=<%= o.Product.IdProduct %>
                        quantity=<%= o.Quantity %>
                        price=<%= o.Product.Price %>/> %>
    </o:orders>
```

You can appreciate the power of this solution, which keeps the XML syntax without losing the stability of typed code and transforms a set of entities selected via LINQ to SQL into an XML *InfoSet*.

 More Info   You will find more information about LINQ to XML syntax and its potential in Chapter 6, "LINQ to XML."

Language Integration

Language integration is a fundamental aspect of LINQ. The most visible part is the query expression feature, which is present in C# 3.0 and Visual Basic 9.0. It allows you to write code such as the following:

```
var query =
    from    c in Customers
    where   c.Country == "Italy"
    orderby c.Name
    select  new { c.Name, c.City };
```

instead of writing this code:

```
var query =
        Customers
        .Where( c => c.Country == "Italy" );
        .OrderBy( c => c.Name )
        .Select( c => new { c.Name, c.City } );
```

Many people call this simplification *syntax sugaring* because it is just a simpler way to write code that defines a query over data. However, there is more to it than that. Many language constructs and syntaxes are necessary to support what seems to be just a few lines of code that query data. Under the cover of this simple query expression are local type inference, extension methods, lambda expressions, object initialization expressions, and anonymous types. All of these features are useful by themselves, but if you look at the overall picture you should see that there is a big step in two directions: one moving to a more declarative style of coding, and one lowering the impedance mismatch between data and code.

Declarative Programming

What are the differences between an SQL query and an equivalent C# 2.0 or Visual Basic 8.0 program that filters data contained in native storage (such as a table for SQL or an array for C# or Visual Basic)?

In SQL, you can write the following:

```
SELECT * FROM Customers WHERE Country = 'Italy'
```

In C#, you would probably write this:

```
public List<Customer> ItalianCustomers( Customer customers[] )
  {
    List<Customer> result = new List<Customer>();
    foreach( Customer c in customers ) {
        if (c.Country == "Italy") result.Add( c );
    }
    return result;
}
```

C# code takes longer to write and read. But the most important consideration is expressivity. In SQL, you describe *what* you want. In C#, you describe *how* to obtain the expected result. In SQL, the selection of the best algorithm to implement the *how* (which is more explicitly dealt with in C#) is the responsibility of the query engine. This is because the SQL query engine has more freedom to apply optimizations than a C# compiler, which has many more constraints on the *how*.

Note The previous C# code sample could be written in .NET 2.0 using a *Find* predicate, but for many developers the required anonymous delegate syntax is not very easy to use. However, the samples are merely illustrative of the different programming paradigms.

LINQ enables a more declarative style of coding for C# and Visual Basic. A LINQ query describes operations on data through a declarative construct instead of an iterative one. LINQ allows the intentions of programmers to be made more explicit, and this knowledge of programmer intent is fundamental to obtaining a higher level of services from the underlying framework. For example, think about parallelization. An SQL query can be split into several concurrent operations, simply because it does not place any constraint on the kind of table scan algorithm applied. A C# *foreach* loop is harder to split into several loops over different parts of an array that could be executed in parallel by different processors.

> **More Info**   Parallel LINQ (PLINQ) is a research project on the parallelism that can be obtained by writing code with LINQ.

Declarative programming can take advantage of services offered by compilers and frameworks, and in general it is easier to read and maintain. This single "feature" can be the most important one because it boosts programmers' productivity. For example, suppose that you want to get a list of all static methods available in the current application domain that return an *IEnumerable<T>* interface. You can use LINQ to write a query over Reflection:

```
var query =
    from    assembly in AppDomain.CurrentDomain.GetAssemblies()
    from    type in assembly.GetTypes()
    from    method in type.GetMethods()
    where   method.IsStatic
            && method.ReturnType.GetInterface( "IEnumerable`1" ) != null
    orderby method.DeclaringType.Name, method.Name
    group   method by new { Class = method.DeclaringType.Name,
                            Method = method.Name };
```

The equivalent C# code that handles data is longer to write, harder to read, and probably more error prone. You can see a possible version that is not particularly optimized in Listing 1-10.

Listing 1-10   C# code equivalent to a LINQ query over Reflection

```
List<String> results = new List<string>();
foreach( var assembly in AppDomain.CurrentDomain.GetAssemblies()) {
    foreach( var type in assembly.GetTypes() ) {
        foreach( var method in type.GetMethods()) {
            if (method.IsStatic &&
                method.ReturnType.GetInterface("IEnumerable`1") != null) {
                string fullName = String.Format( "{0}.{1}",
                                        method.DeclaringType.Name,
                                        method.Name );
                if (results.IndexOf( fullName ) < 0) {
                    results.Add( fullName );
                }
            }
        }
    }
}
results.Sort();
```

Type Checking

Another important aspect of language integration is type checking. Whenever data is manipulated by LINQ, no unsafe cast is necessary. The short syntax of a query expression has no compromises with type checking: data is always strongly typed, including both the queried collections and the single entities that are read and returned.

The type checking of the languages that support LINQ (currently C# 3.0 and Visual Basic 9.0) is preserved even when LINQ-specific features are used. This enables the use of Visual Studio features such as IntelliSense and Refactoring, even with LINQ queries. These Visual Studio features are very important for programmers' productivity.

Transparency Across Different Type Systems

When you think about the type system of the Microsoft .NET Framework and the type system of SQL Server, you realize that they are different. Using LINQ, you give precedence to the .NET type system because it is the one supported by any language that hosts a LINQ query. However, most of your data will be saved in a relational database, and it is necessary to convert many types of data between these two worlds. LINQ handles this conversion for you automatically, making the differences in type systems almost completely transparent to the programmer.

> **More Info**   Some limitations exist in the capability to perform conversions between different type systems and LINQ. You will find some information about this topic in Chapter 5, and you can find a more detailed type system compatibilities table in the product documentation.

LINQ Flavors

LINQ is a technology that covers many data domains. Some of these domains are included in those "LINQ Flavors" that Microsoft provides as part of the .NET 3.5 Framework, as shown in Figure 1-1.

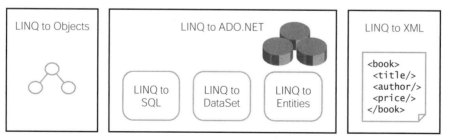

Figure 1-1   LINQ implementations provided by Microsoft within .NET 3.5

Each of these implementations is defined through a set of extension methods that implement the operators needed by LINQ to run over a particular data domain. The access to these features is controlled by the imported namespaces.

> **More Info**   Namespaces are imported in the current scope of a program through the keywords *using* in C# and *Imports* in Visual Basic.

LINQ to Objects

LINQ to Objects has the goal of manipulating collections of objects, which can be related to each other to form a hierarchy or a graph. From a certain point of view, LINQ to Objects is the default implementation used by a LINQ query. LINQ to Objects is enabled including the *System.Linq* namespace.

> **More Info**   The base concepts of LINQ are explained using LINQ to Objects as a reference implementation in Chapter 4, "LINQ Syntax Fundamentals."

It would be a mistake to think that LINQ to Objects queries are limited to collections of user-generated data. You can see why this is not true by analyzing Listing 1-11, which shows you a LINQ query over information extracted from the file system. The list of all files in a given directory is read in memory before being filtered by the LINQ query.

Listing 1-11   LINQ query that gets temporary files greater than 10,000 bytes, ordered by size

```
string tempPath = Path.GetTempPath();
DirectoryInfo dirInfo = new DirectoryInfo( tempPath );
var query =
    from    f in dirInfo.GetFiles()
    where   f.Length > 10000
    orderby f.Length descending
    select  f;
```

LINQ to ADO.NET

LINQ to ADO.NET includes different LINQ implementations that share the need to manipulate relational data. It includes other technologies that are specific to each particular persistence layer:

- **LINQ to SQL**   Handles the mapping between custom types in C# and the physical table schema.

- **LINQ to Entities**   Is in many ways similar to LINQ to SQL. However, instead of using the physical database as a persistence layer, it uses a conceptual Entity Data Model (EDM). The result is an abstraction layer that is independent from the physical data layer.

- **LINQ to DataSet**   Makes it possible to query a *DataSet* using LINQ.

LINQ to SQL and LINQ to Entities have similarities because they both access information stored in a relational database and operate on object entities that represent external data in memory. The main difference is that they operate at a different level of abstraction. While LINQ to SQL is tied to the physical database structure, LINQ to Entities operates over a conceptual model (business entities) that might be far from the physical structure (database tables).

The reason for these different options for accessing relational data through LINQ is that different models for database access are in use today. Some organizations implement all access through stored procedures, including any kind of database query, without using dynamic queries. Many others use stored procedures to insert, update, or delete data and dynamically built SELECT statements to query data. Some see the database as a simple object persistence layer, while others put some business logic into the database using triggers, stored procedures, or both. LINQ tries to offer help and improvements in database access without forcing everyone to adopt a single comprehensive model.

More Info   The use of any LINQ to ADO.NET feature depends on the inclusion of particular namespaces in the scope. LINQ to ADO.NET implementations and similar details are investigated in Chapter 5.

LINQ to XML

LINQ to XML offers a slightly different syntax that operates on XML data, allowing query and data manipulation. A particular type of support for LINQ to XML is offered by Visual Basic 9.0, which includes XML literals in the language. This enhanced support simplifies the code necessary to manipulate XML data. In fact, you can write such a query in Visual Basic 9.0:

```
Dim book = _
    <Book Title="Introducing LINQ">
        <%= From person In team _
            Where person.Role = "Author" _
            Select <Author><%= person.Name %></Author> %>
    </Book>
```

This query corresponds to the following C# 3.0 syntax:

```
dim book =
    new XElement( "Book",
        new XAttribute( "Title", "Introducing LINQ" ),
        from    person in team
        where   person.Role == "Author"
        select new XElement( "Author", person.Name ) );
```

More Info   You can find more information about XML support in Visual Basic in Chapter 3. The general LINQ to XML implementation is discussed in Chapter 6.

Present State and Future Direction of LINQ

At the time of this writing, LINQ is still in a beta stage. LINQ made its first appearance in September 2005 as a technical preview. Since then, it has evolved from an extension of Visual Studio 2005 to an integrated part of the next .NET Framework release (version 3.5) and the next Visual Studio release (code-named "Orcas").

> **This Book Is Based on Beta Code!**   Because the entire book is based on beta code, some features might be changed, removed, or added in the final release. This could invalidate some of the examples shown in the book. We tried to keep the book updated and aligned with the most recent information we had. In any case, we will publish news, book corrections, and updated code samples at *http://www.introducinglinq.com.*

The first released version of LINQ will directly support some data domains, as we saw in the "LINQ Flavors" section that appeared earlier. However, LINQ can be extended to support other data domains. Possible extensions could be something like LINQ to SharePoint, LINQ to Exchange, and LINQ to OLAP, just to name a few examples. Actually, some possible implementations are already available using LINQ to Objects—we have already seen a possible LINQ to Reflection query in the "LINQ to Objects" section.

Another point of extensibility of LINQ is the provider model included in LINQ to SQL and LINQ to Entities. Beta versions of LINQ support only SQL Server databases, but it is possible to implement a provider for any other relational database. We can expect that many providers will be written by developer communities and third parties.

LINQ is likely to have an impact on the way applications are coded. It would be an error to think that LINQ will change application architectures, because its goal is to provide a set of tools that improve code implementation by adapting to several different architectures. However, we cannot avoid speculating that LINQ might affect some critical parts of the layers of an *n*-tier solution. For example, we envision the use of LINQ in a SQLCLR stored procedure, with a direct transfer of the query expression to the SQL engine instead of using an SQL statement.

Many possible evolutions could originate from LINQ, and we should not forget that SQL is a widely adopted standard that cannot be easily replaced by another, just for performance reasons. Nevertheless, LINQ is an interesting step in the evolution of current mainstream programming languages. The declarative nature of its syntax might be interesting for uses other than data access. We already cited PLINQ, a research project that is an example of the current studies in this direction. Many other services can be offered by an execution framework to a program written using a higher level of abstraction such as the one offered by LINQ. A good understanding of this new technology might be important today, but it could become fundamental tomorrow!

Summary

In this chapter, we introduced LINQ and discussed how it works. We also examined how different data domains can be queried and manipulated by using a uniform syntax that is integrated into current mainstream programming languages such as C# and Visual Basic. We took a look at the benefits offered by language integration, including declarative programming, type checking, and transparency across different type systems. We briefly presented the LINQ implementations available in .NET 3.5—LINQ to Objects, LINQ to ADO.NET and LINQ to XML—and we will cover them in more detail in later chapters of the book. Finally, we made some observations about the present state and the future direction of LINQ.

Chapter 2
C# Language Features

A full knowledge of the C# 3.0 language enhancements is not necessary to use Language Integrated Query (LINQ). For example, none of the new language features require a modification of the common language runtime (CLR). LINQ relies on new compilers (C# 3.0 or Microsoft Visual Basic 9.0), and these compilers generate intermediate code that works well on Microsoft .NET 2.0, given that you have the LINQ libraries available.

However, in this chapter, we provide short descriptions of C# features (ranging from C# 1.*x* to C# 3.0) that you need to clearly understand to work with LINQ most effectively. If you decide to skip this chapter, you can come back to it later when you want to understand what is really going on within LINQ syntax.

C# 2.0 Revisited

C# 2.0 improved the original C# language in many ways. For example, the introduction of generics enabled developers to use C# to define methods and classes having one or more type parameters. Generics are a fundamental pillar of LINQ.

In this section, we will describe several C# 2.0 features that are important to LINQ: generics, anonymous methods (which are the basis of lambda expressions in C# 3.0), the *yield* keyword, and the *IEnumerable* interface. You need to understand these concepts well to best understand LINQ.

Generics

Many programming languages handle variables and objects by defining specific types and strict rules about converting between types. Code that is written in a strongly typed language lacks something in terms of generalization, however. Consider the following code:

```
int Min( int a, int b ) {
    if (a < b) return a;
    else return b;
}
```

To use this code, we need a different version of *Min* for each type of parameter we want to compare. Developers who are accustomed to using objects as placeholders for a generic type (which is common with collections) might be tempted to write a single *Min* function such as this:

```
object Min( object a, object b ) {
    if (a < b) return a;
    else return b;
}
```

Unfortunately, the *less than* operator (<) is not defined for the generic object type. We need to use a common (or "generic") interface to do that:

```
IComparable Min( IComparable a, IComparable b ) {
    if (a.CompareTo( b ) < 0) return a;
    else return b;
}
```

However, even if we solve this problem, we are faced with a bigger issue: the indeterminate result type of the *Min* function. A caller of *Min* that passes two integers should make a type conversion from *IComparable* to *int*, but this might raise an exception and surely would involve a CPU cost:

```
int a = 5, b = 10;
int c = (int) Min( a, b );
```

C# 2.0 solved this problem with generics. The basic principle of generics is that type resolution is moved from the C# compiler to the jitter. Here is the generic version of the *Min* function:

```
T Min<T>( T a, T b ) where T : IComparable<T> {
    if (a.CompareTo( b ) < 0) return a;
    else return b;
}
```

Note   The jitter is the run-time compiler that is part of the .NET runtime. It translates intermediate language (IL) code to machine code. When you compile .NET source code, the compiler generates an executable image containing IL code, which is compiled in machine code instructions by the jitter at some point before the first execution.

Moving type resolution to the jitter is a good compromise: the jitter can generate many versions of the same code, one for each type that is used. This approach is similar to a macro expansion, but it differs in the optimizations used to avoid code proliferation—all versions of a generic function that use reference types as generic types share the same compiled code, while the difference is maintained against callers.

With generics, instead of this:

```
int a = 5, b = 10;
int c = (int) Min( a, b );
```

you can write code such as this:

```
int a = 5, b = 10;
int c = Min<int>( a, b );
```

The cast for *Min* results has disappeared, and the code will run faster. Moreover, the compiler can infer the generic *T* type of the *Min* function from the parameters, and we can write this simpler form:

```
int a = 5, b = 10;
int c = Min( a, b );
```

Type Inference   Type inference is a key feature. It allows you to write more abstract code, making the compiler handle details about types. Nevertheless, the C# implementation of type inference does not remove type safety and can intercept wrong code (for example, a call that uses incompatible types) at compile time.

Generics can also be used with type declarations (as classes and interfaces) and not only to define generic methods. As we said earlier, a detailed explanation of generics is not the goal of this book, but we want to emphasize that you have to be comfortable with generics to work well with LINQ.

Delegates

A delegate is a class that encapsulates one or more methods. Internally, one delegate stores a list of method pointers, each of which can be paired with a reference to an instance of the class containing an instance method.

A delegate can contain a list of several methods, but our attention in this section is on delegates that contain only one method. From an abstract point of view, a delegate of this type is like a "code container." The code in that container is not modifiable, but it can be moved along a call stack or stored in a variable until its use is no longer necessary. It stores a context of execution (the object instance), extending the lifetime of the object until the delegate is valid.

The syntax evolution of delegates is the foundation for anonymous methods, which we will cover in the next section. The declaration of a delegate actually defines a type that will be used to create instances of the delegate itself. The delegate declaration requires a complete method signature. In the code in Listing 2-1, we declare three different types: each one can be instantiated only with references to methods with the same signatures.

Listing 2-1   Delegate declaration

```
delegate void SimpleDelegate();
delegate int ReturnValueDelegate();
delegate void TwoParamsDelegate( string name, int age );
```

Delegates are a typed and safe form of old-style C function pointers. With C# 1.x, a delegate instance can be created only through an explicit object creation, such as those shown in Listing 2-2.

Listing 2-2   Delegate instantiation (C# 1.x)

```
public class DemoDelegate {
    void MethodA() { … }
    int MethodB() { … }
    void MethodC( string x, int y ) { … }

    void CreateInstance() {
        SimpleDelegate a = new SimpleDelegate( MethodA );
        ReturnValueDelegate b = new ReturnValueDelegate ( MethodB );
        TwoParamsDelegate c = new TwoParamsDelegate( MethodC );
        // …
    }
}
```

The original syntax needed to create a delegate instance is tedious: you always have to know the name of the delegate class, even if the context forces the requested type, because it does not allow any other. This requirement means, however, that the delegate type can be safely inferred from the context of an expression.

C# 2.0 is aware of this capability and allows you to skip part of the syntax. The previous delegate instances we have shown can be created without the *new* keyword. You only need to specify the method name. The compiler infers the delegate type from the assignment. If you are assigning a *SimpleDelegate* type variable, the *new SimpleDelegate* code is automatically generated by the C# compiler, and the same is true for any delegate type. The code for C# 2.0 shown in Listing 2-3 produces the same compiled IL code as the C# 1.x sample code.

Listing 2-3   Delegate instantiation (C# 2.0)

```
public class DemoDelegate {
    void MethodA() { … }
    int MethodB() { … }
    void MethodC( string x, int y ) { … }

    void CreateInstance() {
        SimpleDelegate a = MethodA;
        ReturnValueDelegate b = MethodB;
        TwoParamsDelegate c = MethodC;
        // …
    }
    // …
}
```

You can also define a generic delegate type, which is useful when a delegate is defined in a generic class and is an important capability for many LINQ features.

The common use for a delegate is to inject some code into an existing method. In Listing 2-4, we assume that *Repeat10Times* is an existing method that we do not want to change.

Listing 2-4   Common use for a delegate

```
public class Writer {
    public string Text;
    public int Counter;
    public void Dump() {
        Console.WriteLine( Text );
        Counter++;
    }
}

public class DemoDelegate {
    void Repeat10Times( SimpleDelegate someWork ) {
        for (int i = 0; i < 10; i++) someWork();
    }

    void Run1() {
        Writer writer = new Writer();
        writer.Text = "C# chapter";
        this.Repeat10Times( writer.Dump );
        Console.WriteLine( writer.Counter );
    }
    // …
}
```

The existing callback is defined as *SimpleDelegate*, but we want to pass a string to the injected method and we want to count how many times the method is called. We define the *Writer* class, which contains instance data that acts as a sort of parameter for the *Dump* method. As you can see, we need to define a separate class just to put together code and data that we want to use. A simpler way to code a similar pattern is to use the anonymous method syntax.

Anonymous Methods

In the previous section, we illustrated a common use for a delegate. C# 2.0 established a way to write the code shown in Listing 2-4 more concisely by using an anonymous method. Listing 2-5 shows an example.

Listing 2-5   Using an anonymous method

```
public class DemoDelegate {
    void Repeat10Times( SimpleDelegate someWork ) {
        for (int i = 0; i < 10; i++) someWork();
    }
```

```
void Run2() {
    int counter = 0;
    this.Repeat10Times( delegate {
        Console.WriteLine( "C# chapter" );
        counter++;
    } );
    Console.WriteLine( counter );
}
// ...
}
```

In this code, we no longer declare the *Writer* class. The compiler does this for us automatically with a hidden and automatically generated class name. Instead, we define a method inside the *Repeat10Times* call, which might seem as though we are really passing a piece of code as a parameter. Nevertheless, the compiler converts this code into a pattern similar to the common delegate example with an explicit *Writer* class. The only evidence for this conversion in our source code is the *delegate* keyword before the code block. This syntax is called an *anonymous method*.

> **Note** Remember that you cannot pass code into a variable. You can only pass a pointer to some code. Repeat this to yourself a couple of times before going on.

The *delegate* keyword for anonymous methods precedes the code block. When we have a method signature for a delegate that contains one or more parameters, this syntax allows us to define the names of the parameters for the delegate. The code in Listing 2-6 defines an anonymous method for the *TwoParamsDelegate* delegate type.

Listing 2-6 Parameters for an anonymous method

```
public class DemoDelegate {

    void Repeat10Times( TwoParamsDelegate callback ) {
        for (int i = 0; i < 10; i++) callback( "Linq book", i );
    }

    void Run3() {
        Repeat10Times( delegate( string text, int age ) {
            Console.WriteLine( "{0} {1}", text, age );
        } );
    }
    // ...
}
```

We are now passing two implicit parameters to the delegate inside the *Repeat10Times* method. Think about it: if you were to remove the declaration for the *text* and *age* parameters, the delegate block would generate two errors of undefined names.

Important   You will (indirectly) use delegates and anonymous methods in C# 3.0, and for this reason, it is important to understand the concepts behind them. Only in this way can you master this higher level of abstraction that hides growing complexity.

Enumerators and Yield

C# 1.*x* defines two interfaces to support enumeration. The namespace *System.Collections* contains these declarations, shown in Listing 2-7.

Listing 2-7   *IEnumerator* and *IEnumerable* declarations

```
public interface IEnumerator {
     bool MoveNext();
     object Current { get; }
     void Reset();
}

public interface IEnumerable {
     IEnumerator GetEnumerator();
}
```

An object that implements *IEnumerable* can be enumerated through an object that implements *IEnumerator*. The enumeration can be performed by calling the *MoveNext* method until it returns *false*.

The code in Listing 2-8 defines a class that can be enumerated in this way. As you can see, the *CountdownEnumerator* class is more complex, and it implements the enumeration logic in a single place. In this sample, the enumerator does not really enumerate anything but simply returns descending numbers starting from the *StartCountdown* number defined in the *Countdown* class (which is also the enumerated class).

Listing 2-8   Enumerable class

```
public class Countdown : IEnumerable {
    public int StartCountdown;

    public IEnumerator GetEnumerator() {
        return new CountdownEnumerator( this );
    }
}

public class CountdownEnumerator : IEnumerator {
    private int _counter;
    private Countdown _countdown;
```

```
        public CountdownEnumerator( Countdown countdown ) {
            _countdown = countdown;
            Reset();
        }

        public bool MoveNext() {
            if (_counter > 0) {
                _counter--;
                return true;
            }
            else {
                return false;
            }
        }

        public void Reset() {
            _counter = _countdown.StartCountdown;
        }

        public object Current {
            get {
                return _counter;
            }
        }
    }
}
```

The real enumeration happens only when the *CountdownEnumerator* is used by a code block. For example, one possible use is shown in Listing 2-9.

Listing 2-9   Sample enumeration code

```
public class DemoEnumerator {
    public static void DemoCountdown() {
        Countdown countdown = new Countdown();
        countdown.StartCountdown = 5;

        IEnumerator i = countdown.GetEnumerator();
        while (i.MoveNext()) {
            int n = (int) i.Current;
            Console.WriteLine( n );
        }
        i.Reset();
        while (i.MoveNext()) {
            int n = (int) i.Current;
            Console.WriteLine( "{0} BIS", n );
        }
    }
    // …
}
```

The *GetEnumerator* call provides the enumerator object. We make two loops on it just to show the use of the *Reset* method. We need to cast the *Current* return value to *int* because we are using the nongeneric version of the enumerator interfaces.

> **Note**   C# 2.0 introduced enumeration support through generics. The namespace
> *System.Collections.Generic* contains generic *IEnumerable<T>* and *IEnumerator<T>* declarations.
> These interfaces eliminate the need to convert data in and out from an *object* type. This
> capability is important when enumerating value types because there are no more box or
> unbox operations that might affect performance.

Since C# 1.*x*, enumeration code can be simplified by using the *foreach* statement. The code
in Listing 2-10 produces a result equivalent to the previous example.

Listing 2-10   Enumeration using a *foreach* statement

```
public class DemoEnumeration {
    public static void DemoCountdownForeach() {
        Countdown countdown = new Countdown();
        countdown.StartCountdown = 5;

        foreach (int n in countdown) {
            Console.WriteLine( n );
        }
        foreach (int n in countdown) {
            Console.WriteLine( "{0} BIS", n );
        }
    }
    // ...
}
```

Using *foreach*, the compiler generates an initial call to *GetEnumerator* and a call to *MoveNext*
before each loop. The real difference is that the code generated by *foreach* never calls the *Reset*
method: two instances of *CountdownEnumerator* objects are created instead of one.

> **Note**   The *foreach* statement can also be used with classes that do not expose an *IEnumerable*
> interface but that have a public *GetEnumerator* method.

C# 2.0 introduced the *yield* statement through which the compiler automatically generates a
class that implements the *IEnumerator* interface returned by the *GetEnumerator* method. The
yield statement can be used only immediately before a *return* or *break* keyword. The code in
Listing 2-11 generates a class equivalent to the previous *CountdownEnumerator*.

Listing 2-11   Enumeration using a *yield* statement

```
public class CountdownYield : IEnumerable {
    public int StartCountdown;

    public IEnumerator GetEnumerator() {
        for (int i = StartCountdown - 1; i >= 0; i--) {
            yield return i;
        }
    }
}
```

From a logical point of view, the *yield return* statement is equivalent to suspending execution, which is resumed at the next *MoveNext* call. Remember that the *GetEnumerator* method is called only once for the whole enumeration, and it returns a class that implements an *IEnumerator* interface. Only that class really implements the behavior defined in the method that contains the *yield* statement.

A method that contains *yield* statements is called an *iterator*. An iterator can include many *yield* statements. The code in Listing 2-12 is perfectly valid and is functionally equivalent to the previous *CountdownYield* class with a *StartCountdown* value of 5.

Listing 2-12   Multiple *yield* statements

```
public class CountdownYieldMultiple : IEnumerable {
    public IEnumerator GetEnumerator() {
        yield return 4;
        yield return 3;
        yield return 2;
        yield return 1;
        yield return 0;
    }
}
```

By using the generic version of *IEnumerator*, it is possible to define a strongly typed version of the *CountdownYield* class, shown in Listing 2-13.

Listing 2-13   Enumeration using *yield* (typed)

```
public class CountdownYieldTypeSafe : IEnumerable<int> {
    public int StartCountdown;

    IEnumerator IEnumerable.GetEnumerator() {
        return this.GetEnumerator();
    }
    public IEnumerator<int> GetEnumerator() {
        for (int i = StartCountdown - 1; i >= 0; i--) {
            yield return i;
        }
    }
}
```

The strongly typed version contains two *GetEnumerator* methods: one is for compatibility with nongeneric code (returning *IEnumerable*), and the other is the strongly typed one (returning *IEnumerator<int>*).

The internal implementation of LINQ to Objects makes extensive use of enumerations and *yield*. Even if they work under the covers, keep their behavior in mind while you are debugging code.

C# 3.0 Features

C# 3.0 moves C# in the direction of a functional language, supporting a more declarative style of coding. LINQ makes extensive use of all the new features, which also let you use a higher level of abstraction in your code in areas other than LINQ.

> **Note**   You can read an interesting post about C# and functional languages written by Mads Torgersen, a program manager for the C# language, on his blog at *http://blogs.msdn.com/ madst/archive/2007/01/23/is-c-becoming-a-functional-language.aspx*

Local Type Inference

Type inference is a wonderful feature for any language. It preserves type safety while allowing you to write more "relaxed" code. In other words, you can define variables and use them without worrying too much about their types, leaving it to the compiler to determine the correct type of a variable by inferring it from the expression assigned to the variable itself.

The price for using type inference might be less explicit code against the types you want to use, but in our opinion, this feature simplifies code maintenance of local variables where explicit type declaration is not particularly meaningful.

C# 3.0 offers type inference that allows you to define a variable by using the *var* keyword instead of a specific type. This might seem to be equivalent to defining a variable of type *object*, but it is not. The following code shows you that an *object* type requires the boxing of a value type (see *b* declaration), and in any case it requires a cast operation when you want to operate with the specific type (see *d* assignment):

```
var a = 2;        // a is declared as int
object b = 2;     // Boxing an int into an object
int c = a;        // No cast, no unboxing
int d = (int) b;  // Cast is required, an unboxing is done
```

When *var* is used, the compiler infers the type from the expression used to initialize the variable. The compiled IL code contains only the inferred type. In other words, consider this code:

```
int a = 5;
var b = a;
```

It is perfectly equivalent to this example:

```
int a = 5;
int b = a;
```

Why is this important? The *var* keyword calls to mind the Component Object Model (COM) type VARIANT, which was used pervasively in Visual Basic 6.0, but in reality it is *absolutely* different because it is a type-safe declaration. In fact, it infers the type just as you wrote it.

To some, *var* might seem to be a tool for the lazy programmer. Nevertheless, *var* is the only way to define an anonymous type variable, as we will describe later.

> **Note** Variants were a way in COM to implement late binding with the type of a variable. There was no compile check using variants, and this caused a lot of nasty bugs that were revealed only when code was executed (most of the time, only when it was executed by end users).

The *var* keyword can be used only within a local scope. In other words, a local variable can be defined in this way, but not a member or a parameter. The following code shows some examples of valid uses of *var*: *x*, *y*, and *r* are *double* types; *d* and *w* are *decimal*; *s* and *p* are *string*; and *l* is an *int*. Please note that the constant 2.3 defines the type inferred by three variables, and the *default* keyword is a "typed" *null* that infers the correct type to *p*.

```
public void ValidUse( decimal d ) {
    var x = 2.3;            // double
    var y = x;             // double
    var r = x / y;         // double
    var s = "sample";      // string
    var l = s.Length;      // int
    var w = d;             // decimal
    var p = default(string); // string
}
```

The next sample shows some cases in which the *var* keyword is not allowed:

```
class VarDemo {
    // invalid token 'var' in class, struct or interface member declaration
    var k = 0;

    // type expected in parameter list
    public void InvalidUseParameter( var x ) {}

    // type expected in result type declaration
    public var InvalidUseResult() {
        return 2;
    }
    public void InvalidUseLocal() {
        var x;             // Syntax error, '=' expected
        var y = null;      // Cannot infer local variable type from 'null'
    }
    // ...
}
```

The *k* type can be inferred by the constant initializer, but *var* is not allowed on type members. The result type of *InvalidUseResult* could be inferred by the internal *return* statement, but even this syntax is not allowed.

This simple language feature allows us to write code that virtually eliminates almost all local variable type declarations. Although this simplifies code writing, it can make reading code more difficult. For example, if you are going to call an overloaded method with versions of the method that differ in parameter types, it could be unclear which version of the method is being called by reading the code. Anyway, similar problems are generated from the poor use of method overloading: you should use different method names when the behavior (and the meaning) of the methods is different.

Lambda Expressions

C# 2.0 introduced the capability to "pass a pointer to some code" as a parameter by using anonymous methods. This concept is a powerful one, but what you really pass in this way is a reference to a method, not exactly a piece of code. That reference points to strongly typed code that is generated at compile time. Using generics, you can obtain more flexibility, but it is hard to apply standard operators to a generic type.

C# 3.0 introduces lambda expressions, which allow the definition of anonymous methods using more concise syntax. Lambda expressions can also optionally postpone code genera-tion by creating an *expression tree* that allows further manipulation before code is actually generated, which happens at execution time. An expression tree can be generated only for the particular "pieces of code" that are expressions.

The following code shows a simple use of an anonymous method:

```csharp
public class AggDelegate {
    public List<int> Values;
    delegate T Func<T>( T a, T b );

    static T Aggregate<T>( List<T> l, Func<T> f ) {
        T result = default(T);
        bool firstLoop = true;
        foreach( T value in l ) {
            if (firstLoop) {
                result = value;
                firstLoop = false;
            }
            else {
                result = f( result, value );
            }
        }
        return result;
    }

    public static void Demo() {
        AggDelegate l = new AggDelegate();
        int sum;
        sum = Aggregate(
                l.Values,
                delegate( int a, int b ) { return a + b; }
            );
        Console.WriteLine( "Sum = {0}", sum );
    }

    // …
}
```

In the following examples, we use similar versions of the *Aggregate* method, so we will not reproduce it each time. The anonymous method passed as a parameter to *Aggregate* defines the aggregate operation that is executed for each element of the *List* object that is used.

Using lambda expression syntax, we can write the *Aggregate* call as shown in Listing 2-14.

Listing 2-14   Explicitly typed parameter list

```
sum = Aggregate(
        l.Values,
        ( int a, int b ) => { return a + b; }
    );
```

You can read this formula as "given a and b, both integers, return a+b that is the sum of a and b."

We removed the *delegate* keyword before the parameter list and added the => token between the parameter list and the method code. At this stage, the difference is only syntactical because the compiled code is identical to the result of the anonymous method syntax. However, lambda expression syntax allows you to write the same code as shown in Listing 2-15.

Listing 2-15   Implicitly typed parameter list

```
sum = Aggregate(
        l.Values,
        ( a, b ) => { return a + b; }
    );
```

> **Note**   The pronunciation of the => token has no official definition. A few developers use "such that" when the lambda expression is a predicate and "becomes" when it is a projection. Other developers say generically "goes to."

You can read this formula as "given a and b, return a+b, whatever '+' means for the type of a and b." (The "+" operator must exist for the concrete type of a and b–inferred from the context–otherwise, the code will not compile.)

Although we removed parameter types from the parameter list, the compiler will infer parameter types from the *Aggregate* call. We are calling a generic method, but the generic type *T* is defined from the *l.Values* parameter, which is a *List<int>* type. In this call, *T* is an *int*; therefore, the *Func<T>* delegate is a *Func<int>*, and both *a* and *b* are of type *int*.

You can think of this syntax as more similar to a *var* declaration than to another form of generic use. The type resolution is made at compile time. If a parameter type is generic, you cannot access operators and members other than those allowed by type constraints. If it is a regular type, you have full access to operators (such as the "+" operator we are using) and members eventually defined on that type.

A lambda expression can define a body in two ways. We have seen the statement body, which requires brackets like any other block of code and a *return* statement before the expression that has to be returned. The other form is the expression body, which can be used when the code inside the block is only a *return* followed by an expression. You can simply omit the brackets and the *return* statement, as shown in Listing 2-16.

Listing 2-16   Expression body

```
sum = Aggregate(
        1.Values,
        ( a, b ) => a + b
    );
```

When we worked with lambda expressions for the first time, we felt some confusion until we realized that they are only a more powerful syntax with which to write an anonymous method. This is an important concept to remember, because you can always access identifiers that are not defined in the parameter list. In other words, remember that the parameter list defines the parameters of the anonymous method. Any other identifier inside the body (either a statement or an expression) of a lambda expression has to be resolved within the anonymous method definition. The following code shows an example of this. (The *AggregateSingle<T>* method uses a slightly different delegate for the second parameter, declared as delegate *T FuncSingle<T>(T a)*).

```
int sum = 0;
sum = AggregateSingle(
        1.Values,
        ( x ) => sum += x
    );}
```

This lambda expression has only the *x* parameter; *sum* is a local variable of the containing method, and its lifetime is extended over the lifetime of the delegate instance that points to the anonymous method defined by the lambda expression itself. Remember that the result of the corresponding *return sum += x* statement will be the value of *sum* after the sum of *x*.

When a lambda expression has only one parameter, the parentheses can be omitted from the parameter list, as in this example:

```
int sum = 0;
sum = AggregateSingle(
        1.Values,
        x => sum += x
    );}
```

If there are no parameters for a lambda expression, two parentheses are required before the => token. The code in Listing 2-17 shows some of the possible syntaxes.

Listing 2-17   Lambda expression examples

```
( int a, int b ) => { return a + b; } // Explicitly typed, statement body
( int a, int b ) => a + b;            // Explicitly typed, expression body
( a, b ) => { return a + b; }         // Implicitly typed, statement body
( a, b ) => a + b                     // Implicitly typed, expression body
( x ) => sum += x                     // Single parameter with parentheses
x => sum += x                         // Single parameter no parentheses
() => sum + 1                         // No parameters
```

Predicate and Projection

Some lambda expressions have a particular name based on their purpose:

- A *predicate* is a Boolean expression that is intended to indicate membership of an element in a group. For example, it is used to define how to filter items inside a loop:

```
// Predicate
( age ) => age > 21
```

- A *projection* is an expression that returns a type different from the type of its single parameter:

```
// Projection: takes a string and returns an int
( s ) => s.Length
```

A practical use of lambda expressions is in writing small pieces of code inside the parameter list of a method call. The following code shows an example of a predicate passed as a parameter to a generic *Display* method that iterates an array of elements and displays only those that make the predicate true. The predicate and its use are highlighted in the code. The *Func* delegate shown in Listing 2-18 is explained in the following pages.

Listing 2-18   Lambda expression as a predicate

```
public static void Demo() {
    string[] names = { "Marco", "Paolo", "Tom" };
    Display( names, s => s.Length > 4 );
}

public static void Display<T>( T[] names, Func<T, bool> filter ) {
    foreach( T s in names) {
        if (filter( s )) Console.WriteLine( s );
    }
}
```

The execution results in a list of names having more than four characters. The conciseness of this syntax is one reason for using lambda expressions in LINQ; the other reason is the potential to create an expression tree.

To this point, we have considered the difference between the statement body and the expression body only as a different syntax that can be used to retrieve the same code, but there is something more. A lambda expression can also be assigned to a variable of these delegate types:

```
public delegate T Func< T >();
public delegate T Func< A0, T >( A0 arg0 );
public delegate T Func<A0, A1, T> ( A0 arg0, A1 arg1 );
public delegate T Func<A0, A1, A2, T >( A0 arg0, A1 arg1, A2 arg2 );
public delegate T Func<A0, A1, A3, T> ( A0 arg0, A1 arg1, A2 arg2, A3 arg3 );
```

There are no requirements for defining these delegates in a particular way. LINQ defines such delegates within the *System.Linq* namespace, but lambda expression functionality does not depend on these declarations. You can make your own, even with a name other than *Func*, except in one case: if you convert a lambda expression to an expression tree, the compiler emits a binary representation of the lambda expression that can be manipulated and converted into executable code at execution time. An expression tree is an instance of a *System.Linq.Expressions.Expression<T>* class, where *T* is the delegate that the expression tree represents.

In many ways, the use of lambda expressions to create an expression tree makes lambda expressions similar to generic methods. The difference is that generic methods are already described as IL code at compile time (only the type parameters used are not completely specified), while an expression tree becomes IL code only at execution time. Only lambda expressions with an expression body can be converted into an expression tree, and this conversion is not possible if the lambda expression contains a statement body.

Listing 2-19 shows how the same lambda expression can be converted into either a delegate or an expression tree. The highlighted lines show the assignment of the expression tree and its use.

Listing 2-19   Use of an expression tree

```
class ExpressionTree {
    delegate T Func<T>( T a, T b );
    public static void Demo() {
        Func<int> x = (a, b) => a + b;
        Expression<Func<int>> y = (a, b) => a + b;
        Console.WriteLine( "Delegate" );
        Console.WriteLine( x.ToString() );
        Console.WriteLine( x( 29, 13 ) );
        Console.WriteLine( "Expression tree" );
        Console.WriteLine( y.ToString() );
        Console.WriteLine( y.Compile()( 29, 13 ) );
    }
}
```

Here is the output of *Demo* execution. The result of the invocation is the same (42), but the output of the *ToString()* invocation is different.

```
Delegate ExpressionTree+Func`1[System.Int32]
42
Expression tree (a, b) => (a + b)
42
```

The expression tree maintains a representation of the expression in memory. You cannot use the compact delegate invocation on an expression tree as we did on the *x* delegate syntax. When you want to evaluate the expression, you need to compile it. The invocation of the *Compile* method returns a delegate that can be invoked through the *Invoke* method (or the compact delegate invocation syntax we used in the preceding example). We do not have space here for a deeper investigation of deferred query evaluation, but it is an important foundation for many parts of LINQ. For example, LINQ to SQL has methods that navigate an expression tree and convert it into an SQL statement. That conversion is made at execution time and not at compile time.

Extension Methods

C# is an object-oriented programming language that allows the extension of a class through inheritance. Nevertheless, designing a class that can be inherited in a safe way and maintaining that class in the future is hard work. A safe way to write such code is to declare all classes as sealed, unless they are designed as inheritable. In that case, safety is set against agility.

> **More Info**   Microsoft .NET allows class A in assembly X.DLL to be inherited by class B in assembly Y.DLL. This implies that a new version of X.DLL should be designed to be compatible even with older versions of Y.DLL. C# and .NET have many tools to help in this effort. However, we can say that a class has to be designed as inheritable if you want to allow its derivation; otherwise, you run the risk that making a few changes in the base classes will break existing code in derived classes. If you do not design a class to be inheritable, it is better to make the class *sealed*, or at least *private* or *internal*.

C# 3.0 introduces a syntax that conceptually extends an existing type (either reference or value) by adding new methods without deriving it into a new type. Some might consider the results of this change to be only syntactic sugar, but this capability makes LINQ code more readable and easier to write. The methods that extend a type can use only the public members of the type itself, just as you can do from any piece of code outside the target type.

The following code shows a traditional approach to writing two methods (*FormattedUS* and *FormattedIT*) that convert a *decimal* value into a string formatted with a specific culture:

```
static class Traditional {
    public static void Demo() {
        decimal x = 1234.568M;
        Console.WriteLine( FormattedUS( x ) );
        Console.WriteLine( FormattedIT( x ) );
    }
```

```
public static string FormattedUS( decimal d ) {
    return String.Format( formatIT, "{0:#,0.00}", d );
}

public static string FormattedIT( decimal d ) {
    return String.Format( formatUS, "{0:#,0.00}", d );
}

static CultureInfo formatUS = new CultureInfo( "en-US" );
static CultureInfo formatIT = new CultureInfo( "it-IT" );
}
```

There is no link between these methods and the *decimal* type other than the methods'
parameters. We can change this code to extend the *decimal* type. It is a value type and not
inheritable, but we can add the *this* keyword before the first parameter type of our methods,
and in this way use the method as if it was defined inside the decimal type. Changes are
highlighted in the code shown in Listing 2-20.

Listing 2-20   Extension methods declaration

```
static class ExtensionMethods {
    public static void Demo() {
        decimal x = 1234.568M;
        Console.WriteLine( x.FormattedUS() );
        Console.WriteLine( x.FormattedIT() );
        Console.WriteLine( FormattedUS( x ) ); // Traditional call allowed
        Console.WriteLine( FormattedIT( x ) ); // Traditional call allowed
    }

    static CultureInfo formatUS = new CultureInfo( "en-US" );
    static CultureInfo formatIT = new CultureInfo( "it-IT" );
    public static string FormattedUS( this decimal d ) {
        return String.Format( formatIT, "{0:#,0.00}", d );
    }

    public static string FormattedIT( this decimal d ) {
        return String.Format( formatUS, "{0:#,0.00}", d );
    }
}
```

An extension method must be *static* and *public*, must be declared inside a *static* class, and must
have the keyword *this* before the first parameter type, which is the type that the method
extends. Extension methods are public because they can be (and normally are) called from
outside the class where they are declared.

Although this is not a big revolution, one advantage could be Microsoft IntelliSense support,
which could show all extension methods accessible to a given identifier. However, the result
type of the extension method might be the extended type itself. In this case, we can extend
a type with many methods, all working on the same data. LINQ very frequently uses
extension methods in this way.

We can write a set of extension methods to *decimal* as shown in Listing 2-21.

Listing 2-21   Extension methods for native value types

```
static class ExtensionMethods {
    public static decimal Double( this decimal d ) {
        return d + d;
    }
    public static decimal Triple( this decimal d ) {
        return d * 3;
    }
    public static decimal Increase( this decimal d ) {
        return ++d;
    }
    public static decimal Decrease( this decimal d ) {
        return --d;
    }
    public static decimal Half( this decimal d ) {
        return d / 2;
    }
    // …
}
```

In Listing 2-22, we can compare the two calling syntaxes, the classical one (*y*) and the new one (*x*).

Listing 2-22   Extension methods call order

```
decimal x = 14M, y = 14M;
x = Half( Triple( Decrease( Decrease( Double( Increase( x ) ) ) ) ) );
y = y.Increase().Double().Decrease().Decrease().Triple().Half();
```

The result for both *x* and *y* is 42. The classical syntax requires several nested calls that have to be read from the innermost to the outermost. The new syntax acts as though our new methods are members of the decimal class. The call order follows the read order (left to right) and is much easier to understand.

Note   It is important to recognize that extension methods come at a price. When you call an instance method of a type, you can expect that the instance state can be modified by your call. But keep in mind that an extension method can do that only by calling public members of the extended type, as we already said. When the extension method returns the same type as it extends, you can assume that the instance state of the type should not be changed. This might be a recommendation for extending value types, but we cannot assume the same for any reference type because the related cost (creating a copy of an object for each call) could be too high.

An extension method is not automatically considered. Its resolution follows some rules. Here is the order of evaluation used to resolve a method for an identifier:

1.   **Instance method:** If an instance method exists, it has priority.

2.   **Extension method:** The search for an extension method is made through all static classes in the "current namespace" and in all namespaces included in active *using* directives. (*Current namespace* refers to the closest enclosing namespace declaration. This is the namespace that contains the static class with the extension method declaration.) If two types contain the same extension method, the compiler raises an error.

The most common use of extension methods is to define them in static classes in specific namespaces, importing them into the calling code by specifying one or more *using* directives in the module.

These precedence rules used to resolve a method call define a feature that is not apparent at first sight. When you call an extension method on a class, it can always be replaced by a specific version of the method defined as a member method for a particular type. In other words, the extension method represents a "default" implementation for a method, which can always be overridden by a specialized version for specific classes.

We can see this behavior in a few examples. The first code example contains an extension method for the *object* type; in this way, you can call *Display* on an instance of any type. We call it on our own *Customer* class instance:

```
public class Customer {
    protected int Id;
    public string Name;

    public Customer( int id ) {
        this.Id = id;
    }
}

static class Visualizer {
    public static void Display( this object o ) {
        string s = o.ToString();
        Console.WriteLine( s );
    }
}

static class Program {
    static void Main() {
        Customer c = new Customer( 1 );
        c.Name = "Marco";
        c.Display();
    }
}
```

The result of executing this code is the class name *Customer*.

We can customize the behavior of the *Display* method for the *Customer* class, defining an overloaded extension method, as shown in Listing 2-23. (We could define an overloaded extension method in another namespace if this namespace had a higher priority in the resolution order.)

Listing 2-23   Extension methods overload

```
static class Visualizer {
    public static void Display( this object o ) {
        string s = o.ToString();
        Console.WriteLine( s );
    }
    public static void Display( this Customer c ) {
        string s = String.Format( "Name={0}", c.Name );
        Console.WriteLine( s );
    }
}
```

This time the more specialized version is executed, as we can see from the execution output, shown here:

```
Name=Marco
```

Without removing these extension methods, we can add other special behavior to *Display* by implementing it as an instance method in the *Customer* class. This implementation, shown in Listing 2-24, will have precedence over any other extension method for a type equal to or derived from *Customer*.

Listing 2-24   Instance method over extension methods

```
public class Customer {
    protected int Id;
    public string Name;

    public Customer( int id ) {
        this.Id = id;
    }
    public void Display() {
        string s = String.Format( "{0}-{1}", Id, Name );
        Console.WriteLine( s );
    }
}
```

The execution output, shown here, illustrates that the instance method is now called:

```
1-Marco
```

At first glance, this behavior seems to overlap functionality provided by virtual methods. It does not, however, because an extension method has to be resolved at compile time, while virtual methods are resolved at execution time. This means that if you call an extension method on an object defined as a base class, the instance type of the contained object is not relevant.

If a compatible extension method exists (even if it is a derived class), it is used in place of the instance method. The code in Listing 2-25 illustrates this concept.

Listing 2-25   Extension methods resolution

```
public class A {
    public virtual void X() {}
}
public class B : A {
    public override void X() {}
    public void Y() {}
}

static public class E {
    static void X( this A a ) {}
    static void Y( this A b ) {}

    public static void Demo() {
        A a = new A();
        B b = new B();
        A c = new B();

        a.X(); // Call A.X
        b.X(); // Call B.X
        c.X(); // Call B.X

        a.Y(); // Call E.Y
        b.Y(); // Call B.Y
        c.Y(); // Call E.Y
    }
}
```

The *X* method is always resolved by the instance method. It is a virtual method, and for this reason *c.X()* calls the *B.X* overridden implementation. The extension method *E.X* is never called on these objects.

The *Y* method is defined only on the *B* class. It is an extension method for the *A* class, and therefore only *b.Y()* calls the *B.Y* implementation. Note that *c.Y()* calls *E.Y* because the *c* identifier is defined as an *A* type, even if it contains an instance of type *B*, because *Y* is not defined in class *A*.

A final point to consider regarding a generic extension method is that when you use a generic type as the parameter that you mark with the *this* keyword, you are extending not only a class but a whole set of classes. We found that this operation is not very intuitive when you are designing a components library, but it is a comfortable approach when you are writing the code that uses them. The following code is a slightly modified version of a previous example of lambda expressions. We added the *this* keyword to the *names* parameter and changed the invocation of the *Display* method. Important changes are highlighted in the code shown in Listing 2-26.

Listing 2-26 Lambda expression as predicate

```
public static void Display<T>( this T[] names, Func<T, bool> filter ) {…}

public static void Demo() {
    string[] names = { "Marco", "Paolo", "Tom" };
    names.Display( s => s.Length > 4 );
    // It was: Display( names, s => s.Length > 4 );
}
```

The *Display* method can be used with a different class (for example, an array of type *int*), and it will always require a predicate with a parameter that is the same type as the array. The following code uses the same *Display* method, showing only the even values:

```
int[] ints = { 19, 16, 4, 33 };
ints.Display( i => i % 2 == 0 );
```

As you learn more about extension methods, you can start to see a language that is more flexible but still strongly typed.

Object Initialization Expressions

C# 1.x allows the initialization of a field or a local variable in a single statement. The syntax shown here can initialize a single identifier:

```
int i = 3;
string name = 'Unknown';
Customer c = new Customer( "Tom", 32 );
```

When an initialization statement of this kind is applied to a reference type, it requires a call to a class constructor that has parameters that specify how to initialize the inner state of the instance created. You can use an object initializer on both reference and value types.

When you want to initialize an object (either a reference or value type), you need a constructor with enough parameters to specify the initial state of the object you want to initialize. Consider this code:

```
public class Customer {
    public int Age;
    public string Name;
    public string Country;
    public Customer( string name, int age ) {
        this.Name = name;
        this.Age = age;
    }
    // …
}
```

The *customer* instance is initialized through the *Customer* constructor, but we set only the *Name* and *Age* fields. If we want to set *Country* but not *Age*, we need to write code such as that shown in Listing 2-27.

Listing 2-27   Standard syntax for object initialization

```
Customer customer = new Customer();
customer.Name = "Marco";
customer.Country = "Italy";
```

C# 3.0 introduces a shorter form of object initialization syntax that generates functionally equivalent code, shown in Listing 2-28.

Listing 2-28   Object initializer

```
// Implicitly calls default constructor before object initialization
Customer customer = new Customer { Name = "Marco", Country = "Italy" };
```

Note   The syntaxes used to initialize an object (standard and object initializers) are equivalent after code is compiled. Object initializer syntax produces a call to a constructor for the specified type (either a reference or value type): this is the default constructor whenever you do not place a parenthesis between the type name and the open bracket. If that constructor makes assignments to the member fields successively initialized, the compiler still performs that work, although the assignment might not be used. An object initializer does not have an additional cost if the called constructor of the initialized type is empty.

The names assigned in an initialization list can correspond to either fields or properties that are public members of the initialized object. The syntax also allows for specifying a call to a nondefault constructor, which might be necessary if the default constructor is not available for a type. Listing 2-29 shows an example.

Listing 2-29   Explicit constructor call in object initializer

```
// Explicitly specify constructor to call before object initialization
Customer c1 = new Customer() { Name = "Marco", Country = "Italy" };

// Explicitly specify nondefault constructor
Customer c2 = new Customer( "Paolo", 21 ) { Country = "Italy" };
```

The *c2* assignment above is equivalent to this one:

```
Customer c2 = new Customer( "Paolo", 21 );
c2.Country = "Italy";
```

> **Note**   The real implementation of an object initializer creates and initializes the object into a temporary variable and, only at the end, it copies the reference to the destination variable. In this way, the object is not visible to another thread until it is not completely initialized.

One of the advantages of the object initializer is that it allows for writing a complete initialization in a functional form: you can put it inside an expression without using different statements. Therefore, the syntax can also be nested, repeating the syntax for the initial value of a member into an initialized object. The classic *Point* and *Rectangle* class example shown in Listing 2-30 (part of the C# 3.0 specification document) illustrates this.

Listing 2-30   Nested object initializers

```
public class Point {
    int x, y;
    public int X { get { return x; } set { x = value; } }
    public int Y { get { return y; } set { y = value; } }
}

public class Rectangle {
    Point tl, br;
    public Point TL { get { return tl; } set { tl = value; } }
    public Point BR { get { return br; } set { br = value; } }
}

// Possible code inside a method
Rectangle r = new Rectangle {
    TL = new Point { X = 0, Y = 1 },
    BR = new Point { X = 2, Y = 3 }
};
```

The compiled initialization code for *r* is equivalent to the following:

```
Rectangle rectangle2 = new Rectangle();
Point point1 = new Point();
point1.X = 0;
point1.Y = 1;
rectangle2.TL = point1;
Point point2 = new Point();
point2.X = 2;
point2.Y = 3;
rectangle2.BR = point2;
Rectangle rectangle1 = rectangle2;
```

Now that you have seen this code, it should be clear when using the shortest syntax has a true advantage in terms of code readability. The two temporary variables, *point1* and *point2*, are also created in the object initializer form, but we do not need to explicitly define them.

The previous example used the nested object initializers with reference types. The same syntax also works for value types, but you have to remember that a copy of a temporary *Point* object is made when the *TL* and *BR* members are initialized.

Note   Copying value types can have performance implications on large value types, but this is not related to the use of object initializers.

The object initializer syntax can be used only for assignment of the initial value of a field or variable. The *new* keyword is required only for the final assignment. Inside an initializer, you can skip the *new* keyword in an object member's initialization. In this case, the code uses the object instance created by the constructor of the containing object, as shown in Listing 2-31.

Listing 2-31   Initializers for owned objects

```
public class Rectangle {
    Point tl = new Point();
    Point br = new Point();
    public Point TL { get { return tl; } }
    public Point BR { get { return br; } }
    }

// Possible code inside a method
Rectangle r = new Rectangle {
    TL = { X = 0, Y = 1 },
    BR = { X = 2, Y = 3 }
};
```

The *TL* and *BR* member instances are implicitly created by the *Rectangle* class constructor. The object initializer for *TL* and *BR* does not have the *new* keyword. In this way, the initializer works on the existing instance of *TL* and *BR*.

In the examples so far, we have used some constant within the object initializers. You can also use other calculated values, as shown here:

```
Customer c3 = new Customer{
        Name = c1.Name, Country = c2.Country, Age = c2.Age };
```

C# 1.*x* included the concept of initializers that used a similar syntax, but it was limited to arrays:

```
int[] integers = { 1, 3, 9, 18 };
string[] customers = { "Jack", "Paolo", "Marco" };
```

The same new object initializer syntax can also be used for collections. The internal list can be made of constants, expressions, or other initializers, like any other object initializer we have already shown. If the collection class implements the *System.Collections.Generic.ICollection<T>* interface, for each element in the initializer a call to *ICollection<T>.Add(T)* is made with the same order of the elements. If the collection class implements the *IEnumerable* interface, the *Add()* method is called for each element in the initializer. The code in Listing 2-32 shows some examples of using collection initializers.

Listing 2-32 Collection initializers

```
// Collection classes that implement ICollection<T>
List<int> integers = new List<int> { 1, 3, 9, 18 };

List<Customer> list = new List<Customer> {
    new Customer( "Jack", 28 ) { Country = "USA"},
    new Customer { Name = "Paolo" },
    new Customer { Name = "Marco", Country = "Italy" },
};

// Collection classes that implement IEnumerable
ArrayList integers = new ArrayList() { 1, 3, 9, 18 };

ArrayList list = new ArrayList {
    new Customer( "Jack", 28 ) { Country = "USA"},
    new Customer { Name = "Paolo" },
    new Customer { Name = "Marco", Country = "Italy" },
};
```

In summary, object and collection initializers allow the creation and initialization of a set of objects (eventually nested) within a single function. LINQ makes extensive use of this feature, especially through anonymous types.

Anonymous Types

An object initializer can also be used without specifying the class that will be created with the *new* operator. Doing that, a new class—an anonymous type—is created. Consider the example shown in Listing 2-33.

Listing 2-33 Anonymous types definition

```
Customer c1 = new Customer { Name = "Marco" };
var c2 = new Customer { Name = "Paolo" };
var c3 = new { Name = "Tom", Age = 31 };
var c4 = new { c2.Name, c2.Age };
var c5 = new { c1.Name, c1.Country };
var c6 = new { c1.Country, c1.Name };
```

The variables *c1* and *c2* are of the *Customer* type, but the type of variables *c3*, *c4*, *c5*, and *c6* cannot be inferred simply by reading the printed code. The *var* keyword should infer the variable type from the assigned expression, but this one has a *new* keyword without a type specified. As you might expect, that kind of object initializer generates a new class.

The generated class has a public property and an underlying private field for each argument contained in the initializer: its name and type are inferred from the object initializer itself. When the name is not explicit, it is inferred from the initialization expression, as in the definitions for *c4*, *c5*, and *c6*. This shorter syntax is called a *projection initializer* because it projects not just a value but also the name of the value.

That class is the same for all possible anonymous types whose properties have the same names and types in the same order. We can see the type names used and generated in this code:

```
Console.WriteLine( "c1 is {0}", c1.GetType() );
Console.WriteLine( "c2 is {0}", c2.GetType() );
Console.WriteLine( "c3 is {0}", c3.GetType() );
Console.WriteLine( "c4 is {0}", c4.GetType() );
Console.WriteLine( "c5 is {0}", c5.GetType() );
Console.WriteLine( "c6 is {0}", c6.GetType() );
```

The following is the output that is generated:

```
c1 is Customer
c2 is Customer
c3 is <>f__AnonymousType0`2[System.String,System.Int32]
c4 is <>f__AnonymousType0`2[System.String,System.Int32]
c5 is <>f__AnonymousType5`2[System.String,System.String]
c6 is <>f__AnonymousTypea`2[System.String,System.String]
```

The anonymous type name cannot be referenced by the code (you do not know the generated name), but it can be queried on an object instance. The variables *c3* and *c4* are of the same anonymous type because they have the same fields and properties. Even if *c5* and *c6* have the same properties (type and name), they are in a different order, and that is enough for the compiler to create two different anonymous types.

> **Important**   Usually in C# the order of members inside a type is not important; even standard object initializers are based on member names and not on their order. The need for LINQ to get a different type for two classes that differ only in the order of their members derives from the need to represent an ordered set of fields, as in a SELECT statement.

The syntax to initialize a typed array has been enhanced in C# 3.0. Now you can declare an array initializer and infer the type from the initializer content. This mechanism can be combined with anonymous types and object initializers, as in the code shown in Listing 2-34.

Listing 2-34 Implicitly typed arrays

```
var ints = new[] { 1, 2, 3, 4 };
var ca1 = new[] {
    new Customer { Name = "Marco", Country = "Italy" },
    new Customer { Name = "Tom", Country = "USA" },
    new Customer { Name = "Paolo", Country = "Italy" }
};
var ca2 = new[] {
    new { Name = "Marco", Sports = new[] { "Tennis", "Spinning"} },
    new { Name = "Tom", Sports = new[] { "Rugby", "Squash", "Baseball" } },
    new { Name = "Paolo", Sports = new[] { "Skateboard", "Windsurf" } }
};
```

> **Note**   The syntax of C# 1.*x* needs the assigned variable to be a definite type. The syntax of C# 3.0 allows the use of the *var* keyword to define the variable initialized in such a way.

While *ints* is an array of *int* and *ca1* is an array of *Customers*, *ca2* is an array of anonymous types, each containing a string (*Name*) and an array of strings (*Sports*). You do not see a type in the *ca2* definition because all types are inferred from the initialization expression. Once again, note that the *ca2* assignment is a single expression, which could be embedded in another one.

Query Expressions

C# 3.0 also introduces *query expressions*, which have a syntax similar to the SQL language and are used to manipulate data. This syntax is converted into regular C# 3.0 syntax that makes use of specific classes, methods, and interfaces that are part of the LINQ libraries. We would not cover all the keywords in detail because it is beyond the scope of this chapter. We will cover the syntax of query expressions in more detail in Chapter 4, "LINQ Syntax Fundamentals."

In this section, we want to introduce the transformation that the compiler applies to a query expression, just to describe how the code is interpreted.

Here is a typical LINQ query:

```
// Declaration and initialization of an array of anonymous types
var customers = new []{
    new {  Name = "Marco", Discount = 4.5 },
    new {  Name = "Paolo", Discount = 3.0 },
    new {  Name = "Tom", Discount = 3.5 }
};

 var query =
    from c in customers
    where c.Discount > 3
    orderby c.Discount
    select new { c.Name, Perc = c.Discount / 100 };

foreach( var x in query ) {
    Console.WriteLine( x );
}
```

A query expression begins with a *from* clause (in C#, all query expression keywords are case sensitive) and ends with either a *select* or *group* clause. The *from* clause specifies the object on which LINQ operations are applied, which must be an instance of a class that implements the *IEnumerable<T>* interface.

That code produces the following results:

```
{ Name = Tom, Perc = 0.035 }
{ Name = Marco, Perc = 0.045 }
```

C# 3.0 interprets the *query* assignment as if it was written in this way:

```
var query = customers
            .Where( c => c.Discount > 3)
            .OrderBy( c => c.Discount )
            .Select( c=> new { c.Name, Perc = c.Discount / 100 } );
```

Each query expression clause corresponds to a generic method, which is resolved through the same rules that apply to an extension method. Therefore, the query expression syntax is similar to a macro expansion, even if it is a more intelligent one because it infers many definitions, like the names of parameters in lambda expressions.

At this point, it should be clear why the features of C# 3.0 that allow you to write complex actions into a single expression are so important to LINQ. A query expression calls many methods in a chain, where each call uses the result of the previous call as a parameter. Extension methods simplify the syntax, avoiding nested calls. Lambda expressions define the logic for some operations (such as *where*, *orderby*, and so on). Anonymous types and object initializers define how to store the results of a query. Local type inference is the glue that holds these pieces together.

Summary

In this chapter, we reviewed some C# 1.*x* and 2.0 concepts, such as generics, anonymous methods, and iterators and yield. These concepts are all very important to understanding the C# 3.0 extensions. We also covered the new features of C# 3.0 that are the basis for LINQ: local type inference, lambda expressions, extension methods, object initializers, and anonymous types.

The more visible changes in C# 3.0 are the query expressions. We will cover their syntax in more detail in Chapter 4, together with an explanation of the LINQ architecture.

Chapter 3

Visual Basic 9.0 Language Features

The release of Microsoft Visual Basic 9.0 introduces enhancements to the language to better support Language Integrated Query (LINQ). As with C# 3.0, the changes to Visual Basic 9.0 do not require modification of the common language runtime (CLR).

More Info   For more information about C# 3.0, see Chapter 2, "C# Language Features."

In this chapter, we will examine the new syntax available in Visual Basic 9.0, comparing it to the C# equivalent whenever possible. As you will see, there are some differences between these languages, and some features are not present in both. Even if you are a C# programmer, please take a look at this chapter. You will discover that sometimes you can take advantage of Visual Basic 9.0 rather than C#, or at least you will be able to read Visual Basic code for LINQ.

If you prefer to use Visual Basic, remember that knowledge of the whole set of Visual Basic 8.0 features is necessary to effectively use the new Visual Basic 9.0 syntax. The ability to read C# code is also important for reading the rest of this book (because LINQ examples are written in C#) and for understanding differences between C# 3.0 and Visual Basic 9.0.

Visual Basic 9.0 and Nullable Types

Visual Basic 9.0 includes features that have been available in C# since version 2.0. One of these features—nullable types—is often useful with LINQ; therefore, we want to quickly describe nullable types here.

Since the introduction of generics in Microsoft .NET 2.0, the CLR offered the generic class *Nullable(Of T As Struct)* to programmers who wanted to add the semantic of NULL to a value type. Declaring a variable of this type, you can assign the NULL "value" without having to define a new type for this sole purpose. In this way, handling NULLs in data becomes similar to how it is done in SQL.

C# 2.0 added direct support in the language to enable the use of this type: if you simply add the *?* suffix to the name of the type, your compiled code will use the *Nullable* generic class instantiated for the requested type. Visual Basic 9.0 offers the same capabilities with a similar syntax, as you can see in Listing 3-1.

Listing 3-1   Nullable type declarations

```
Dim a As Integer? = 18
Dim b As Integer? = 24
Dim c As Integer? = Nothing
Dim d As Integer?
d = a + c   ' d = 18 + Nothing = Nothing
c = a + b   ' c = 18 + 24 = 42
```

A regular *Integer* variable cannot be assigned to *Nothing*, because *Integer* is a value type. In Listing 3-1, we assigned *c* to *Nothing*, and we used it in a calculation to assign *d*. The result of *a + c* is *Nothing*, showing the three-valued logic that is typical of the nullable types. The NULL "value" (represented by *Nothing* in Visual Basic) is propagated into an expression, with some exceptions using logical operators.

A nullable value cannot be assigned to the corresponding non-nullable type. The code in Listing 3-2 shows the required conversions.

Listing 3-2   Nullable type conversions

```
Dim k As Integer? = 16
Dim p As Integer = k     ' Compiler error
Dim q As Integer = DirectCast( k, Integer ) ' Ok
Dim r As Integer = CType( k, Integer )      ' Ok
```

Please refer to the Visual Basic documentation for more information about the nullable types in Visual Basic 9.0. We expect this feature to be used extensively in code that manipulates data back and forth from a relational database.

Visual Basic 9.0 Features Corresponding to C# 3.0

Most of the new Visual Basic 9.0 features have a C# 3.0 equivalent. For the sake of conciseness, this section will concentrate on the specific Visual Basic 9.0 syntax. The considerations about implications and possible uses of new features are the same that we offered in Chapter 2 for the corresponding C# 3.0 features.

Local Type Inference

The local type inference feature is also called *implicitly typed local variables*. It allows the definition of variables by inferring types from the assigned expression. At first sight, a Visual Basic developer might think that this is the same behavior that is obtained with *Option Strict*

Off. In fact, you still get a strongly typed variable if you assign a value in the declaration state-ment. The example in Listing 3-3 shows you this syntax; the comments indicate the effective type of the variable declared.

Listing 3-3   Local type inference

```
Dim x = 2.3        ' Double
Dim y = x          ' Double
Dim r = x / y      ' Double
Dim s = "sample"   ' String
Dim l = s.Length   ' Integer
Dim w = d          ' Decimal
Dim o              ' Object - allowed only with Option Strict Off
```

We see the same behavior here that we have seen in C#. The syntax for Visual Basic simply omits the *As type* part of the declaration. The declaration of *o* is not valid if you enable *Option Strict On*. Note that even with *Option Strict Off* active, all variables types are those inferred by the initialization expression. In fact, that setting would compile the example even with Visual Basic 8.0, but all variables would be of the *Object* type, boxing the value assigned in the initialization expression.

> **Note**   We recommend that you use *Option Strict On* unless you have a good reason to avoid it. For example, when you access a Component Object Model (COM) object through interop without having a primary interop assembly, the late-binding behavior of *Option Strict Off* could be useful to call methods implemented only through the *IDispatch* interface that are not exposed in the type library of the COM object.

The use of *Option Strict On* can help you avoid some possible errors. For example, consider the code in Listing 3-4.

Listing 3-4   Changed behavior from Visual Basic 8.0 to Visual Basic 9.0

```
Option Strict Off
Module LocalTypeInference
    Sub BeCareful()
        Dim a = 10
        a = "Hello"
        Console.WriteLine(a)
    End Sub
    ' ...
End Module
```

In Visual Basic 8.0, the *a* variable is of type *Object*; therefore, we can always change the assigned value type because it is eventually boxed. Executing the *BeCareful* method in Visual Basic 8.0, we display the string *Hello*. In Visual Basic 9.0, using *Option Strict Off*, we get an exception when trying to assign a *String* (that does not contain a number) to an *Integer* variable:

```
Unhandled Exception: System.InvalidCastException: Conversion from string "Hello" to type
'Integer' is not valid. ---> System.FormatException: Input string was not in a correct format
```

If you use *Option Strict On*, you get a compile error for the code in Listing 3-4. Visual Basic 8.0 does not accept the *a* declaration; Visual Basic 9.0 does not like the *Hello* string to be assigned to an integer variable. Be careful when you migrate existing Visual Basic code to LINQ if you have always used *Option Strict Off*.

> **Important**   You can disable local type inference by specifying *Option Infer Off*. By default, a new Visual Basic 9.0 project uses *Option Infer On*. To avoid possible issues in code migration, use *Option Infer Off* when you are migrating code from a previous version of Visual Basic.

Extension Methods

Extension methods can be defined in Visual Basic 9.0 with a technique that produces results like those obtained in C#. We will concentrate our attention only on syntax differences here. The code in Listing 3-5 uses traditional method declarations and calls to convert a *decimal* value into a string formatted with a specific culture.

Listing 3-5   Standard method declaration and use

```
Module Demo
    Sub DemoTraditional()
        Dim x As Decimal = 1234.568
        Console.WriteLine(FormattedIT(x))
        Console.WriteLine(FormattedUS(x))
    End Sub
End Module

Public Class TraditionalMethods
    Shared Function FormattedIT(ByVal d As Decimal) As String
        Return String.Format(formatIT, "{0:#,0.00}", d)
    End Function

    Shared Function FormattedUS(ByVal d As Decimal) As String
        Return String.Format(formatUS, "{0:#,0.00}", d)
    End Function

    Shared formatUS As CultureInfo = New CultureInfo("en-US")
    Shared formatIT As CultureInfo = New CultureInfo("it-IT")
End Class
```

As with C#, we can change this Visual Basic code to extend the *decimal* type. Instead of adding a keyword (as in C#, which uses *this* before the first argument), in Visual Basic we decorate both the extension method and the containing class with the attribute *System.Runtime .CompilerServices.Extension*.

> **Note**   The *Extension* attribute is automatically generated by the C# compiler when it encounters the *"this"* keyword before the first argument in a method declaration. Visual Basic assigns this task to the programmer.

To use a shorter attribute name, we can add the *Imports System.Runtime.CompilerServices* statement, as you can see in Listing 3-6.

Listing 3-6   Extension method declaration

```
Imports System.Runtime.CompilerServices
<Extension()> _
Public Module ExtensionMethods
    <Extension()> _
    Public Function FormattedIT(ByVal d As Decimal) As String
        Return String.Format(formatIT, "{0:#,0.00}", d)
    End Function

    <Extension()> _
    Public Function FormattedUS(ByVal d As Decimal) As String
        Return String.Format(formatUS, "{0:#,0.00}", d)
    End Function

    Private formatUS As CultureInfo = New CultureInfo("en-US")
    Private formatIT As CultureInfo = New CultureInfo("it-IT")
End Module
```

An extension method must be defined in a *Module*, and both the method and the containing module must be decorated with the *Extension* attribute. The first parameter type is the type that the method extends. Usually, extension methods and containing modules are public because they can be (and normally are) called even from outside the assembly in which they are declared.

> **Note**   At this point, the compiled code for the *ExtensionMethods* module contains metadata, as we would have defined a class with both *MustInherit* and *NotInheritable* keywords, which is a syntax that is not allowed by the compiler. When decompiling the code with ILDASM (Intermediate Language Disassembler) or Reflector, you have to interpret this condition as the equivalent of a static class in C#. ILDASM is a tool that is part of the .NET Framework SDK. Reflector is a free decompiler that supports several languages, including C# and Visual Basic, and is available at *http://www.aisto.com/roeder/dotnet/*.

Using an extension method from Visual Basic code requires that the class containing extension methods be used as a parameter of an *Imports* statement. This is different from C#, which requires a *using* statement for the containing namespace and not of the specific class. In Listing 3-7, you can see the call of the extension methods we declared in the previous sample. We use *Imports ExtensionVB.ExtensionMethods* because the containing namespace is

ExtensionVB (it is either the name of our assembly or the name of the root namespace), and *ExtensionMethods* is the name of the class containing our extension methods.

Listing 3-7   Extension method use

```
Imports ExtensionVB.ExtensionMethods

Module Demo
    Sub DemoExtension()
        Dim x As Decimal = 1234.568
        Console.WriteLine(x.FormattedIT())
        Console.WriteLine(x.FormattedUS())
    End Sub
End Module
```

Almost all the considerations about extension methods that we covered in Chapter 2 are valid here, with the only exceptions being the syntax differences that we have highlighted.

Object Initialization Expressions

Visual Basic 9.0 offers a new syntax to initialize multiple members of the same type instance. The *With* syntax does the same work, but the object initializer in Visual Basic 9.0 allows the initialization of multiple members in a single expression. This functionality is necessary to initialize anonymous types, as we will see later.

We will consider the class shown in Listing 3-8 in our examples.

Listing 3-8   Sample class for object initializers

```
Public Class Customer
    Public Age As Integer
    Public Name As String
    Public Country As String
    Public Sub New(ByVal name As String, ByVal age As Integer)
        Me.Age = age
        Me.Name = name
    End Sub
    ' ...
End Class
```

If we want to initialize *Country* but not *Age* on a new instance for *Customer*, in Visual Basic 8.0, we can write the code based on the *With* statement shown in Listing 3-9.

Listing 3-9   Initialization using *With* statement

```
Dim customer As New Customer
With customer
    .Name = "Marco"
    .Country = "Italy"
End With
```

The new object initializer syntax of Visual Basic 9.0 allows initialization in a different form, as we can see in Listing 3-10.

Listing 3-10   Object initializer syntax

```
Dim customer As Customer
customer = New Customer With {.Name = "Marco", .Country = "Italy"}
```

The object initializer syntax expects the keyword *With* after the object creation, followed by brackets containing a list of members to initialize. Each member is assigned by specifying its name prefixed by a dot, followed by an equals sign (=) and then the initialization expression. Multiple members are separated by a comma (,).

If you are a C# developer, you should be aware that splitting an expression on multiple lines in Visual Basic always requires the line continuation notation, which is a special character (an underscore) at the end of each line. You can see how to use them in Listing 3-11.

Listing 3-11   Object initializer syntax on multiple lines

```
Dim customer As Customer = _
    New Customer With { _
        .Name = "Marco", _
        .Country = "Italy"}
```

The use of line continuations can negate the benefits of object initializers. We generally prefer to use the new object initializer syntax rather than the traditional *With* statement in cases in which we can write everything on a single line. For example, we can leverage local type inference to write the code in Listing 3-12.

Listing 3-12   Object initializer syntax and local type inference

```
Dim customer = New Customer With {.Name = "Marco", .Country = "Italy"}
```

Object initializers can use constants or other expressions for the assigned values. Moreover, you can use a nondefault constructor followed by an object initializer. The example in Listing 3-13 illustrates these concepts.

Listing 3-13   Object initializers using expressions

```
Dim c1 = New Customer With {.Name = "Marco", .Country = "Italy"}
Dim c2 = New Customer("Paolo", 21) With {.Country = "Italy"}
Dim c3 = New Customer With {.Name = "Paolo", .Age = 21, .Country = "Italy"}
Dim c4 = New Customer With {.Name = c1.Name, .Country = c2.Country, .Age = c2.Age}
```

Because an object initializer is an expression, it can be nested. Listing 3-14 shows a possible use.

Listing 3-14   Nested object initializers

```
' In Point and Rectangle classes, we collapsed parts of implementation
Public Class Point
    Private _x, _y As Integer
    Public Property X ... ' Integer - implementation collapsed
    Public Property Y ... ' Integer - implementation collapsed
End Class

Public Class Rectangle
    Private _tl, _br As Point
    Public Property TL() ... ' Point - implementation collapsed
    Public Property BR() ... ' Point - implementation collapsed
End Class

' Possible code inside a method
    Dim r = New Rectangle With { _
                .TL = New Point With {.X = 0, .Y = 1}, _
                .BR = New Point With {.X = 2, .Y = 3} _
            }
```

Anonymous Types

An anonymous type is a type that is declared without an identifier. Anonymous types in Visual Basic 9.0 are aligned with the corresponding C# 3.0 features. You can use object initializers without specifying the class that will be created with the *New* operator. When you do this, a new class (an anonymous type) is created. Consider Listing 3-15.

Listing 3-15   Anonymous type definition

```
Dim c1 As New Customer With {.Name = "Marco"}
Dim c2 = New Customer With {.Name = "Paolo"}
Dim c3 = New With {.Name = "Tom", .Age = 31}
Dim c4 = New With {c2.Name, c2.Age}
Dim c5 = New With {c1.Name, c1.Country}
Dim c6 = New With {c1.Country, c1.Name}
```

The variables *c1* and *c2* are of the *Customer* type, but the type of variables *c3*, *c4*, *c5*, and *c6* cannot be inferred simply by reading the printed code. The local type inference should infer the variable type from the assigned expression, but we do not have an explicit type after the *New* keyword for these expressions. That kind of object initializer generates a new class.

The generated class has a public property and an underlying private field for each argument contained in the initializer; the property's name and type are inferred from the object initializer. That class is the same for all possible anonymous types that have the same names and types in the same order for their properties. We can see the type names used and generated with this code:

```
Console.WriteLine("c1 is {0}", c1.GetType())
Console.WriteLine("c2 is {0}", c2.GetType())
Console.WriteLine("c3 is {0}", c3.GetType())
Console.WriteLine("c4 is {0}", c4.GetType())
Console.WriteLine("c5 is {0}", c5.GetType())
Console.WriteLine("c6 is {0}", c6.GetType())
```

The output generated is the following:

```
c1 is AnonymousTypes.Customer
c2 is AnonymousTypes.Customer
c3 is VB$AnonymousType_0`2[System.String,System.Int32]
c4 is VB$AnonymousType_0`2[System.String,System.Int32]
c5 is VB$AnonymousType_1`2[System.String,System.String]
c6 is VB$AnonymousType_2`2[System.String,System.String]
```

The anonymous type name cannot be referenced by the code (because you do not know the generated name), but it can be queried on an object instance. The variables *c3* and *c4* are of the same anonymous type because they have the same fields and properties. Even if *c5* and *c6* have the same properties (type and name), they are in a different order—that is enough for the compiler to create two different anonymous types.

If you use the syntax for a collection initializer, you can create an array of anonymous types, as shown in Listing 3-16.

Listing 3-16   Array of anonymous types

```
Dim ca = {New With {.Name = "Marco", .Country = "Italy"}, _
          New With {.Name = "Tom", .Country = "USA"}, _
          New With {.Name = "Paolo", .Country = "Italy"} _
          }

Dim cs = {New With {.Name = "Marco", .Sports = {"Tennis", "Spinning"}}, _
          New With {.Name = "Tom", .Sports = {"Rugby", "Squash", "Baseball"}}, _
          New With {.Name = "Paolo", .Sports = {"Skateboard", "Windsurf"}} _
          }
```

The first array, *ca*, is made by instances of an anonymous type that have two members of type *String*. The second array, *cs*, is an array of a different anonymous type, which is formed by a string *Name* and an array of strings named *Sports*.

Query Expressions

Visual Basic 9.0 supports the concept of query expressions (a syntax similar to the SQL language used to manipulate data) just as C# 3.0 does. Preliminary documentation of Visual Basic 9.0 talks about query comprehensions to identify this language-integrated syntax for queries. A detailed explanation of all the keywords valid in a query expression will be shown in Chapter 4, "LINQ Syntax Fundamentals." This section illustrates the main syntax differences in query expressions between C# and Visual Basic 9.0. Some of the specific details will be more clear after you read Chapter 4.

A LINQ query can be written in Visual Basic using the *From... Where... Select...* pattern, as shown in Listing 3-17.

Listing 3-17   Simple LINQ query

```
Dim customers() = { _
    New With {.Name = "Marco", .Discount = 4.5}, _
    New With {.Name = "Paolo", .Discount = 3.0}, _
    New With {.Name = "Tom", .Discount = 3.5} _
}

Dim query = _
    From c In customers _
    Where c.Discount > 3 _
    Select New With {c.Name, .Perc = c.Discount / 100}
```

The *Where* clause is optional, but *From* and *Select* are mandatory. If the *Where* clause is present, the predicate used as the *Where* condition is transformed into a lambda expression (as shown in the next section) by the compiler. Another nested function is generated for the projection (the code that follows the *Select* keyword).

In the case of an *Order By* clause, the order of keywords is different than in C# 3.0. For example, consider the C# 3.0 code shown in Listing 3-18.

Listing 3-18   *Order By* in C# 3.0

```
var query =
    from    c in customers
    where   c.Discount > 3
    orderby perc
    select  new {c.Name, Perc = c.Discount / 100)
```

The code in Listing 3-18 can be written in Visual Basic 9.0, as shown in Listing 3-19.

Listing 3-19   *Order By* in Visual Basic 9.0

```
Dim query = _
    From c In customers _
    Where c.Discount > 3 _
    Select r = New With {c.Name, .Perc = c.Discount / 100} _
    Order By r.Perc
```

Note that *Order By* precedes *select* in C# 3.0, but it is immediately after *Select* in Visual Basic 9.0.

Lambda Expressions

C# 3.0 allows you to explicitly write a lambda expression using this syntax:

```
(c) => c.Country == "USA"
( a, b ) => a + b
```

The corresponding syntax in Visual Basic 9.0 is based on the keyword *Function*, as you can see in Listing 3-20.

Listing 3-20   Lambda expressions in Visual Basic 9.0

```
Function(c) c.Country = "USA"
Function( a, b ) a + b
```

Using lambda expressions, you can write more complex query expressions, as shown in Listing 3-21.

Listing 3-21   Use of lambda expressions in query expressions

```
Dim customers As List(Of Customer) = New List(Of Customer)
Dim query = customers.FindAll( Function(c) c.Country = "USA" );
```

Closures

When a query expression contains a delegate as a parameter, in C# 3.0 we use a lambda expression to define the delegate in a shorter and easier way. We can use lambda expressions even in Visual Basic 9.0, and the compiler produces a similar result by creating *closures*, which are delegates that capture their surrounding context and pass them to the underlying method call. For example, with the query in Listing 3-22, the compiler generates two lambda expressions that represent the delegate to be passed to the *Select* and *Where* functions.

Listing 3-22   Closures with query expressions

```
Dim maxPlayers = 2
Dim players = _
    From customer In customers _
    Where customer.Sports.Count > maxPlayers _
    Select customer.Name
```

The two lambda expressions generate two corresponding closures. These closures have the same scope as the method that contains the *players* variable assignment, which uses the lambda expressions. This setup is necessary to access the *maxPlayers* variable. The generated code is equivalent to the following:

```
Dim maxPlayers = 2
Dim players = _
    Enumerable.Select(
        Enumerable.Where( customers,
            Function(customer) customer.Sports.Count > maxPlayers ),
            Function(customer) customer.Name );
```

Visual Basic 9.0 Features Without C# 3.0 Counterparts

Visual Basic 9.0 has some features that do not have an equivalent counterpart in C# 3.0. These features are partially related to LINQ. XML support has a big impact only if you use LINQ to XML. Dynamic interfaces and dynamic identifiers are not necessary to support LINQ from Visual Basic 9.0.

XML Support

Visual Basic 9.0 is a language that implements a particular syntax support for LINQ to XML, consisting of XML literals and late binding over XML. To describe these features, we will use some classes that are part of LINQ to XML: *XDocument*, *XElement*, and *XAttribute*. We will cover these classes in more detail in Chapter 6, "LINQ to XML." For the purpose of describing XML support, it is sufficient to know that these classes represent an XML document, element, and attribute, respectively.

XML Literals

In Visual Basic 9.0, an *XML literal* is considered an expression. If you want to assign a value to an object representing an XML tree, you can simply write that value as an assigned expression, as shown in Listing 3-23.

Listing 3-23   XML literal used as a constant

```
Dim ourBook As XElement
ourBook = _
    <Book Title="Introducing LINQ">
        <Author>Marco Russo</Author>
        <Author>Paolo Pialorsi</Author>
    </Book>
```

We have assigned to *ourBook* an *XElement* instance named *Book* that has an attribute *Title* containing "Introducing LINQ" and two inner *Author* elements containing our names.

The code in Listing 3-23 is translated by the compiler into the following calls:

```
Dim book As XElement
book = New XElement("Book", _
            New XAttribute("Title", "Introducing LINQ"), _
            New XElement("Author", "Marco Russo"), _
            New XElement("Author", "Paolo Pialorsi"))
```

> **Important**   As we said before, XML literals are expressions in Visual Basic 9.0. These expressions do not require a line continuation when defined across multiple lines. More important, either an underscore character or a comment in an XML literal is considered part of the XML and not a line continuation or a comment. This is a big exception against Visual Basic syntax. The end of the expression is defined by the closing tag matching the initial tag.

As usual, we can infer the variable type by placing the initial assignment into the declaration. In the next assignment, we can also see an XML literal defined in a single line:

```
Dim book = <Book Title="Introducing LINQ"></Book>
```

It is important to understand that XML literals are converted into method calls by the compiler. The compiler expects a valid XML syntax. An invalid XML literal produces a compiler error. As you can see in Listing 3-24, the XML literal assigned to *a* has an invalid *Title* attribute (it's missing a "), and the one assigned to *b* has a missing closing tag (it should be *</Book>* instead of *<Book>*).

Listing 3-24   Invalid XML literals

```
Dim a = <Book Title="Invalid Title></Book> ' Error
Dim b = <Book Title="Good Title"><Book>    ' Error
```

Visual Basic 9.0 leverages XML literals, thereby enabling the calls for other expressions. In other words, an XML literal can be an expression that will be evaluated at execution time and not only a constant in the code. For example, imagine that we want to generate an XML literal dynamically for a book and use a string to assign the book title attribute. To do that, we need to "break" the XML literal with a regular Visual Basic 9.0 expression, using the special <%= and %> tags. The code in Listing 3-25 shows how to assign attributes and element content with regular Visual Basic 9.0 expressions.

Listing 3-25   XML literal in a dynamic expression

```
Dim bookTitle = "Introducing LINQ"
Dim author1 = "Marco Russo"
Dim author2 = "Paolo Pialorsi"
Dim book = _
    <Book Title=<%= bookTitle %>>
        <Author><%= author1 %></Author>
        <Author><%= author2 %></Author>
    </Book>
```

> **Warning**   Leave a space after <%= tags and before %> tags; otherwise, the compiler cannot interpret the expression correctly.

The <%= and %> tags define a "hole" into an XML literal that embeds an expression, which is evaluated and substituted into the hole at execution time. These holes are placeholders equivalent to the parameters of an *XElement*, *XAttribute*, or *XDocument* constructor. You can place into holes an expression that is valid in those contexts.

For example, we can define in a dynamic way not only the element and attribute content, but also their names, as shown in Listing 3-26. We also use a string concatenation to assign the *Authors* element, combining two strings with our names, divided by a comma.

Listing 3-26   Dynamic XML tags in an XML literal

```
Dim bookTitle = "Introducing LINQ"
Dim author1 = "Marco Russo"
Dim author2 = "Paolo Pialorsi"
Dim tagBook = "Book"
Dim attrName = "Title"
Dim tagAuthors = "Authors"
Dim book = _
    <<%= tagBook %> <%= attrName %>=<%= bookTitle %>>
        <<%= tagAuthors %>><%= author1 & ", " & author2 %></>
    </>
```

In our opinion, the example in Listing 3-26 is not the best way to use XML literals. Filling the code with angular brackets and "holes" is not the best way to make code readable. The same *book* assignment is more explicit and clear if written with the code shown in Listing 3-27 (for the sake of brevity, we skipped variable declarations).

Listing 3-27   Dynamic XML tags in explicit method calls

```
Dim book = _
    New XElement(tagBook, _
        New XAttribute(attrName, bookTitle), _
        New XElement(tagAuthors, author1 & ", " & author2))
```

> **Note**   We are not saying that you should not use expressions to assign a tag name in an XML literal. Our intention is to emphasize that expressions embedded in XML literals are convenient when the resulting XML structure is immediately understandable. At the extreme, you could define an XML literal without any constant inside (as we did before), but we do not think this is significantly more readable than regular method calls.

If you use an embedded expression to define XML element names, you have to be careful with the syntax required for the closing tag. In such a case, the closing tag must not have the tag name inside. As you can see in Listing 3-28, the closing tag is only </>, without the dynamic tag name defined by the *tagElement* variable.

Listing 3-28   Closing tag for dynamic XML tags

```
Dim tagElement = "Description"
Dim sample = <<%= tagElement %>>Sample element</>
```

A hole in an XML literal can embed just one expression. Because an XML literal is an expression, you can write this apparently useless syntax:

```
Dim book = _
    <Book Title="Introducing LINQ">
        <%= <Publisher>Microsoft Press</Publisher> %>
    </Book>
```

In this case, the *Publisher* element is an XML literal embedded into a hole of the external *Book* element, another XML literal. This example is useful for observing an important syntax detail. The <%= tag must have the evaluated expression in the same line; otherwise, it requires a line continuation. The %> tag must be in the same line as the end of the evaluated expression; otherwise, we need a line continuation in the preceding line.

In other words, the following code is not valid:

```
Dim book = _
    <Book Title="Introducing LINQ">
        <%=
            <Publisher>Microsoft Press</Publisher>
        %>
    </Book>
```

But we can separate code in different lines by using line continuation, as in the following sample. Note that line continuation is always external to XML literals.

```
Dim book = _
    <Book Title="Introducing LINQ">
        <%= _
            <Publisher>Microsoft Press</Publisher> _
        %>
    </Book>
```

If you want to put more expressions into a single hole, you must define an array of elements. For example, to put two separate *Author* elements into a single hole, we can enclose a list of XML literals between brackets, as shown in Listing 3-29. Note the use of a line continuation character after the first element in the array initializer.

Listing 3-29 Nested list of XML literals

```
Dim book = _
    <Book Title="Introducing LINQ">
        <%= { <Author>Marco Russo</Author>, _
            <Author>Paolo Pialorsi</Author> } %>
    </Book>
```

We just used an array to put a list of *Author* elements into a *Book* element. Therefore, we can leverage other methods that generate an *IEnumerable* object to put a list of XML elements into another XML element.

In the statements shown in Listing 3-30, we use a LINQ query to get the list of authors from an array of people. As you can see, an XML literal can embed a query expression that returns a sequence of XML literals, which are built with another embedded expression that references each row returned from the query.

Listing 3-30 Query embedded into an XML literal

```
Dim team = {New {Name := "Marco Russo", Role := "Author"}, _
            New {Name := "Paolo Pialorsi", Role := "Author"}, _
            New {Name := "Roberto Brunetti", Role := "Reviewer"}}
Dim book = _
    <Book Title="Introducing LINQ">
        <%= From person In team _
            Where person.Role = "Author" _
            Select <Author><%= person.Name %></Author> %>
    </Book>
```

By combining LINQ syntax and XML literals, you can generate simple and complex XML data structures containing query results in an easy and efficient way.

Late Binding over XML

When you want access to XML data, you probably need to navigate into an object tree that represents the hierarchical structure of the XML document. Visual Basic 9.0 offers some syntax that simplifies this kind of operation—that is, late-binding operations over XML.

We start by considering an XML list of movies. Each movie item must have one *Title* (as an attribute) and one *Director* (as an element), plus one list of genres for each movie. The following code shows part of the initialization in our sample code:

```
Dim movies = _
<Movies>
    <Movie Title="Fight Club">
        <Genre>Crime</Genre>
        <Genre>Drama</Genre>
```

```
            <Genre>Thriller</Genre>
            <Director>David Fincher</Director>
        </Movie>
        <!-other movies not shown here -->
    </Movies>
```

The first dedicated XML syntax that we show is the *child axis*. If we write *movie.<Genre>*, we get all the genres of the chosen *movie*, as we can see in Listing 3-31.

Listing 3-31   Child axis

```
    Dim fightClub = _
        (From movie In movies.<Movie> _
        Where movie.@Title = "Fight Club" _
        Select movie).First()

    ' Get the first genre
    Dim firstGenre = fightClub.<Genre>(0).Value
    ' Corresponds to: firstGenre = fightClub.Elements("Genre")(0).Value
    Console.WriteLine("First = {0}", firstGenre)

    ' Display all genres
    ' Corresponds to: fightClub.Elements("Genre")
    For Each g In fightClub.<Genre>
        Console.WriteLine(g.Value)
    Next
```

If the query provides only one row, or if we are interested only in the first row of results, we can access the first element of the collection. For example, *fightClub.<Genre>(0)* allows access to a corresponding *XElement* instance. If we need the value of an element or an attribute, we need to read the *Value* property. However, this syntax might return more than one row. In such a case, a loop that iterates over all rows in the sequence might access all of them.

The child axis syntax is translated into a call to *Elements*, specifying the name of the element as an argument. For syntax details, refer to the comments in Listing 3-31.

You can access an attribute through the *attribute axis*. If you write *fightClub.@Title*, you get a string with the value of the attribute, as shown in Listing 3-32.

Listing 3-32   Attribute axis

```
    ' Display the Title attribute of Fight Club movie
    Console.WriteLine(fightClub.@Title)
    ' Corresponds to: Console.WriteLine(fightClub.Attribute("Title").Value)
```

The attribute axis syntax is translated into a call to *Attribute*, specifying the name of the attribute as an argument.

The last operation introduced here is the *descendants axis*. It allows you to get all children of an element, regardless of their position in the hierarchy. You can see in Listing 3-33 that the syntax is similar to the one for the child axis, but there are three dots instead of one.

Listing 3-33   Descendants axis

```
' List of Directors
Dim directors = movies...<Director>
For Each director In directors
    Console.WriteLine(director)
Next
```

In this case, the output of Listing 3-33 (the descendants axis) shows possible duplicates. We could use the *Distinct* operator to "clean up" the output. We will provide more details about this when we discuss LINQ operators in Chapter 4.

We will further analyze the integration with XML of .NET compilers in Chapter 6.

Relaxed Delegates

In Visual Basic version 8.0 and earlier, if you wanted to bind a method to a delegate, the two signatures (method and delegate) had to be exactly the same. This is not necessary in C#—the method simply needs a "compatible" signature. For example, less specialized types in parameters are allowed. Visual Basic 9.0 removes the previous limitation, and you can now legally write code such as that shown in Listing 3-34.

Listing 3-34   Relaxed delegates

```
Public Delegate Sub EventHandler(ByVal s As Object, ByVal e As EventArgs)

Public Class DemoEvent
    Public Event Click As EventHandler
End Class

Module Application
    Public WithEvents A As DemoEvent

    Sub DemoOnClick(ByVal s As Object, ByVal e As Object) Handles A.Click
        Console.WriteLine("Hello World")
    End Sub
    ' ...
End Module
```

In Listing 3-34, we highlighted the line that produces a compilation error in Visual Basic 8.0. To be compiled with Visual Basic 8.0, it should have been written as shown in the following code (in which we have highlighted the changed type of the second parameter):

```
Sub DemoOnClick(ByVal s As Object, ByVal e As EventArgs) Handles A.Click
```

If you do not use the parameters inside the method bound to a delegate, you can skip the whole parameter list from the method declaration. The *Handles* keyword infers the real signature of the method from the corresponding delegate declaration. In Listing 3-35, you can see an alternative way to write the previous *DemoOnClick* method. C# does not permit such syntax, because C# does not have an equivalent to the *Handles* keyword that can be used to infer the missing signature.

Listing 3-35   Relaxed delegates with signature inference

```
Sub RelaxedOnClick2() Handles A.Click
    Console.WriteLine("Hello World from")
End Sub
```

C# 3.0 Features Without Visual Basic 9.0 Counterparts

C# 3.0 has some features that do not have an equivalent in Visual Basic 9.0. These features are the *yield* keyword and *anonymous methods*. Neither of these features is fundamental to supporting LINQ, even if they are useful in many situations that are common when writing code that uses LINQ.

The *yield* Keyword

Visual Basic 9.0 does not have a feature that corresponds to the C# 2.0 *yield* keyword. You can implement iterators in Visual Basic 9.0 by using an iterator design pattern. Remember that *yield* does not require support from the CLR. It is implemented by the compiler that generates the code necessary for implementing the iterator.

 More Info   For more information about closures, see the section called "Closures," earlier in this chapter.

Anonymous Methods

Anonymous methods are not available in Visual Basic 9.0 as a stand-alone feature, but sometimes lambda expressions can be used as a substitute. Closures for lambda expressions are generated by the compiler in a way that is similar to that used by the C# compiler with anonymous methods. However, lambda expressions cannot replace anonymous delegates in every situation.

Summary

In this chapter, we covered the most important new features of Visual Basic 9.0, dividing them into four main sections. The first was about nullable types, which have been part of C# since version 2.0. The second section discussed features matching C# 3.0: local type inference, extension methods, object initialization expressions, anonymous types, query expressions, lambda expressions, and closures. The third section covered features present only in Visual Basic 9.0: XML literals, late binding over XML, and relaxed delegates. Finally, the last section was dedicated to features present in C# 3.0 but not in Visual Basic 9.0: the *yield* keyword and anonymous methods. In the next chapter, you will learn about some of the fundamentals of LINQ syntax.

Chapter 4
LINQ Syntax Fundamentals

Modern programming languages and software development architectures are based more and more on object-oriented design and development. As a result, quite often we need to query and manage objects and collections of items, rather than records and data tables. We also need tools and languages independent from specific data sources or persistence layers. Language Integrated Query (LINQ) allows developers to query and manage sequences of items (objects, entities, database records, XML nodes, and so on) within their software solutions, using a unique programming language independent from their original persistence media. The key feature of LINQ is its integration with widely used programming languages, made possible by the use of a syntax common to all kinds of content.

In this chapter, we will describe the main classes and operators on which LINQ is based as a means of understanding its architecture and to learn its syntax. As we described in Chapter 1, "LINQ Introduction," LINQ provides a basic infrastructure for many different implementations of querying engines, such as LINQ to Objects, LINQ to SQL, LINQ to DataSet, LINQ to Entities, LINQ to XML, and so on. All the query extensions are based on extension methods specialization, which you will read about in this chapter. The examples in this chapter mainly use LINQ to Objects so that we can focus on queries and operators rather than on specific internal implementations of the various flavors of LINQ. In Chapter 5, "LINQ to ADO.NET," and Chapter 6, "LINQ to XML," we will explore some of the query operators further to cover the different implementations of LINQ.

LINQ Queries

LINQ is based on a set of query operators, defined as extension methods, that mainly work with any object that implements *IEnumerable<T>*. (For more details about extension methods, see Chapter 2, "C# Language Features," and Chapter 3, "Microsoft Visual Basic 9.0 Language Features.") This approach makes LINQ a general-purpose querying framework because many lists implement *IEnumerable<T>*, and any developer can implement his or her own. This query infrastructure is also very extensible. Given the architecture of extension methods, developers can specialize a method's behavior based on the type of data they are querying. For instance, LINQ to SQL and LINQ to XML have specialized LINQ operators to handle relational data and XML nodes, respectively.

Query Syntax

To understand query syntax, we will start with a simple example. Consider the following *Developer* type:

```
public class Developer {
    public string Name;
    public string Language;
    public int Age;
}
```

Imagine that you need to query an array of objects of the *Developer* type, using LINQ to Objects, extracting the developers who use C# as their main programming language. The code you might use is shown in Listing 4-1.

Listing 4-1   A simple LINQ query

```
using System;
using System.Linq;
using System.Collections.Generic;

class app {
    static void Main() {
        Developer[] developers = new Developer[] {
            new Developer {Name = "Paolo", Language = "C#"},
            new Developer {Name = "Marco", Language = "C#"},
            new Developer {Name = "Frank", Language = "VB.NET"}};

        IEnumerable<string> developersUsingCsharp =
            from    d in developers
            where   d.Language == "C#"
            select d.Name;

        foreach (string item in developersUsingCsharp) {
            Console.WriteLine(item);
        }
    }
}
```

The result of running this code would be the developers *Paolo* and *Marco*.

The syntax of this query (shown in bold in Listing 4-1) reads something like an SQL statement, although its style is a bit different. To understand it and become familiar with this new syntax, we will try to deconstruct its definition.

Query Expression   A query expression is an expression tree that operates on one or more information sources by applying one or more query operators from either the group of standard query operators or domain-specific operators. In general, the evaluation of a query expression results in a sequence of values. A query expression is evaluated only when its contents are enumerated.

The expression is defined by a selection command:

```
select d.Name
```

applied to a set of items:

```
from d as developers
```

where the *from* clause targets any instance of a class that implements the *IEnumerable<T>* interface. The selection applies a specific filtering condition:

```
where d.Language == "C#"
```

The filtering condition simply translates to an invocation of the *Where* extension method of the *Enumerable* class, defined in the *System.Linq* namespace. The *select* statement is another extension method, named *Select*, provided by the *Enumerable* class.

Tip   The *Enumerable* class, defined in the *System.Linq* namespace, provides many query operators for the LINQ to Objects implementation, defining them as extension methods for types that implement *IEnumerable<T>*.

Starting from the considerations just mentioned, we can rewrite the query expression and resolve its definition into basic elements:

```
IEnumerable<string> expr =
    developers
    .Where(d => d.Language == "C#")
    .Select(d => d.Name);
```

The *Where* method and the *Select* method both receive lambda expressions as arguments. (See Chapter 2 for more information about lambda expressions and their definition and syntax.) These lambda expressions translate to predicates that are based on a set of generic delegate types, defined within the *System.Linq* namespace.

Here is the entire family of generic delegate types available:

```
public delegate T Func< T >();
public delegate T Func< A0, T >( A0 arg0 );
public delegate T Func< A0, A1, T > ( A0 arg0, A1 arg1 );
public delegate T Func< A0, A1, A2, T >( A0 arg0, A1 arg1, A2 arg2 );
public delegate T Func< A0, A1, A3, T > ( A0 arg0, A1 arg1, A2 arg2, A3
    arg3 );
```

Many extension methods of the *Enumerable* class accept these delegates as arguments, and we will use them throughout the examples in this chapter. A final deconstruction of our initial query might be something like Listing 4-2.

Listing 4-2   The first LINQ query translated into basic elements

```
Func<Developer, bool> filteringPredicate = d => d.Language == "C#";
Func<Developer, string> selectionPredicate = d => d.Name;
IEnumerable<string> expr =
    developers
    .Where(filteringPredicate)
    .Select(selectionPredicate);
```

The C# 3.0 compiler, like the Visual Basic 9.0 compiler, translates the LINQ statement (Listing 4-1) into something like the statement shown in Listing 4-2. When you have become familiar with the LINQ syntax (Listing 4-1), it is simpler and easier to write and manage, even if it is optional, and you can always use the equivalent, more verbose version. Nevertheless, sometimes it is necessary to use the direct call to an extension method because query syntax does not cover all possible extension methods.

Full Query Syntax

In the previous section, we defined and deconstructed a simple query over a list of objects. However, LINQ query syntax is more complete and articulated. Every query starts with a *from* clause and ends with either a *select* clause or a *group* clause. The reason to start with a *from* clause instead of a *select* statement, as in SQL syntax, is related to the need to provide Microsoft IntelliSense capabilities within the remaining part of the query, which makes writing conditions, selections, and any other LINQ query clauses easier. A *select* clause projects the result of an expression into an enumerable object. A *group* clause projects the result of an expression into a set of groups, based on a grouping condition, where each group is an enumerable object. The following code shows a prototype of the full syntax of a LINQ query expression:

```
query-expression ::= from-clause query-body

query-body ::=
join-clause*
(from-clause join-clause* | let-clause | where-clause)*
orderby-clause?
(select-clause | groupby-clause)
    query-continuation?

from-clause ::= from itemName in srcExpr

select-clause ::= select selExpr

groupby-clause ::= group selExpr by keyExpr
```

The first *from* clause can be followed by zero or more *from*, *let*, or *where* clauses. A *let* clause applies a name to the result of an expression, while a *where* clause defines a filter that will be applied to include specific items in the results. Each *from* clause is a generator that represents an iteration over a sequence on which query operators (such as the extension methods of *System.Linq.Enumerable*) are applied.

```
let-clause ::= let itemName = selExpr
```

```
where-clause ::= where predExpr
```

A *from* clause can be followed by any number of *join* clauses. The final *select* or *group* clause can be preceded by an *orderby* clause that applies an ordering to the results:

```
join-clause ::=
join itemName in srcExpr on keyExpr equals keyExpr
(into itemName)?
```

```
orderby-clause ::= orderby (keyExpr (ascending | descending)?)*
```

```
query-continuation ::= into itemName query-body
```

We will use query expressions throughout this chapter. Refer to this section when you want to check the syntax of a LINQ query.

Sample Data for Examples

We need to define some data that we will use in the examples in this chapter. We will use a set of customers, each of which has ordered products. The following code defines types and initial values of our sample data.

```csharp
public enum Countries {
    USA,
    Italy,
}

public class Customer {
    public string Name;
    public string City;
    public Countries Country;
    public Order[] Orders;
}

public class Order {
    public int Quantity;
    public bool Shipped;
```

```
    public string Month;
    public int IdProduct;
}

public class Product {
    public int IdProduct;
    public decimal Price;
}

// ------------------------------------------------------
// Initialize a collection of customers with their orders:
// ------------------------------------------------------
customers = new Customer[] {
  new Customer {Name = "Paolo", City = "Brescia", Country = Countries.Italy, Orders =
  new Order[] {
    new Order {Quantity = 3, IdProduct = 1 , Shipped = false, Month = "January"},
    new Order {Quantity = 5, IdProduct = 2 , Shipped = true, Month = "May"}}},
  new Customer {Name = "Marco", City = "Torino", Country = Countries.Italy, Orders =
  new Order[] {
    new Order {Quantity = 10, IdProduct = 1 , Shipped = false, Month = "July"},
    new Order {Quantity = 20, IdProduct = 3 , Shipped = true, Month = "December"}}},
  new Customer {Name = "James", City = "Dallas", Country = Countries.USA, Orders =
  new Order[] {
    new Order {Quantity = 20, IdProduct = 3 , Shipped = true, Month = "December"}}},
  new Customer {Name = "Frank", City = "Seattle", Country = Countries.USA, Orders =
  new Order[] {
    new Order {Quantity = 20, IdProduct = 5 , Shipped = false, Month = "July"}}}};

products = new Product[] {
    new Product {IdProduct = 1, Price = 10 },
    new Product {IdProduct = 2, Price = 20 },
    new Product {IdProduct = 3, Price = 30 },
    new Product {IdProduct = 4, Price = 40 },
    new Product {IdProduct = 5, Price = 50 },
    new Product {IdProduct = 6, Price = 60 }};
```

Query Operators

The remaining sections of this chapter describe the main methods and generic delegates provided by the *System.Linq* namespace to query items with LINQ.

The *Where* Operator

Imagine that you need to list the names and cities of customers from Italy. To filter a set of items, you can use the *Where* operator, which is also called a restriction operator because it restricts a set of items. Listing 4-3 shows a simple example.

Listing 4-3   A query with a restriction

```
var expr =
    from   c in customers
    where  c.Country == Countries.Italy
    select new { c.Name, c.City };
```

Here are the signatures of the *Where* operator:

```
public static IEnumerable<T> Where<T>(
    this IEnumerable<T> source,
    Func<T, bool> predicate);
public static IEnumerable<T> Where<T>(
    this IEnumerable<T> source,
    Func<T, int, bool> predicate);
```

As you can see, two signatures are available. In Listing 4-3, we used the first signature, which enumerates items of the *source* sequence and yields those that verify the predicate (*c.Country == Countries.Italy*). The second signature accepts an additional parameter of type *Integer* for the predicate. This argument is used as a zero-based index of the elements within the *source* sequence. Keep in mind that if you pass null arguments to the predicates, an *ArgumentNullException* error will be thrown. You can use the index parameter to start filtering by a particular index, as shown in Listing 4-4.

Listing 4-4   A query with a restriction and an index-based filter

```
var expr =
    customers
    .Where((c, index) => (c.Country == Countries.Italy && index >= 1))
    .Select(c => c.Name);
```

> **Important**   In Listing 4-4, we cannot use the LINQ query syntax because the *Where* version that we want to call is not supported by an equivalent LINQ query clause. We will use both syntaxes from here onward.

The result of Listing 4-4 will be the list of Italian customers, skipping the first one. The capability to filter items of the *source* sequence by using their positional index is useful when you want to extract a specific page of data from a large sequence of items. Listing 4-5 shows an example.

Listing 4-5   A query with a paging restriction

```
int start = 5;
int end = 10;

var expr =
    customers
    .Where((c, index) => ((index >= start) && (index < end)))
    .Select(c => c.Name);
```

Keep in mind that it is generally not a good practice to store large sequences of data loaded from a database persistence layer in memory; usually, it is better to page data at the persistence layer level. Therefore, use this paging technique only if you have already loaded data into memory. Reloading the current page from a persistence layer is less efficient than directly accessing the sequence already loaded "in memory."

Projection Operators

The following sections describe how to use projection operators. These operators are used to select (or "project") contents from the source enumeration into the result.

Select

In Listing 4-3, you saw an example of defining the result of the query by using the *Select* operator. The signatures for the *Select* operator are shown here:

```
public static IEnumerable<S> Select<T, S>(
    this IEnumerable<T> source,
    Func<T, S> selector);
public static IEnumerable<S> Select<T, S>(
    this IEnumerable<T> source,
    Func<T, int, S> selector);
```

The *Select* operator is one of the projection operators because it projects the query results, making them available through an object that implements *IEnumerable<T>*. This object will enumerate items identified by the *selector* predicate. Like the *Where* operator, *Select* enumerates the *source* sequence and yields the result of the *selector* predicate. Consider the following predicate:

```
var expr = customers.Select(c => c.Name);
```

This predicate's result will be a sequence of customer names (*IEnumerable<string>*). Now consider this example:

```
var expr = customers.Select(c => new { c.Name, c.City });
```

This predicate projects a sequence of an anonymous type, defined as a tuple of *Name* and *City*, for each customer object. With the second overload of *Select*, we can also provide an argument of type *Integer* for the predicate. This zero-based index is used to define the positional index of each item inserted in the resulting sequence.

SelectMany

Imagine that you want to select all the orders of customers from Italy. You could write the query shown in Listing 4-6 using the verbose method.

Listing 4-6   The list of orders made by Italian customers

```
var orders =
    customers
    .Where(c => c.Country == Countries.Italy)
    .Select(c => c.Orders);

foreach(var item in orders) { Console.WriteLine(item); }
```

Because of the behavior of the *Select* operator, the resulting type of this query will be *IEnumerable<Order[]>*, where each item in the resulting sequence represents the array of orders of a single customer. In fact, the *Orders* property of a *Customer* instance is of type *Order[]*. The output of the code in Listing 4-6 would be the following:

```
DevLeap.Linq.Ch4.Operators.Order[]
DevLeap.Linq.Ch4.Operators.Order[]
```

To have a "flat" *IEnumerable<Order>* result type, we need to use the *SelectMany* operator:

```
public static IEnumerable<S> SelectMany<T, S>(
    this IEnumerable<T> source,
    Func<T, IEnumerable<S>> selector);
public static IEnumerable<S> SelectMany<T, S>(
    this IEnumerable<T> source,
    Func<T, int, IEnumerable<S>> selector);
public static IEnumerable<S> SelectMany<T, C, S>(
    this IEnumerable<T> source,
    Func<T, IEnumerable<C>> collectionSelector,
    Func<T, C, S> resultSelector);
```

This operator enumerates the *source* sequence and merges the resulting items, providing them as a single enumerable sequence. The second overload available is analogous to the equivalent overload for *Select*, which allows a zero-based integer index for indexing purposes. Listing 4-7 shows an example.

Listing 4-7   The flattened list of orders made by Italian customers

```
IEnumerable<Order> orders =
    customers
    .Where(c => c.Country == Countries.Italy)
    .SelectMany(c => c.Orders);
```

Using the query expression syntax, the query in Listing 4-7 can be written with the code shown in Listing 4-8.

Listing 4-8   The flattened list of orders made by Italian customers, written with a query expression

```
IEnumerable<Order> orders =
    from   c in customers
    where  c.Country == Countries.Italy
        from   o in c.Orders
        select o;
```

The *select* keyword in query expressions, for all but the initial *from* clause, is translated to invocations of *SelectMany*. In other words, every time you see a query expression with more than one *from* clause, you can apply this rule: the *select* over the first *from* clause is converted to an invocation of *Select*, and the other *select* commands are translated into a *SelectMany* call.

The third overload of *SelectMany* is useful whenever you need to select a custom result from the source set of sequences instead of simply merging their items, as with the two previous overloads. This overload invokes the *collectionSelector* predicate over the *source* sequence and returns the result of the *resultSelector* predicate, applied to each item in the collections selected by *collectionSelector*. In Listing 4-9, you can see an example of this method, used to extract a new anonymous type made from the *Quantity* and *IdProduct* of each order of Italian customers.

Listing 4-9   The list of *Quantity* and *IdProduct* of orders made by Italian customers

```
var items = customers
    .Where(c => c.Country == Countries.Italy)
    .SelectMany(c => c.Orders,
        (c, o) => new {o.Quantity, o.IdProduct});
```

The query in Listing 4-9 can be written with the query expression shown in Listing 4-10.

Listing 4-10   The list of *Quantity* and *IdProduct* of orders made by Italian customers, written with a query expression

```
IEnumerable<Order> orders =
    from   c in customers
    where  c.Country == Countries.Italy
        from   o in c.Orders
        select new {o.Quantity, o.IdProduct};
```

Ordering Operators

Another useful set of operators is the ordering operators group. Ordering operators are used to determine the ordering and direction of elements in output sequences.

OrderBy and OrderByDescending

Sometimes it is helpful to apply an order to the results of a database query. LINQ can order the results of queries, in ascending or descending order, by using ordering operators, just as we do in SQL syntax. For instance, if you need to select the *Name* and *City* of all Italian customers in descending order by *Name*, you can write the corresponding query expression shown in Listing 4-11.

Listing 4-11   A query expression with a descending *orderby* clause

```
var expr =
    from    c in customers
    where   c.Country == Countries.Italy
    orderby c.Name descending
    select  new { c.Name, c.City };
```

The query expression syntax will translate the *orderby* keyword into one of the following ordering extension methods:

```
public static IOrderedSequence<T> OrderBy<T, K>(
    this IEnumerable<T> source,
    Func<T, K> keySelector);
public static IOrderedSequence<T> OrderBy<T, K>(
    this IEnumerable<T> source,
    Func<T, K> keySelector,
    IComparer<K> comparer);
public static IOrderedSequence<T> OrderByDescending<T, K>(
    this IEnumerable<T> source,
    Func<T, K> keySelector);
public static IOrderedSequence<T> OrderByDescending<T, K>(
    this IEnumerable<T> source,
    Func<T, K> keySelector,
    IComparer<K> comparer);
```

As you can see, the two main extension methods, *OrderBy* and *OrderByDescending*, both have two overloads. The methods' names suggest their objective: *OrderBy* is for ascending order, and *OrderByDescending* is for descending order. The *keySelector* argument represents a function that extracts a key, of type *K*, from each item of type *T*, taken from the *source* sequence. The extracted key represents the typed content to be compared by the comparer while ordering, and the *T* type describes the type of each item of the *source* sequence. Both methods have an overload that allows you to provide a custom comparer. If no comparer is provided or the *comparer* argument is null, a default comparer is used (*Comparer<K>.Default*). It is important to emphasize that these ordering methods return not just *IEnumerable<T>* but *IOrderedSequence<T>*, which is an interface that implements *IEnumerable<T>* internally.

The code sample in Listing 4-11 will be translated to the following:

```
var expr =
    customers
    .Where(c => c.Country == Countries.Italy)
```

```
.OrderByDescending(c => c.Name)
.Select(c => new { c.Name, c.City } );
```

ThenBy and ThenByDescending

When you need to order data by many different keys, you can take advantage of the *ThenBy* and *ThenByDescending* operators. Here are their signatures:

```
public static IOrderedSequence<T> ThenBy<T, K>(
    this IOrderedSequence<T> source,
    Func<T, K> keySelector);
public static IOrderedSequence<T> ThenBy<T, K>(
    this IOrderedSequence<T> source,
    Func<T, K> keySelector,
    IComparer<K> comparer);
public static IOrderedSequence<T> ThenByDescending<T, K>(
    this IOrderedSequence<T> source,
    Func<T, K> keySelector);
public static IOrderedSequence<T> ThenByDescending<T, K>(
    this IOrderedSequence<T> source,
    Func<T, K> keySelector,
    IComparer<K> comparer);
```

These operators have signatures similar to *OrderBy* and *OrderByDescending*. The difference is that *ThenBy* and *ThenByDescending* can be applied only to *IOrderedSequence<T>* and not to any *IEnumerable<T>*. Therefore, you can use the *ThenBy* or *ThenByDescending* operator just after the first use of *OrderBy* or *OrderByDescending*. Here is an example:

```
var expr = customers
    .Where(c => c.Country == Countries.Italy)
    .OrderByDescending(c => c.Name)
    .ThenBy(c => c.City)
    .Select(c => new { c.Name, c.City } );
```

In Listing 4-12, you can see the corresponding query expression.

Listing 4-12   A query expression with *orderby* and *thenby*

```
var expr =
    from    c in customers
    where   c.Country == Countries.Italy
    orderby c.Name descending, c.City
    select  new { c.Name, c.City };
```

> **Important**   In the case of multiple occurrences of the same key within a sequence to be ordered, the result is not guaranteed to be "stable." In such conditions, the original ordering cannot be preserved by the comparer.

A custom comparer might be useful when the items in your *source* sequence need to be ordered using custom logic. For instance, imagine that you want to select all the orders of your customers ordered by month:

```
var expr =
    from c in customers
        from    o in c.Orders
        orderby o.Month
        select  o;
```

If you apply the default comparer to the *Month* property of the orders, you will get a result alphabetically ordered. The result is wrong because the *Month* property is just a string and not a number or a date:

```
20 - True - December - 3
20 - True - December - 3
3 - False - January - 1
20 - False - July - 5
10 - False - July - 1
5 - True - May - 2
```

You should use a custom *MonthComparer* that correctly compares months:

```
using System.Globalization;

private class MonthComparer: IComparer<string> {
    public int Compare(string x, string y) {
        DateTime xDate = DateTime.ParseExact(x, "MMMM", new CultureInfo("en-US"));
        DateTime yDate = DateTime.ParseExact(y, "MMMM", new CultureInfo("en-US"));
        return(Comparer<DateTime>.Default.Compare(xDate, yDate));
} }
```

The newly defined custom *MonthComparer* could be passed as a parameter while invoking the *OrderBy* extension method, as in Listing 4-13.

Listing 4-13   A custom comparer used with an *OrderBy* operator

```
IEnumerable<Order> orders =
    customers
    .SelectMany(c => c.Orders)
    .OrderBy(o => o.Month, new MonthComparer());
```

Reverse Operator

Sometimes you need to reverse the result of a query, listing the last item in the result first. LINQ provides a last-ordering operator, called *Reverse*, that allows you to perform this operation:

```
public static IEnumerable<T> Reverse<T>(
    this IEnumerable<T> source);
```

The implementation of *Reverse* is quite simple. It just yields each item in the *source* sequence in reverse order. Listing 4-14 shows an example of its use.

Listing 4-14   The *Reverse* operator applied

```
var expr =
    customers
    .Where(c => c.Country == Countries.Italy)
    .OrderByDescending(c => c.Name)
    .ThenBy(c => c.City)
    .Select(c => new { c.Name, c.City } )
    .Reverse();
```

The *Reverse* operator, like many other operators, does not have a short "alias" in LINQ query expressions. However, we can merge query expression syntax with operators, as shown in Listing 4-15.

Listing 4-15   The *Reverse* operator applied to a query expression with *orderby* and *thenby*

```
var expr =
    (from    c in customers
    where   c.Country == Countries.Italy
    orderby c.Name descending, c.City
    select  new { c.Name, c.City }
    ).Reverse();
```

As you can see, we apply the *Reverse* operator to the expression resulting from Listing 4-11. Under the covers, the inner query expression is first translated to the resulting list of extension methods, and then the *Reverse* method is applied. It is just like Listing 4-14, but easier to write.

Grouping Operators

Now you have seen how to select, filter, and order sequences of items. Sometimes when querying contents, you also need to group results based on specific criteria. To realize content groupings, you use a grouping operator.

The *GroupBy* operator, also called a grouping operator, is the only operator of this family and provides the following overloads:

```
public static IEnumerable<IGrouping<K, T>> GroupBy<T, K>(
    this IEnumerable<T> source, Func<T, K> keySelector);
public static IEnumerable<IGrouping<K, T>> GroupBy<T, K>(
    this IEnumerable<T> source, Func<T, K> keySelector,
    IEqualityComparer<K> comparer);
public static IEnumerable<IGrouping<K, E>> GroupBy<T, K, E>(
    this IEnumerable<T> source, Func<T, K> keySelector,
    Func<T, E> elementSelector);
```

```
public static IEnumerable<IGrouping<K, E>> GroupBy<T, K, E>(
    this IEnumerable<T> source, Func<T, K> keySelector,
    Func<T, E> elementSelector, IEqualityComparer<K> comparer);
```

All of these overloads return *IEnumerable<IGrouping<K, T>>*, where the *IGrouping<K, T>* generic interface is a specialized implementation of *IEnumerable<T>*. This implementation can return a specific *Key* of type *K* for each item within the enumeration:

```
public interface IGrouping<K, T> : IEnumerable<T> {
    K Key { get; }
}
```

From a practical point of view, a type that implements this generic interface is simply a typed enumeration with an identifying type *Key* for each item. All the *GroupBy* methods work on a *source* sequence as usual, and they call the *keySelector* function to extract the *Key* value from each item to group results based on the different *Key* values. The *elementSelector* argument, if present, defines a function that maps the source element within the *source* sequence to the destination element of the resulting sequence. If you do not specify the *elementSelector*, elements are mapped directly from the source to the destination. (You will see an example of this later in the chapter, in Listing 4-18.)

The *GroupBy* method selects pairs of keys and items for each item in *source*, using the *keySelector* predicate and, if present, the *elementSelector* argument. Then it yields a sequence of *IGrouping<K, T>* objects, where each group consists of a sequence of items with a common *Key* value. The last optional argument you can pass to the method is a custom *comparer*, which is useful when you need to compare key values and define group membership. If no custom *comparer* is provided, the *EqualityComparer<K>.Default* is used. The order of keys and items within each group corresponds to their occurrence within the *source*. Listing 4-16 shows an example of using the *GroupBy* operator.

Listing 4-16   The *GroupBy* operator used to group customers by *Country*

```
var expr = customers.GroupBy(c => c.Country);

foreach(IGrouping<Countries, Customer> customerGroup in expr) {
    Console.WriteLine("Country: {0}", customerGroup.Key);
    foreach(var item in customerGroup) {
        Console.WriteLine(item);
    }
}
```

As Listing 4-16 shows, you need to enumerate all group keys before iterating over the items contained within each group. Every group is an instance of a type that implements *IGrouping<Countries, Customer>*, because we are using the default *elementSelector* that directly projects the source *Customer* instances into the result. In query expressions, the *GroupBy* operator can be defined using the *group ... by ...* syntax, which is shown in Listing 4-17.

Listing 4-17   A query expression with a *group by* syntax

```
var expr =
    from  c in customers
    group c by c.Country;

foreach(IGrouping<Countries, Customer> customerGroup in expr) {
    Console.WriteLine("Country: {0}", customerGroup.Key);
    foreach(var item in customerGroup) {
        Console.WriteLine(item);
    }
}
```

The code defined in Listing 4-17 is semantically equivalent to the code shown in Listing 4-16.

Listing 4-18 is another example of grouping, this time with a custom *elementSelector*.

Listing 4-18   The *GroupBy* operator used to group customer names by *Country*

```
var expr =
    customers
    .GroupBy(c => c.Country, c => c.Name);

foreach(IGrouping<Countries, string> customerGroup in expr) {
    Console.WriteLine("Country: {0}", customerGroup.Key);
    foreach(var item in customerGroup) {
        Console.WriteLine("  {0}", item);
    }
}
```

Here is the result of this code:

```
Country: Italy
  Paolo
  Marco
Country: USA
  James
  Frank
```

In this last example, the result is a class that implements *IGrouping<Countries, string>*, because the *elementSelector* predicate projects only the customers' names (of type *string*) into the output sequence.

Join Operators

Join operators are used to define relationships within sequences in LINQ queries. From a SQL and relational point of view, almost every query requires joining one or more tables. In LINQ, a set of join operators is defined to implement this behavior.

Join

The first operator of this group is of course the *Join* method, which is defined by the following signatures:

```
public static IEnumerable<V> Join<T, U, K, V>(
    this IEnumerable<T> outer,
    IEnumerable<U> inner,
    Func<T, K> outerKeySelector,
    Func<U, K> innerKeySelector,
    Func<T, U, V> resultSelector);
public static IEnumerable<V> Join<T, U, K, V>(
    this IEnumerable<T> outer,
    IEnumerable<U> inner,
    Func<T, K> outerKeySelector,
    Func<U, K> innerKeySelector,
    Func<T, U, V> resultSelector,
    IEqualityComparer<K> comparer);
```

Join requires a set of four generic types. The *T* type represents the type of the *outer* source sequence, and the *U* type describes the type of the *inner* source sequence. The predicates *outerKeySelector* and *innerKeySelector* define how to extract the identifying keys from the *outer* and *inner* source sequence items, respectively. These keys are both of type *K*, and their equivalence defines the join condition. The *resultSelector* predicate defines what to project into the result sequence, which will be an implementation of *IEnumerable<V>*. *V* is the last generic type needed by the operator, and it defines the type of each single item in the join result sequence. The second overload of the method has an additional custom equality comparer, used to compare the keys. If the *comparer* argument is NULL or if the first overload of the method is invoked, a default key comparer (*EqualityComparer<TKey>.Default*) will be used.

Here is an example that will make the use of *Join* more clear. Think about our customers, with their orders and products. In Listing 4-19, a query joins orders with their corresponding products.

Listing 4-19   The *Join* operator used to map orders with products

```
var expr =
    customers
    .SelectMany(c => c.Orders)
    .Join( products,
           o => o.IdProduct,
           p => p.IdProduct,
           (o, p) => new {o.Month, o.Shipped, p.IdProduct, p.Price });
```

The following is the result of the query:

```
{Month=January, Shipped=False, IdProduct=1, Price=10}
{Month=May, Shipped=True, IdProduct=2, Price=20}
{Month=July, Shipped=False, IdProduct=1, Price=10}
{Month=December, Shipped=True, IdProduct=3, Price=30}
{Month=January, Shipped=True, IdProduct=3, Price=30}
{Month=July, Shipped=False, IdProduct=4, Price=40}
```

In this example, *orders* represents the outer sequence and *products* is the inner sequence. The *o* and *p* used in lambda expressions are of type *Order* and *Product*, respectively. Internally, the operator collects the elements of the *inner* sequence into a hash table, using their keys extracted with *innerKeySelector*. It then enumerates the *outer* sequence and maps its elements, based on the *Key* value extracted with *outerKeySelector*, to the hash table of items. Because of its implementation, the *Join* operator result sequence keeps the order of the *outer* sequence first, and then uses the order of the *inner* sequence for each *outer* sequence element.

From an SQL point of view, the example in Listing 4-19 can be thought of as an inner equijoin somewhat like the following SQL query:

```
SELECT     o.Month, o.Shipped, p.IdProduct, p.Price
FROM       Orders AS o
INNER JOIN Products AS p
      ON   o.IdProduct = p.IdProduct
```

If you want to translate the SQL syntax into the *Join* operator syntax, you can think about the columns selection in SQL as the *resultSelector* predicate, while the equality condition on *IdProduct* columns (of orders and products) corresponds to the pair of *innerKeySelector* and *outerKeySelector* predicates.

The *Join* operator has a corresponding LINQ syntax, which is shown in Listing 4-20.

Listing 4-20   The *Join* operator query expression syntax

```
var expr =
    from c in customers
        from  o in c.Orders
        join  p in products
              on o.IdProduct equals p.IdProduct
        select new {o.Month, o.Shipped, p.IdProduct, p.Price };
```

Important   The order of items to relate (*o.IdProduct equals p.IdProduct*) in LINQ query syntax must have the outer sequence first and the inner sequence after; otherwise, the LINQ query will not compile. This requirement is different from standard SQL queries, in which item ordering does not matter.

GroupJoin

In cases in which you need to define something similar to a LEFT OUTER JOIN or a RIGHT OUTER JOIN, you need to use the *GroupJoin* operator. Its signatures are quite similar to the *Join* operator:

```
public static IEnumerable<V> GroupJoin<T, U, K, V>(
    this IEnumerable<T> outer,
    IEnumerable<U> inner,
    Func<T, K> outerKeySelector,
```

```
      Func<U, K> innerKeySelector,
      Func<T, IEnumerable<U>, V> resultSelector);
public static IEnumerable<V> GroupJoin<T, U, K, V>(
   this IEnumerable<T> outer,
   IEnumerable<U> inner,
   Func<T, TKey> outerKeySelector,
   Func<U, TKey> innerKeySelector,
   Func<T, IEnumerable<U>, V> resultSelector,
   IEqualityComparer<TKey> comparer);
```

The only difference is the definition of the *resultSelector* predicate. It requires an instance of *IEnumerable<U>*, instead of a single object of type *U*, because it projects a hierarchical result of type *IEnumerable<V>*, made of a selection of each item extracted from the *inner* sequence joined with a group of items, of type *U*, extracted from the *outer* sequence.

As a result of this behavior, the output is not a flattened outer equijoin, which would be produced by using the *Join* operator, but a hierarchical sequence of items. Nevertheless, you can define queries using *GroupJoin* with results equivalent to the *Join* operator, whenever the mapping is a one-to-one relationship. In case of the absence of a corresponding element group in the *inner* sequence, the *GroupJoin* operator extracts the *outer* sequence element paired with an empty sequence (*Count = 0*). In Listing 4-21, you can see an example of this operator.

Listing 4-21   The *GroupJoin* operator used to map products with orders, if present

```
var expr =
    products
     .GroupJoin(
        customers.SelectMany(c => c.Orders),
        p => p.IdProduct,
        o => o.IdProduct,
        (p, orders) => new { p.IdProduct, Orders = orders });

foreach(var item in expr) {
    Console.WriteLine("Product: {0}", item.IdProduct);
    foreach (var order in item.Orders) {
        Console.WriteLine("    {0}", order); }}
```

The following is the result of Listing 4-21:

```
Product: 1
    3 - False - January - 1
    10 - False - July - 1
Product: 2
    5 - True - May - 2
Product: 3
    20 - True - December - 3
    10 - True - January - 3
Product: 4
Product: 5
    20 - False - July - 5
Product: 6
```

You can see that products 4 and 6 have no mapping orders, but the query returns them nonetheless. You can think about this operator like a SELECT ... FOR XML AUTO query in Transact-SQL in Microsoft SQL Server 2000 and 2005. In fact, it returns results hierarchically grouped like a set of XML nodes nested within their parent nodes, similar to the default result of a FOR XML AUTO query.

In a query expression, the *GroupJoin* operator is defined as a *join ... into ...* clause. The query expression shown in Listing 4-22 is equivalent to Listing 4-21.

Listing 4-22   A query expression with a *join into* clause

```
var customersOrders =
    from c in customers
        from o in c.Orders
        select o;

var expr =
    from   p in products
    join   o in customersOrders
               on p.IdProduct equals o.IdProduct
               into orders
    select new { p.IdProduct, Orders = orders };
```

In this example, we first define an expression called *customersOrders* to extract the flat list of orders. (This expression still uses the *SelectMany* operator.) We could also define a single query expression, nesting the *customersOrders* expression within the main query. This approach is shown in Listing 4-23.

Listing 4-23   The query expression of Listing 4-22 in its compact version

```
var expr =
    from   p in products
    join   o in (
           from c in customers
               from   o in c.Orders
               select o
           ) on p.IdProduct equals o.IdProduct
           into orders
    select new { p.IdProduct, Orders = orders };
```

Set Operators

Our journey through LINQ operators continues with a group of methods that are used to handle sets of data, applying common set operations (*union*, *intersect*, and *except*) and selecting unique occurrences of items (*distinct*).

Distinct

Imagine that you want to extract all products that are mapped to orders, avoiding duplicates. This requirement could be solved in standard SQL using a DISTINCT clause within a JOIN query. LINQ provides a *Distinct* operator, a member of the set operators. Its signature is quite simple. It requires just a *source* sequence, from which all the distinct occurrences of items will be yielded. An example of the operator is shown in Listing 4-24.

```
public static IEnumerable<T> Distinct<T>(
    this IEnumerable<T> source);
```

Listing 4-24   The *Distinct* operator applied to the list of products used in orders

```
var expr =
    customers
    .SelectMany(c => c.Orders)
    .Join(products,
          o => o.IdProduct,
          p => p.IdProduct,
          (o, p) => p)
    .Distinct();
```

Distinct does not have an equivalent query expression clause; hence, as we did in Listing 4-15, we can apply this operator to the result of a query expression, as shown in Listing 4-25.

Listing 4-25   The *Distinct* operator applied to a query expression

```
var expr =
    (from c in customers
          from  o in c.Orders
          join  p in products
                on o.IdProduct equals p.IdProduct
          select p
    ).Distinct();
```

By default, *Distinct* compares and identifies elements using their *GetHashCode* and *Equals* methods because, internally, it uses a default comparer of type *EqualityComparer<T>.Default*. We can, if necessary, override our type behavior to change the *Distinct* result, or we can just use the second overload of the *Distinct* method.

```
public static IEnumerable<T> Distinct<T>(
    this IEnumerable<T> source,
    IEqualityComparer<T> comparer);
```

This last overload accepts a *comparer* argument, available to provide a custom comparer for instances of type *T*.

> **Note**   We will see an example of how to compare reference types in the *Union* operator examples in Listing 4-26.

Union, Intersect, and Except

Within the set operators group, three more operators are useful for classic set operations. They are *Union*, *Intersect*, and *Except*, and they share a similar definition:

```
public static IEnumerable<T> Union<T>(
    this IEnumerable<T> first,
    IEnumerable<T> second);
public static IEnumerable<T> Union<T>(
    this IEnumerable<T> first,
    IEnumerable<T> second,
    IEqualityComparer<T> comparer);
public static IEnumerable<T> Intersect<T>(
    this IEnumerable<T> first,
    IEnumerable<T> second);
public static IEnumerable<T> Intersect<T>(
    this IEnumerable<T> first,
    IEnumerable<T> second,
    IEqualityComparer<T> comparer);
public static IEnumerable<T> Except<T>(
    this IEnumerable<T> first,
    IEnumerable<T> second);
public static IEnumerable<T> Except<T>(
    this IEnumerable<T> first,
    IEnumerable<T> second,
    IEqualityComparer<T> comparer);
```

The *Union* operator yields the *first* sequence elements and the *second* sequence elements, skipping duplicates. For instance, in Listing 4-26, you can see how to merge the orders of the second customer with the orders of the third.

Listing 4-26   The *Union* operator applied to the second and third customer orders

```
var expr = customers[1].Orders.Union(customers[2].Orders);
```

As with the *Distinct* operator, in *Union*, *Intersect*, and *Except*, the elements are compared by using the *GetHashCode* and *Equals* methods in the first overload, or by using a custom *comparer* in the second overload. Here is the result of Listing 4-26:

```
10 - False - July - 1
20 - True - December - 3
20 - True - December - 3
```

The result might seem unexpected because we have two rows that appear to be the same. However, if you look at the initialization code used in all of our examples, each order is a different instance of the *Order* reference type. Even if the second order of the second customer is semantically equal to the first order of the third customer, they have two different hash codes. You can see this effect in the following code, where the two semantically equivalent *Order* instances are in bold:

```
customers[1] = new Customer {Name = "Marco", City = "Torino",
    Country = Countries.Italy, Orders = new Order[] {
    new Order {Quantity = 10, IdProduct = 1 ,
      Shipped = false, Month = "July"},
    new Order {Quantity = 20, IdProduct = 3 ,
      Shipped = true, Month = "December"}}};

customers[2] = new Customer {Name = "James", City = "Dallas",
    Country = Countries.USA, Orders = new Order[] {
    new Order {Quantity = 20, IdProduct = 3 ,
      Shipped = true, Month = "December"}}};
```

We have not defined a value type semantic for our *Order* reference type. To get the expected result, we can implement a value type semantic by overriding the *GetHashCode* and *Equals* implementations of the type to be compared. In this situation, it might be useful to do that, as you can see in this new *Order* implementation:

```
public class Order {
    public int Quantity;
    public bool Shipped;
    public string Month;
    public int IdProduct;

    public override string ToString() {
        return String.Format("{0} - {1} - {2} - {3}",
        this.Quantity, this.Shipped, this.Month, this.IdProduct);
    }

    public override bool Equals(object obj) {
        if (!(obj is Order))
            return false;
        else {
            Order o = (Order)obj;
            return(o.IdProduct == this.IdProduct &&
                o.Month == this.Month &&
                o.Quantity == this.Quantity &&
                o.Shipped == this.Shipped); }
    }

    public override int GetHashCode() {
        return String.Format("{0}|{1}|{2}|{3}", this.IdProduct,
          this.Month, this.Quantity, this.Shipped).GetHashCode();
    }
}
```

Another way to get the correct result is to use the second overload of the *Union* method, providing a custom comparer for the *Order* type. A final way to get the expected distinct behavior is to define the *Order* type as a value type, using *struct* instead of *class* in its declaration. By the way, it is not always possible to define a *struct*, because sometimes you need to implement an object-oriented infrastructure using type inheritance.

```
// Using struct instead of class, we get a value type
public struct Order {
    public int Quantity;
    public bool Shipped;
    public string Month;
    public int IdProduct;
}
```

Remember that an anonymous type is defined as a reference type with a value type semantic. In other words, all anonymous types are defined as a class with an override of *GetHashCode* and *Equals* written by the compiler.

In Listing 4-27, you can find an example of using *Intersect* and *Except*.

Listing 4-27   The *Intersect* and *Except* operators applied to the second and third customer orders

```
var expr1 = customers[1].Orders.Intersect(customers[2].Orders);
var expr2 = customers[1].Orders.Except(customers[2].Orders);
```

The *Intersect* operator yields only the elements that occur in both sequences, and the *Except* operator yields all the elements in the *first* sequence that are not present in the *second* sequence. Once again, there are no compact clauses to define set operators in query expressions, but we can apply them to LINQ query results, as in Listing 4-28.

Listing 4-28   Set operators applied to query expressions

```
var expr =
    (from c in customers
        from   o in c.Orders
        where  c.Country == Countries.Italy
        select o
    ).Intersect(
        from c in customers
            from   o in c.Orders
            where  c.Country == Countries.USA
            select o);
```

Value Type vs. Reference Type Semantic   Remember that all the considerations for *Union* and *Distinct* operators are also valid for *Intersect* and *Except*. In general, they are valid for each operation that involves a comparison of two items made by LINQ to Objects. The result of the *Intersect* operation illustrated in Listing 4-28 is an empty set whenever the *Order* type is a reference type with no overload operators defined, like the one defined at the beginning of this chapter, in case we do not provide a custom comparer. If you define *Order* as a value type (using *struct* instead of *class*), you get an order (20 - True - December - 3) as an *Intersection* result. Once again, we want to emphasize that when using LINQ, it is better to use types with a value type semantic, even if they are reference types, so that you get consistent behavior across all regular and anonymous types.

Aggregate Operators

At times, you need to make some aggregations over sequences to make calculations on source items. To accomplish this, LINQ provides the family of aggregate operators that implement the most common aggregate functions: *Count, LongCount, Sum, Min, Max, Average*, and *Aggregate*. Many of these operators are simple to use because their behavior is easy to understand.

Count and LongCount

Imagine that you want to list all customers, each one followed by the number of orders the customer has placed. In Listing 4-29, you can see an equivalent syntax, based on the *Count* operator.

Listing 4-29   The *Count* operator applied to customer orders

```
var expr =
    from  c in customers
    select new {c.Name, c.City, c.Country, OrdersCount = c.Orders.Count() };
```

The *Count* operator provides a couple of signatures, as does the *LongCount* operator:

```
public static int Count<T>(
    this IEnumerable<T> source);
public static int Count<T>(
    this IEnumerable<T> source,
    Func<T, bool> predicate);
public static long LongCount<T>(
    this IEnumerable<T> source);
public static long LongCount<T>(
    this IEnumerable<T> source,
    Func<T, bool> predicate);
```

The signature shown in Listing 4-29 is the common and simpler one that simply counts items in the *source* sequence. The second method overload accepts a non-nullable *predicate*, which is used to filter the items to count. *LongCount* variations simply return a *long* instead of an *integer*.

Sum

The *Sum* operator requires more attention because it has multiple definitions:

```
public static Numeric Sum(
    this IEnumerable<Numeric> source);
public static Numeric Sum<T>(
    this IEnumerable<T> source,
    Func<T, Numeric> selector);
```

We used *Numeric* in the syntax to generalize the return type of the *Sum* operator. In practice, it has many definitions, one for each of the main *Numeric* types: *int, int?, long, long?, float, float?, double, double?, decimal*, and *decimal?*.

> **Important** As you probably know, in C# 2.0 and later, the question mark that appears after a value type name (*T?*) defines a nullable type (*Nullable<T>*) of this type. For instance, *int?* means *Nullable<System.Int32>*.

The first implementation sums the *source* sequence items, assuming that the items are all the same numeric type, and returns the result. In the case of an empty *source* sequence, zero is returned. In the case of nullable types, the result might be null. This implementation can be used when the items can be summed directly. For example, we can sum an array of integers as in this code:

```
int[] values = { 1, 3, 9, 29 };
int   total  = values.Sum();
```

When the sequence is not made up of simple *Numeric* types, we need to extract values to be summed from each item in the *source* sequence. To do that, we can use the second overload, which accepts a *selector* argument. You can see an example of this syntax in Listing 4-30.

Listing 4-30   The *Sum* operator applied to customer orders

```
var customersOrders =
    from c in customers
        from  o in c.Orders
        join  p in products
              on o.IdProduct equals p.IdProduct
        select new { c.Name, OrderAmount = o.Quantity * p.Price };

var expr =
    from   c in customers
    join   o in customersOrders
           on c.Name equals o.Name
           into customersWithOrders
    select new { c.Name,
                 TotalAmount = customersWithOrders.Sum(o => o.OrderAmount) };
```

In Listing 4-30, we join customers with the *customersOrders* sequence, returning for each customer the total number of orders, calculated with the *Sum* operator. As usual, we can collapse the previous code using nested queries, which is the approach shown in Listing 4-31.

Listing 4-31   The *Sum* operator applied to customer orders, with a nested query

```
var expr =
    from   c in customers
    join   o in (
           from c in customers
               from  o in c.Orders
               join  p in products
                     on o.IdProduct equals p.IdProduct
               select new { c.Name, OrderAmount = o.Quantity * p.Price }
           ) on c.Name equals o.Name
           into customersWithOrders
    select new { c.Name,
                 TotalAmount = customersWithOrders.Sum(o => o.OrderAmount) };
```

SQL vs. LINQ Query Syntax

At this point, we want to make a comparison with SQL syntax, because there are similarities but also important differences. The following is an SQL statement similar to the query expression in Listing 4-31, assuming that customer names are unique:

```
SELECT    c.Name, SUM(o.OrderAmount) AS OrderAmount
FROM      customers AS c
INNER JOIN (
    SELECT     c.Name, o.Quantity * p.Price AS OrderAmount
    FROM       customers AS c
    INNER JOIN orders AS o ON c.Name = o.Name
    INNER JOIN products AS p ON o.IdProduct = p.IdProduct
    ) AS o
ON        c.Name = o.Name
GROUP BY c.Name
```

You can see that this SQL syntax is redundant. In fact, we can obtain the same result with this simpler SQL query:

```
SELECT    c.Name, SUM(o.OrderAmount) AS OrderAmount
FROM      customers AS c
INNER JOIN (
    SELECT     o.Name, o.Quantity * p.Price AS OrderAmount
    FROM       orders AS o
    INNER JOIN products AS p ON o.IdProduct = p.IdProduct
    ) AS o
ON        c.Name = o.Name
GROUP BY c.Name
```

But it can be simpler and shorter still, as in the following SQL query:

```
SELECT    c.Name, SUM(o.Quantity * p.Price) AS OrderAmount
FROM      customers AS c
INNER JOIN orders AS o ON c.Name = o.Name
INNER JOIN products AS p ON o.IdProduct = p.IdProduct
GROUP BY    c.Name
```

If we started from this last SQL query and tried to write a corresponding query expression syntax using LINQ, we would probably encounter some difficulties. The reason is that SQL queries data through relationships, but all data is flat (in tables) until it is queried. On the other side, LINQ handles data that can have native hierarchical relationships, just as our Customer/Orders/Products data. This difference implies that sometimes one approach has advantages over the other and vice versa, depending on the kind of query and the kind of data you are working on.

For these reasons, the best expression of a query can appear differently in SQL and in LINQ query expression syntax, even if the query is getting the same results from the same data.

Min and *Max*

Within the set of aggregate operators, *Min* and *Max* calculate the minimum and maximum values of the source sequence, respectively. Both of these extension methods provide a rich set of overloads:

```
public static Numeric Min/Max(
    this IEnumerable<Numeric> source);
public static T Min<T>/Max<T>(
    this IEnumerable<T> source);
public static Numeric Min<T>/Max<T>(
    this IEnumerable<T> source,
    Func<T, Numeric> selector);
public static S Min<T, S>/Max<T, S>(
    this IEnumerable<T> source,
    Func<T, S> selector);
```

The first signature, as in the *Sum* operator, provides many definitions for the main numeric types (*int, int?, long, long?, float, float?, double, double?, decimal,* and *decimal?*), and it computes the minimum or maximum value on an arithmetic basis, using the elements of the *source* sequence. This signature is useful when the source elements are numbers by themselves, as in Listing 4-32.

Listing 4-32   The *Min* operator applied to order quantities

```
var expr =
    (from c in customers
            from  o in c.Orders
            select o.Quantity
    ).Min();
```

The second signature computes the minimum or maximum value of the source elements regardless of their type. The comparison is made using the *IComparable<T>* interface implementation, if supported by the source elements, or the nongeneric *IComparable* interface implementation. If the source type *T* does not implement either of these interfaces, an *ArgumentException* error will be thrown, with an *Exception.Message* equal to "At least one object must implement *IComparable.*" To examine this situation, take a look at Listing 4-33, in which the resulting anonymous type does not implement either of the interfaces required by the *Min* operator.

Listing 4-33   The *Min* operator applied to wrong types (thereby throwing an *ArgumentException*)

```
var expr =
    (from c in customers
            from o in c.Orders
            select new { o.Quantity}
    ).Min();
```

In the case of an empty source or null source values, the result will be null whenever the *Numeric* type is a nullable type; otherwise, *ArgumentNullException* will be thrown. The *selector* predicate, available in the last two signatures, defines the function with which to extract values from the *source* sequence elements. For instance, you can use these overloads to avoid errors related to missing interface implementations (*IComparable<T>/IComparable*), as in Listing 4-34.

Listing 4-34   The *Max* operator applied to custom types, with a value selector

```
var expr =
    (from c in customers
        from o in c.Orders
        select new { o.Quantity}
    ).Min(o => o.Quantity);
```

Average

The *Average* operator calculates the arithmetic average of a set of values, extracted from a source sequence. Like the previous operators, this function works with the source elements themselves or with values extracted using a *selector* predicate:

```
public static Result Average(
    this IEnumerable<Numeric> source);
public static Result Average<T>(
    this IEnumerable<T> source,
    Func<T, Numeric> selector);
```

The *Numeric* type can be *int, int?, long, long?, float, float?, double, double?, decimal*, or *decimal?*. The *Result* type always reflects the "nullability" of the numeric type. When the *Numeric* type is *int* or *long*, the *Result* type is *double*. When the *Numeric* type is *int?* or *long?*, the *Result* type is *double?*. Otherwise, the *Numeric* and *Result* types are the same.

When the sum of the values used to compute the arithmetic average is too large for the result type, an *OverflowException* error is thrown. Because of its definition, the *Average* operator's first signature can be invoked only on a *Numeric* sequence. If you want to invoke it on a source sequence, you need to provide a *selector* predicate. In Listing 4-35, you can see an example of both of the overloads.

Listing 4-35   Both *Average* operator signatures applied to product prices

```
var expr =
    (from p in products
    select p.Price
    ).Average();
var expr =
    (from p in products
    select new { p.Price }
    ).Average(p => p.Price);
```

The second signature is useful when you are defining a query in which the average is just one of the results to extract. An example is shown in Listing 4-36, where we extract all customers and their average order amounts.

Listing 4-36   Customers and their average order amounts

```
var expr =
    from  c in customers
    join  o in (
          from c in customers
              from  o in c.Orders
              join  p in products
                    on o.IdProduct equals p.IdProduct
              select new { c.Name, OrderAmount = o.Quantity * p.Price }
          ) on c.Name equals o.Name
          into customersWithOrders
    select new { c.Name,
                 AverageAmount = customersWithOrders.Average(o =>
  o.OrderAmount) };
```

The results will be similar to the following:

```
{Name=Paolo, AverageAmount=65}
{Name=Marco, AverageAmount=350}
{Name=James, AverageAmount=600}
{Name=Frank, AverageAmount=1000}
```

Aggregate

The last operator in this set is *Aggregate*. Take a look at its definition:

```
public static T Aggregate<T>(
    this IEnumerable<T> source,
    Func<T, T, T> func);
public static U Aggregate<T, U>(
    this IEnumerable<T> source,
    U seed,
    Func<U, T, U> func);
public static V Aggregate<T, U, V>(
    this IEnumerable<T> source,
    U seed,
    Func<U, T, U> func,
    Func<U, V> resultSelector);
```

This operator repeatedly invokes the *func* function, storing the result in an accumulator. Every step calls the function with the current accumulator value as the first argument, starting from *seed*, and with the current element within the *source* sequence as the second argument. At the end of the iteration, the operator returns the final accumulator value.

The only difference between the first two signatures is that the second requires an explicit value for the *seed* of type U. The first signature uses the first element in the *source* sequence as the *seed* and infers the *seed* type from the *source* sequence itself. The third signature looks like the second, but it requires a *resultSelector* predicate to call when extracting the final result.

In Listing 4-37, we use the *Aggregate* operator to extract the most expensive order for each customer.

Listing 4-37   Customers and their most expensive orders

```
var expr =
    from    c in customers
    join    o in (
            from c in customers
                from    o in c.Orders
                join    p in products
                        on o.IdProduct equals p.IdProduct
                select new { c.Name, o.IdProduct,
                                OrderAmount = o.Quantity * p.Price }
            ) on c.Name equals o.Name
            into orders
    select new { c.Name,
                MaxOrderAmount =
                    orders
                    .Aggregate((t, s) => t.OrderAmount > s.OrderAmount ?
                                            t : s)
                    .OrderAmount };
```

As you can see, the function called by the *Aggregate* operator compares the *OrderAmount* property of each order executed by the current customer and accumulates the more expensive one. At the end of each customer aggregation, the accumulator will contain the most expensive order, and its *OrderAmount* property will be projected into the final result, coupled with the customer *Name* property. The following is the output from this query:

```
{Name=Paolo, MaxOrderAmount=100}
{Name=Marco, MaxOrderAmount=600}
{Name=James, MaxOrderAmount=600}
{Name=Frank, MaxOrderAmount=1000}
```

In Listing 4-38, you can see another sample of aggregation. This example calculates the total ordered amount for each product.

Listing 4-38   Products and their ordered amounts

```
var expr =
    from    p in products
    join    o in (
            from c in customers
                from    o in c.Orders
                join    p in products
                        on o.IdProduct equals p.IdProduct
                select new { p.IdProduct, OrderAmount = o.Quantity * p.Price }
            ) on p.IdProduct equals o.IdProduct
            into orders
```

```
select new { p.IdProduct,
              TotalOrderedAmount =
                orders
                .Aggregate(0m, (a, o) => a += o.OrderAmount)};
```

Here is the output of this query:

```
{IdProduct=1, TotalOrderedAmount=130}
{IdProduct=2, TotalOrderedAmount=100}
{IdProduct=3, TotalOrderedAmount=1200}
{IdProduct=4, TotalOrderedAmount=0}
{IdProduct=5, TotalOrderedAmount=1000}
{IdProduct=6, TotalOrderedAmount=0}
```

In this second sample, the aggregate function uses an accumulator of *Decimal* type. It is initialized to zero (*seed = 0m*) and accumulates the *OrderAmount* values for every step. The result of this function will also be a *Decimal* type.

Both of the previous examples could also be defined by invoking the *Max* or *Sum* operators, respectively. They are shown in this section to help you learn about the *Aggregate* operator's behavior. In general, keep in mind that the *Aggregate* operator is useful whenever there are no specific aggregation operators available; otherwise, you should use an operator such as *Min*, *Max*, *Sum*, and so on. For instance, consider the example in Listing 4-39.

Listing 4-39   Customers and their most expensive orders paired with the month of execution

```
var expr =
    from   c in customers
    join   o in (
           from c in customers
               from   o in c.Orders
               join   p in products
                      on o.IdProduct equals p.IdProduct
               select new { c.Name, o.IdProduct, o.Month,
                               OrderAmount = o.Quantity * p.Price }
           ) on c.Name equals o.Name into orders
    select new { c.Name,
                MaxOrder =
                    orders
                    .Aggregate( new { Amount = 0m, Month = String.Empty },
                                (t, s) => t.Amount > s.OrderAmount
                                          ? t
                                          : new { Amount = s.OrderAmount,
                                                  Month = s.Month })};
```

The result of Listing 4-39 is shown here:

```
{Name=Paolo, MaxOrder={Amount=100, Month=May}}
{Name=Marco, MaxOrder={Amount=600, Month=December}}
{Name=James, MaxOrder={Amount=600, Month=December}}
{Name=Frank, MaxOrder={Amount=1000, Month=July}}
```

In this example, the *Aggregate* operator returns a new anonymous type called *MaxOrder*: it is a tuple composed of the amount and month of the most expensive order made by each customer. The *Aggregate* operator used here cannot be replaced by any of the other predefined aggregate operators because of its specific behavior and result type.

> **Note** For further information about anonymous types, refer to Chapter 2, "C# Language Features," or Chapter 3, "Microsoft Visual Basic 9.0 Language Features."

The only way to produce a similar result using standard aggregate operators is to call two different aggregators. That would require two *source* sequence scannings: one to get the max amount and one to get its month. Be sure to pay attention to the *seed* definition, which declares the resulting anonymous type that will be used by the aggregation function as well.

Generation Operators

When working with data by applying aggregates, arithmetic operations, and mathematical functions, sometimes you need to also iterate over numbers or item collections. For example, think about a query that needs to extract orders placed for a particular set of years, between 2000 and 2007, or a query that needs to repeat the same operation over the same data. The generation operators are useful for operations such as these.

Range

The first operator of this set is *Range*. It is a simple extension method that yields a set of *Integer* numbers, selected within a specified range of values, as shown in its signature:

```
public static IEnumerable<int> Range(
    int start,
    int count);
```

The code in Listing 4-40 illustrates a means to filter orders for the years between 2005 and 2007.

> **Important** Please note that in the following example, a *where* condition would be more appropriate because we are iterating *orders* many times. The example in Listing 4-40 is provided only for demonstration and is not the best solution for the specific query.

Listing 4-40 A set of years generated by the *Range* operator, used to filter orders

```
var expr =
    Enumerable.Range(2005, 3)
    .SelectMany(x => (from   o in orders
                      where  o.Year == x
                      select new { o.Year, o.Amount }));
```

The *Range* operator can also be used to implement classical mathematical operations such as square, power, factorial, and so on. Listing 4-41 shows an example of using *Range* and *Aggregate* to calculate the factorial of a number.

Listing 4-41   A factorial of a number using the *Range* operator

```
static int Factorial(int number) {
    return (Enumerable.Range(0, number + 1)
            .Aggregate(0, (s, t) => t == 0 ? 1 : s *= t)); }
```

Repeat

Another generation operator is *Repeat*, which returns a set of *count* occurrences of *element*. When the *element* is an instance of a reference type, each repetition returns a reference to the same instance, not a copy of it.

```
public static IEnumerable<T> Repeat<T>(
    T element,
    int count);
```

The *Repeat* operator is useful for initializing enumerations (using the same element for all instances) or for repeating the same query many times. In Listing 4-42, we repeat the customer name selection two times.

Listing 4-42   The *Repeat* operator, used to repeat the same query many times

```
var expr =
    Enumerable.Repeat( (from   c in customers
                        select c.Name), 2)
    .SelectMany(x => x);
```

Please note that in this example, *Repeat* returns a sequence of sequences, formed by two lists of customer names. For this reason, we used *SelectMany* to get a flat list of names.

Empty

The last of the generation operators is *Empty*, which is used to create an empty enumeration of a particular type *T*. This operation can be useful to initialize empty sequences.

```
public static IEnumerable<T> Empty<T>();
```

Listing 4-43 provides an example that uses *Empty* to fill an empty enumeration of *Customer*.

Listing 4-43   The *Empty* operator used to initialize an empty set of customers

```
IEnumerable<Customer> customers = Enumerable.Empty<Customer>();
```

Quantifiers Operators

Imagine that you need to check for the existence of elements within a sequence, based on conditions or selection rules. First you select items with *Restriction* operators, and then you use aggregate operators such as *Count* to determine whether any item that verifies the condition exists. There is, however, a set of operators, called quantifiers, specifically used to check for existence conditions over sequences.

Any

The first operator we will describe in this group is the *Any* method, which evaluates a *predicate* and returns a *Boolean* result:

```
public static bool Any<T>(
    this IEnumerable<T> source,
    Func<T, bool> predicate);
public static bool Any<T>(
    this IEnumerable<T> source);
```

As you can see from the method's signatures, the method has an overload that requires only the *source* sequence, without a predicate. This method returns *true* when at least one element in the *source* sequence exists or *false* if the *source* sequence is empty. To optimize its execution, *Any* returns as soon as a result is available. In Listing 4-44, you can see an example that determines whether there is any order of product one (*IdProduct == 1*) within all the customer orders.

Listing 4-44   The *Any* operator applied to all customer orders to check orders of *IdProduct == 1*

```
bool result =
    (from c in customers
        from   o in c.Orders
        select o)
    .Any(o => o.IdProduct == 1);

result = Enumerable.Empty<Order>().Any(o => o.IdProduct == 1);
```

In this example, the operator evaluates items only until the first order matching the condition (*IdProduct == 1*) is found. The second example in Listing 4-44 illustrates a trivial example of the *Any* operator with a *false* result, using the *Empty* operator described earlier.

All

When you want to determine whether all of the items of a sequence verify a filtering condition, you can use the *All* operator. It returns a *true* result only if the condition is verified by all the elements in the *source* sequence:

```
public static bool All<T>(
    this IEnumerable<T> source,
    Func<T, bool> predicate);
```

For instance, in Listing 4-45 we determine whether every order has a positive quantity.

Listing 4-45   The *All* operator applied to all customer orders to check the quantity

```
bool result =
    (from c in customers
        from o in c.Orders
        select o)
    .All(o => o.Quantity > 0);

result = Enumerable.Empty<Order>().All(o => o.Quantity > 0);
```

> **Important**   The *All* predicate applied to an empty sequence will always return *true*. The internal operator implementation in LINQ to Objects enumerates all the *source* sequence items. It returns *false* as soon as an element that does not verify the *predicate* is found. If the sequence is empty, the *predicate* is never called and the *true* value is returned.

Contains

The last quantifier operator is the *Contains* extension method, which determines whether a *source* sequence contains a specific item value:

```
public static bool Contains<T>(
    this IEnumerable<T> source,
    T value);
public static bool Contains<T>(
    this IEnumerable<T> source,
    T value,
    IEqualityComparer<T> comparer)
```

In the LINQ to Objects implementation, the method tries to use the *Contains* method of *ICollection<T>* if the *source* sequence implements this interface. In cases when *ICollection<T>* is not implemented, *Contains* enumerates all the items in *source*, comparing each one with the given *value* of type *T* and using a custom *comparer* if provided, the second method overload, or *EqualityComparer<T>.Default* otherwise.

In Listing 4-46, you can see an example of the *Contains* method as it is used to check for the existence of a specific order within the collection of orders of a customer.

Listing 4-46   The *Contains* operator applied to the first customer's orders

```
orderOfProductOne = new Order {Quantity = 3, IdProduct = 1 ,
    Shipped = false, Month = "January"};
bool result = customers[0].Orders.Contains(orderOfProductOne);
```

Because of its behavior, the *Contains* method invoked in Listing 4-46 returns *true* only if you use the same instance of *Order* as the value to compare. Otherwise, you need a custom *comparer* or a value type semantic for *Order* type (a reference type that overloads the *GetHashCode* and *Equals* methods or a value type, as we have already seen) to look for an equivalent order in the sequence.

Partitioning Operators

Selection and filtering operations sometimes need to be applied only to a subset of the elements of the source sequence. For instance, you might need to extract only the first N elements that verify a condition. You can use the *Where* and *Select* operators with the zero-based index argument of their predicate, but this approach is not always useful and intuitive. It is better to have specific operators for these kinds of operations because they are performed quite frequently.

A set of partitioning operators is provided to satisfy these needs. *Take* and *TakeWhile* select the first N items or the first items that verify a predicate, respectively. *Skip* and *SkipWhile* complement the *Take* and *TakeWhile* operators, skipping the first N items or the first items that validate a predicate.

Take

We will start with the *Take* and *TakeWhile* family:

```
public static IEnumerable<T> Take<T>(
    this IEnumerable<T> source,
    int count);
```

The *Take* operator requires a *count* argument that represents the number of items to take from the *source* sequence. Negative values of *count* determine an empty result; values over the sequence size return the full *source* sequence. This method is useful for all queries in which you need the top N items. For instance, you could use this method to select the top N customers based on their order amount, as shown in Listing 4-47.

Listing 4-47   The *Take* operator, applied to extract the two top customers ordered by order amount

```
var topTwoCustomers =
    (from    c in customers
     join    o in (
            from c in customers
                from    o in c.Orders
                join    p in products
                    on o.IdProduct equals p.IdProduct
                select new { c.Name, OrderAmount = o.Quantity * p.Price }
            ) on c.Name equals o.Name
            into customersWithOrders
     let     TotalAmount = customersWithOrders.Sum(o => o.OrderAmount)
     orderby TotalAmount descending
     select  new { c.Name, TotalAmount }
    ).Take(2);
```

As you can see, the *Take* operator clause is quite simple, while the whole query is more articulated. The query contains several of the basic elements and operators we have previously discussed. The *let* clause, in addition to *Take*, is the only clause that we have not already seen in action. The *let* keyword is useful to define an alias for a value or for a variable representing a formula. In this sample, we need to use the sum of all order amounts on a customer basis as a value to project into the resulting anonymous type. At the same time, the same value is used as a sorting condition. Therefore, we defined an alias named *TotalAmount* to avoid duplicate formulas.

TakeWhile

The *TakeWhile* operator works like the *Take* operator, but it checks a formula to extract items instead of using a counter. Here are the method's signatures:

```
public static IEnumerable<T> TakeWhile<T>(
    this IEnumerable<T> source,
    Func<T, bool> predicate);
public static IEnumerable<T> TakeWhile<T>(
    this IEnumerable<T> source,
    Func<T, int, bool> predicate);
```

There are two overloads of the method. The first requires a *predicate* that will be evaluated on each *source* sequence item. The method enumerates the *source* sequence and yields items if the *predicate* is *true*; it stops the enumeration when the *predicate* result becomes *false*, or when the end of the *source* is reached. The second overload also requires a zero-based index for the *predicate* to indicate where the query should start evaluating the *source* sequence.

Imagine that you want to identify your top customers, generating a list that makes up a minimum aggregate amount of orders. The problem looks similar to the one we solved with the *Take* operator in Listing 4-47, but we do not know how many customers we need to examine. *TakeWhile* can solve the problem by using a predicate that calculates the aggregate amount and uses that number to stop the enumeration when the target is reached. The resulting query is shown in Listing 4-48.

Listing 4-48   The *TakeWhile* operator, applied to extract the top customers that form 80 percent of all orders

```
// globalAmount is the total amount for all the orders
var limitAmount = globalAmount * 0.8m;
var aggregated = 0m;
var topCustomers =
    (from    c in customers
     join    o in (
            from c in customers
                from    o in c.Orders
                join    p in products
                    on o.IdProduct equals p.IdProduct
                select new { c.Name, OrderAmount = o.Quantity * p.Price }
            ) on c.Name equals o.Name
            into customersWithOrders
```

```
    let    TotalAmount = customersWithOrders.Sum(o => o.OrderAmount)
    orderby TotalAmount descending
    select  new { c.Name, TotalAmount }
)
.TakeWhile( X => {
                bool result = aggregated < limitAmount;
                aggregated += X.TotalAmount;
                return result;
            } );
```

Skip and SkipWhile

The *Skip* and *SkipWhile* signatures are very similar to those for *Take* and *TakeWhile*:

```
public static IEnumerable<T> Skip<T>(
    this IEnumerable<T> source,
    int count);
public static IEnumerable<T> SkipWhile<T>(
    this IEnumerable<T> source,
    Func<T, bool> predicate);
public static IEnumerable<T> SkipWhile<T>(
    this IEnumerable<T> source,
    Func<T, int, bool> predicate);
```

As we mentioned previously, these operators complement the *Take* and *TakeWhile* couple. In fact, the following code returns the full sequence of customers:

```
var result = customers.Take(3).Union(customers.Skip(3));
var result = customers.TakeWhile(p).Union(customers.SkipWhile(p));
```

The only point of interest is that *SkipWhile* skips the *source* sequence items while the *predicate* evaluates to *true* and starts yielding items as soon as the *predicate* result is *false*, suspending the *predicate* evaluation on all the remaining items.

Element Operators

Element operators are defined to work with single items of a sequence, to extract a specific element by position or by using a predicate, rather than a default value in case of missing elements.

First

We will start with the *First* method, which extracts the first element in the sequence by using a predicate or a positional rule:

```
public static T First<T>(
    this IEnumerable<T> source);
public static T First<T>(
    this IEnumerable<T> source,
    Func<T, bool> predicate);
```

The first overload returns the first element in the *source* sequence, and the second overload uses a *predicate* to identify the first element to return. If there are no elements that verify the *predicate* or there are no elements at all in the *source* sequence, the operator will throw an *InvalidOperationException* error. Listing 4-49 shows an example of the *First* operator.

Listing 4-49   The *First* operator, used to select the first American customer

```
var item = customers.First(c => c.Country == Countries.USA);
```

Of course, this example could be defined by using a *Where* and *Take* operator. However, the *First* method better demonstrates the intention of the query, and it also guarantees a single (partial) scan of the *source* sequence.

FirstOrDefault

If you need to find the first element only if it exists, without any exception in case of failure, you can use the *FirstOrDefault* method. This method works like *First*, but if there are no elements that verify the predicate or if the *source* sequence is empty, it returns a default value:

```
public static T FirstOrDefault<T>(
    this IEnumerable<T> source);
public static T FirstOrDefault<T>(
    this IEnumerable<T> source,
    Func<T, bool> predicate);
```

The default returned is *default(T)* in the case of an empty *source*, where that *default(T)* returns *null* for reference types and nullable types. If no *predicate* argument is provided, the method returns the first element of the *source* if it exists. An example is shown in Listing 4-50.

Listing 4-50   Examples of the *FirstOrDefault* operator syntax

```
var item = customers.FirstOrDefault(c => c.City == "Las Vegas");
Console.WriteLine(item == null ? "null" : item.ToString()); // returns null

IEnumerable<Customer> emptyCustomers = Enumerable.Empty<Customer>();
item = emptyCustomers.FirstOrDefault(c => c.City == "Las Vegas");
Console.WriteLine(item == null ? "null" : item.ToString()); // returns null
```

Last and LastOrDefault

The *Last* and *LastOrDefault* operators are complements of *First* and *FirstOrDefault*. The former have signatures and behaviors that mirror the latter:

```
public static T Last<T>(
    this IEnumerable<T> source);
public static T Last<T>(
    this IEnumerable<T> source,
    Func<T, bool> predicate);
```

```
public static T LastOrDefault<T>(
    this IEnumerable<T> source);
public static T LastOrDefault<T>(
    this IEnumerable<T> source,
    Func<T, bool> predicate);
```

These methods work like *First* and *FirstOrDefault*. The only difference is that they select the last element in *source* instead of the first.

Single

Whenever you need to select a specific and unique item from a *source* sequence, you can use the operators *Single* or *SingleOrDefault*:

```
public static T Single<T>(
    this IEnumerable<T> source);
public static T Single<T>(
    this IEnumerable<T> source,
    Func<T, bool> predicate);
```

If no *predicate* is provided, *single* extracts from the *source* sequence the first single element. Otherwise, it extracts the single element that verifies the *predicate*. If there is no predicate and the source sequence contains more than one item, an *InvalidOperationException* error will be thrown. If there is a *predicate* and there are no matching elements or there is more than one match in the *source*, the method will throw an *InvalidOperationException* error, too. You can see some examples in Listing 4-51.

Listing 4-51   Examples of the *Single* operator syntax

```
// returns Product 1
var item = products.Single(p => p.IdProduct == 1);
Console.WriteLine(item == null ? "null" : item.ToString());

// InvalidOperationException
item = products.Single();
Console.WriteLine(item == null ? "null" : item.ToString());

// InvalidOperationException
IEnumerable<Product> emptyProducts = Enumerable.Empty<Product>();
item = emptyProducts.Single(p => p.IdProduct == 1);
Console.WriteLine(item == null ? "null" : item.ToString());
```

SingleOrDefault

The *SingleOrDefault* operator provides a default result value in the case of an empty sequence or no matching elements in *source*. Its signatures are like those for *Single*:

```
public static T SingleOrDefault<T>(
    this IEnumerable<T> source);
```

```
public static T SingleOrDefault<T>(
    this IEnumerable<T> source,
    Func<T, bool> predicate);
```

The default value returned by this method is *default(T)*, as in the *FirstOrDefault* and *LastOrDefault* extension methods.

> **Important**   The default value is returned only if no elements match the *predicate*. An *InvalidOperationException* error is thrown when the *source* sequence contains more than one matching item.

ElementAt and *ElementAtOrDefault*

Whenever you need to extract a specific item from a sequence based on its position, you can use the *ElementAt* or *ElementAtOrDefault* method:

```
public static T ElementAt<T>(
    this IEnumerable<T> source,
    int index);
public static T ElementAtOrDefault<T>(
    this IEnumerable<T> source,
    int index);
```

The *ElementAt* method requires an *index* argument that represents the position of the element to extract. The *index* is zero based; therefore, you need to provide a value of 2 to extract the third element. When the value of *index* is negative or greater than the size of the *source* sequence, an *ArgumentOutOfRangeException* error is thrown. The *ElementAtOrDefault* method differs from *ElementAt* because it returns a default value—*default(T)* for reference types and nullable types—in the case of a negative *index* or an *index* greater than the size of the *source* sequence. Listing 4-52 shows some examples of how to use these operators.

Listing 4-52   Examples of the *ElementAt* and *ElementAtOrDefault* operator syntax

```
// returns Product 2
var item = products.ElementAt(2);
Console.WriteLine(item == null ? "null" : item.ToString());

// returns null
item = Enumerable.Empty<Product>().ElementAtOrDefault(6);
Console.WriteLine(item == null ? "null" : item.ToString());

// returns null
item = products.ElementAtOrDefault(6);
Console.WriteLine(item == null ? "null" : item.ToString());
```

DefaultIfEmpty

DefaultIfEmpty returns a default element for an empty sequence:

```
public static IEnumerable<T> DefaultIfEmpty<T>(
    this IEnumerable<T> source);
public static IEnumerable<T> DefaultIfEmpty<T>(
    this IEnumerable<T> source,
    T defaultValue);
```

By default, it returns the list of items of a *source* sequence. In the case of an empty source, it returns a default value that is *default(T)* in the first overload or *defaultValue* if you use the second overload of the method.

Defining a specific default value can be helpful in many circumstances. For instance, imagine that you have a public static property named *Empty*, used to return an empty instance of a *Customer*:

```
public static Customer Empty {
    get {
        Customer empty = new Customer();
        empty.Name = String.Empty;
        empty.Country = Countries.Italy;
        empty.City = String.Empty;
        empty.Orders = (new List<Order>(Enumerable.Empty<Order>())).ToArray();
        return(empty);
    }
}
```

Sometime this is useful, especially when unit testing code. Another situation is when a query uses *GroupJoin* to realize a left outer join. The possible resulting NULLs can be replaced by a default value chosen by the query author.

In Listing 4-53, you can see how to use *DefaultIfEmpty*, eventually with a custom default value such as *Customer.Empty*.

Listing 4-53   Example of the *DefaultIfEmpty* operator syntax, both with *default(T)* and a custom default value

```
var expr = customers.DefaultIfEmpty();

var customers = Enumerable.Empty<Customer>(); // Empty array
IEnumerable<Customer> customersEmpty =
    customers.DefaultIfEmpty(Customer.Empty);
```

Other Operators

To complete our coverage of LINQ query operators, we describe a few final extension methods in this section.

Concat

The first one is the concatenation operator, named *Concat*. As its name suggests, it simply appends a sequence to another, as we can see from its signature:

```
public static IEnumerable<T> Concat<T>(
    this IEnumerable<T> first,
    IEnumerable<T> second);
```

The only requirement for *Concat* arguments is that they enumerate the same type *T*. We can use this method to append any *IEnumerable<T>* sequence to another of the same type. Listing 4-54 shows an example of customer concatenation.

Listing 4-54   The *Concat* operator, used to concatenate Italian customers with customers from the United States

```
var italianCustomers =
    from   c in customers
    where  c.Country == Countries.Italy
    select c;

var americanCustomers =
    from   c in customers
    where  c.Country == Countries.USA
    select c;

var expr = italianCustomers.Concat(americanCustomers);
```

SequenceEqual

Another useful operator is the equality operator, which corresponds to the *SequenceEqual* extension method:

```
public static bool SequenceEqual<T>(
    this IEnumerable<T> first,
    IEnumerable<T> second);
public static bool SequenceEqual<T>(
    this IEnumerable<T> first,
    IEnumerable<T> second,
    IEqualityComparer<T> comparer);
```

This method compares each item in the first sequence with each corresponding item in the second sequence. If the two sequences have exactly the same number of items with equal items in every position, the two sequences are considered equal. Remember the possible issues of reference type semantics in this kind of comparison. You can consider overriding *GetHashCode* and *Equals* to drive the result of this operator, or you can use the second method overload, providing a custom implementation of *IEqualityComparer<T>*.

Deferred Query Evaluation and Extension Methods Resolution

Conversion operators (which will be described in the last section of this chapter) allow the results of a query to be represented in different ways. To provide context for understanding the need for these operators, we want to examine two behaviors of a LINQ query: deferred query evaluation and extension methods resolution. Both of these concepts are important for all LINQ implementations, so read the following sections carefully.

Deferred Query Evaluation

A LINQ query is not evaluated when it is defined but when it is used. Consider the following query definition:

```
List<Customer> customersList = new List<Customer>(customers);

var expr =
    from   c in customersList
    where  c.Country == Countries.Italy
    select c;
```

This code declares a very simple query that contains just two items, as shown by the result of the following line of code:

```
Console.WriteLine("\nItems after query definition: {0}", expr.Count());
```

Now we want to change the content of the source sequence by adding a new customer:

```
customersList.Add(
  new Customer {Name = "Roberto", City = "Firenze",
    Country = Countries.Italy, Orders = new Order[] {
    new Order {Quantity = 3, IdProduct = 1 , Shipped = false,
      Month = "March"}}});
```

If you enumerate the *expr* variable again or just check its item count, you will find a result different than before, as you can see when executing the code in Listing 4-55.

Listing 4-55   Example that shows when expression trees are evaluated

```
Console.WriteLine("\nItems after source sequence modification: {0}", expr.Count());

foreach (var item in expr) {
    Console.WriteLine(item);
}
```

The result of the code in Listing 4-55 looks like the following. The new customer, Roberto, is included in the result, even though it has been added after the *expr* query definition:

```
Items after source sequence modification: 3
Paolo - Brescia - Italy
Marco - Torino - Italy
Roberto - Firenze - Italy
```

> **Important** From a logical point of view, a LINQ query describes a kind of "query plan" because it is not executed until it is used and will be executed again and again, every time you run it. Some LINQ implementations—such as LINQ to Objects—implement this behavior through delegates, while others—such as LINQ to SQL—might use expression trees. (See Chapter 2 for a definition of an expression tree.) We call this behavior "deferred query evaluation," and it is a fundamental concept in LINQ, regardless of its implementation.

Deferred query evaluation is useful because you can define queries once and apply them several times. Regardless of whether the source sequence has been changed, the result will always be updated to the last sequence content. However, consider a situation in which you want a snapshot of the result at a particular "safe point" to use many times, even if the source sequence changes in the meantime. You need to make a copy of the result, and conversion operators will help you do that.

Extension Methods Resolution

Extension methods resolution is one of the most important concepts to understand if you want to master LINQ. Consider the following code. In it, we define a custom list of type *Customer*, called *Customers*, and a class, *CustomersEnumerable*, that provides an extension method, called *Where*, which applies specifically to instances of the *Customers* type:

```
public sealed class Customers: List<Customer> {
    public Customers(IEnumerable<Customer> items): base(items) {}
}

public static class CustomersEnumerable {
    public static IEnumerable<Customer> Where(
        this Customers source, Func<Customer, bool> predicate) { ... }

    public static IEnumerable<Customer> Where(
        this Customers source, Func<Customer, int, bool> predicate) { ... }
}
```

If we use our usual *customers* array, the behavior of the query in Listing 4-56 is quite interesting.

Listing 4-56 A query expression over a custom list of type *Customers*

```
Customers customersList = new Customers(customers);

var expr =
    from   c in customersList
    where  c.City == "Brescia"
    select c;

foreach (var item in expr) {
    Console.WriteLine(item);
}
```

The query expression will be converted by the compiler into the following code, as we saw early in this chapter:

```
var expr =
    customersList
    .Where(c => c.City == "Brescia")
    .Select(c => c);
```

As a result of the presence of the *CustomersEnumerable* class, the extension method *Where* will be the one defined by *CustomersEnumerable*, instead of the general-purpose one defined in *System.Linq.Enumerable*. (To be considered as an extension method container class, the *CustomersSequence* class must be in the current namespace or in any namespace included in active *using* directives.) Now we are experiencing the real power of LINQ. Using extension methods, we are able to define custom behaviors for specific types. In the following chapters, we will discuss LINQ to SQL, LINQ to XML, and other implementations of LINQ. These implementations are just specific implementations of query operators, thanks to the extension methods resolution realized by the compilers.

At this time, everything looks fine, and it is, of course! By the way, imagine that you need to query the custom list of type *Customers* with the standard *Where* extension method rather than with the specialized one. You should convert the custom list to a more generalized one to divert the extension method resolution made by the compiler. This is another scenario that can benefit from conversion operators.

Conversion Operators

The methods included in the conversion operator set are *AsEnumerable*, *ToArray*, *ToList*, *ToDictionary*, *ToLookup*, *OfType*, and *Cast*. Conversion operators are mainly defined to solve the problems and the needs that we illustrated in the previous two sections. Sometimes you might need a stable and immutable result from a query expression, or you might want to use a generic extension method operator instead of a more specialized one. In the following sections, we will describe the conversion operators in more detail.

AsEnumerable

The signature for *AsEnumerable* is shown here:

```
public static IEnumerable<T> AsEnumerable<T>(
    this IEnumerable<T> source);
```

The *AsEnumerable* operator simply returns the *source* sequence as an object of type *IEnumerable<T>*. This kind of "conversion on the fly" makes it possible to call the general-purpose extension methods over *source*, even if its type has specific implementations of them. You can see an example in Listing 4-57.

Listing 4-57   A query expression over a list of *Customers* converted with the *AsEnumerable* operator

```
Customers customersList = new Customers(customers);

var expr =
    from   c in customersList.AsEnumerable()
    where  c.City == "Brescia"
    select c;

foreach (var item in expr) {
    Console.WriteLine(item);
}
```

The code in Listing 4-57 will use the standard *Where* operator defined for *IEnumerable<T>* within *System.Linq.Enumerable.*

ToArray and ToList

Two other useful conversion operators are *ToArray* and *ToList*. They convert a source sequence of type *IEnumerable<T>* into an array of *T* (*T[]*) or into a generic list of *T* (*List<T>*), respectively:

```
public static T[] ToArray<T>(
    this IEnumerable<T> source);
public static List<T> ToList<T>(
    this IEnumerable<T> source);
```

The results of these operators are snapshots of the sequence. When they are applied inside a query expression, the result will be stable and unchanged, even if the *source* sequence does change. Listing 4-58 shows an example of using *ToList.*

Listing 4-58   A query expression over an immutable list of *Customers* obtained by the *ToList* operator

```
List<Customer> customersList = new List<Customer>(customers);

var expr =
    from   c in customersList.ToList()
    where  c.Country == Countries.Italy
    select c;

foreach (var item in expr) {
    Console.WriteLine(item);
}
```

These methods are also useful whenever you need to enumerate the result of a query many times, executing the query only once for performance reasons. Consider the sample in Listing 4-59. It would probably be inefficient to refresh the list of products to join with orders every time. Therefore, you can create a "copy" of the products query.

Listing 4-59   A query expression that uses *ToList* to copy the result of a query over products

```
var productsQuery =
    (from p in products
     where p.Price >= 30
     select p)
    .ToList();

var ordersWithProducts =
    from c in customers
        from  o in c.Orders
        join  p in productsQuery
              on o.IdProduct equals p.IdProduct
        select new { p.IdProduct, o.Quantity, p.Price,
                    TotalAmount = o.Quantity * p.Price};

foreach (var order in ordersWithProducts) {
    Console.WriteLine(order);
}
```

Every time you enumerate the *ordersWithProducts* expression—for instance, in a *foreach* block—the *productsQuery* expression will not be evaluated again.

ToDictionary

Another operator in this set is the *ToDictionary* extension method. It creates an instance of *Dictionary<K, T>*. The *keySelector* predicate identifies the key of each item. The *elementSelector*, if provided, is used to extract each single item. These predicates are defined through the available signatures:

```
public static Dictionary<K, T> ToDictionary<T, K>(
    this IEnumerable<T> source,
    Func<T, K> keySelector);
public static Dictionary<K, T> ToDictionary<T, K>(
    this IEnumerable<T> source,
    Func<T, K> keySelector,
    IEqualityComparer<K> comparer);
public static Dictionary<K, E> ToDictionary<T, K, E>(
    this IEnumerable<T> source,
    Func<T, K> keySelector,
    Func<T, E> elementSelector);
public static Dictionary<K, E> ToDictionary<T, K, E>(
    this IEnumerable<T> source,
    Func<T, K> keySelector,
    Func<T, E> elementSelector,
    IEqualityComparer<K> comparer);
```

When the method constructs the resulting dictionary, it assumes the uniqueness of each key extracted by invoking the *keySelector*. In cases of duplicate keys, an *ArgumentException* error will be thrown. The key values are compared using the *comparer* argument if provided or

EqualityComparer<K>.Default if not. In Listing 4-60, we use this operator to create a dictionary of customers.

Listing 4-60   An example of the *ToDictionary* operator, applied to customers

```
var customersDictionary =
    customers
    .ToDictionary(c => c.Name,
                  c => new {c.Name, c.City});
```

The first argument of the operator is the *keySelector* predicate, which extracts the customer *Name* as the key. The second argument is *elementSelector*, which creates an anonymous type that consists of customer *Name* and *City* properties. Here is the result of the query in Listing 4-60:

```
[Paolo, {Name=Paolo, City=Brescia}]
[Marco, {Name=Marco, City=Torino}]
[James, {Name=James, City=Dallas}]
[Frank, {Name=Frank, City=Seattle}]
```

Important   Like the *ToList* and *ToArray* operators, *ToDictionary* copies the *source* sequence items rather than creating references to them. The *ToDictionary* method in Listing 4-60 effectively evaluates the query expression and creates the output dictionary. Therefore, *customersDictionary* does not have a deferred query evaluation behavior; it is the result produced by a statement execution.

ToLookup

Another conversion operator is *ToLookup*, which can be used to create enumerations of type *Lookup<K, T>*, whose definition follows:

```
public class Lookup<K, T> : IEnumerable<IGrouping<K, T>> {
    public int Count { get; }
    public IEnumerable<T> this[K key] { get; }
    public bool Contains(K key);
    public IEnumerator<IGrouping<K, T>> GetEnumerator();
}
```

Each object of this type represents a one-to-many dictionary, which defines a tuple of keys and sequences of items, somewhat like the result of a *GroupJoin* method. Here are the available signatures:

```
public static Lookup<K, T> ToLookup<T, K>(
    this IEnumerable<T> source,
    Func<T, K> keySelector);
public static Lookup<K, T> ToLookup<T, K>(
    this IEnumerable<T> source,
    Func<T, K> keySelector,
    IEqualityComparer<K> comparer);
```

```
public static Lookup<K, E> ToLookup<T, K, E>(
    this IEnumerable<T> source,
    Func<T, K> keySelector,
    Func<T, E> elementSelector);
public static Lookup<K, E> ToLookup<T, K, E>(
    this IEnumerable<T> source,
    Func<T, K> keySelector,
    Func<T, E> elementSelector,
    IEqualityComparer<K> comparer);
```

As in *ToDictionary*, there is a *keySelector* predicate, an *elementSelector* predicate, and a *comparer*. The sample in Listing 4-61 demonstrates how to use this method to extract all orders for each product.

Listing 4-61   An example of the *ToLookup* operator, used to group orders by product

```
var ordersByProduct =
    (from c in customers
         from   o in c.Orders
         select o)
    .ToLookup(o => o.IdProduct);

Console.WriteLine( "\n\nNumber of orders for Product 1: {0}\n",
                   ordersByProduct[1].Count());

foreach (var product in ordersByProduct) {
    Console.WriteLine("Product: {0}", product.Key);
    foreach(var order in product) {
        Console.WriteLine("  {0}", order);
    }
}
```

As you can see, *Lookup<K, T>* is accessible through an item key (*ordersByProduct[1]*) or through enumeration (the *foreach* loop). The following is the output of this example:

```
Number of orders for Product 1: 2

Product: 1
  3 - False - January - 1
  10 - False - July - 1
Product: 2
  5 - True - May - 2
Product: 3
  20 - True - December - 3
  20 - True - December - 3
Product: 5
  20 - False - July - 5
```

OfType and *Cast*

The last two operators of this set are *OfType* and *Cast*. The first filters the source sequence, yielding only items of type *T*. It is useful in the case of sequences with items of different types. For instance, working with an object-oriented approach, you might have an object with a common base class and particular specialization in derived classes:

```
public static IEnumerable<T> OfType<T>(
    this IEnumerable source);
```

If you provide a type *T* that is not supported by any of the source items, the operator will return an empty sequence.

The *Cast* operator enumerates the source sequence and tries to yield each item, cast to type *T*. In the case of failure, an *InvalidCastException* error will be thrown.

```
public static IEnumerable<T> Cast<T>(
    this IEnumerable source);
```

Because of its signature, which accepts any *IEnumerable* sequence, this method can be used to convert old nongeneric types to newer *IEnumerable<T>* types. This conversion makes it possible to query these types with LINQ even if the types are unaware of LINQ.

> **Important**   Each item returned by *OfType* and *Cast* is a reference to the original object and not a copy. *OfType* does not create a snapshot of a source; instead, it evaluates the source every time you enumerate the operator's result. This behavior is different from other conversion operators.

Summary

In this chapter, we discussed the principles of LINQ queries and the syntax rules behind them. We covered query operators and conversion operators. We also discussed two important LINQ features, deferred query evaluation and extension methods resolution. We used LINQ to Objects as a reference implementation, but all of the concepts are also valid for other LINQ implementations that we will cover in the following chapters.

Chapter 5
LINQ to ADO.NET

Language Integrated Query (LINQ) is available in several "flavors." The intrinsic extensibility of LINQ makes it useful in many situations where data manipulation is required. At the time of this writing, Microsoft has announced LINQ to SQL, LINQ to DataSet, LINQ to Entities, and LINQ to XML implementations. Other LINQ integrations will soon be available from both Microsoft and third parties.

LINQ to ADO.NET includes several LINQ implementations that operate with Microsoft ADO.NET:

- LINQ to SQL allows querying a relational structure by converting the LINQ query into a native SQL query.

- LINQ to DataSet interacts with data already in ADO.NET *DataSet* structures.

- LINQ to Entities leverages the ADO.NET Entity Framework to query a logical model that usually has a higher-level representation of data information compared to direct access to relational data sources.

LINQ to SQL

The first and most obvious application of LINQ is for querying an external relational database. LINQ to SQL is a component of the LINQ Project that provides the capability to query a relational database, offering you an object model based on available entities. In other words, you can define a set of objects that represents a thin abstraction layer over the relational data, and you can query this object model using LINQ queries that are converted into corresponding SQL queries by the LINQ to SQL component.

In LINQ to SQL, we can write a simple query like the following:

```
var query =
    from    c in Customers
    where   c.Country == "USA"
            && c.State == "WA"
    select  new {c.CustomerID, c.CompanyName, c.City };
```

This query is converted into an SQL query that is sent to the relational database:

```
SELECT CustomerID, CompanyName, City
FROM   Customers
WHERE  Country = 'USA'
  AND  Region = 'WA'
```

> **Important**   The SQL queries generated by LINQ that we show in this chapter are only illus-
> trative. Microsoft reserves the right to change the SQL that is generated by LINQ, and at
> times we use simplified queries in the text. Thus, you should not rely on the SQL that is
> shown.

At this point, you might be asking a few questions. First, how can the LINQ query be written using object names that are validated by the compiler? Second, when is the SQL query generated from the LINQ query? Third, when is the SQL query executed? To understand the answers to these questions, you need to understand the entity model in LINQ to SQL and then the deferred query evaluation.

Entities in LINQ to SQL

Any external data must be described with appropriate metadata bound to class definitions. Each table must have a corresponding class decorated with particular attributes, which corresponds to a row of data and describes all columns in terms of data members of the defined type. The type can be a complete or partial description of an existing physical table, view, or stored procedure result. Only the described fields can be used inside a LINQ query for both projection and filtering. Listing 5-1 shows a small and simple entity definition.

Listing 5-1   Entity definition for LINQ to SQL

```
[Table(Name="Customers")]
public class Customer {
    [Column] public string CustomerID;
    [Column] public string CompanyName;
    [Column] public string City;
    [Column(Name="Region")] public string State;
    [Column] public string Country;
}
```

The *Customer* type defines the content of a row, and each field or property decorated with *Column* corresponds to a column of the relational table. The *Name* parameter can specify a column name that is different from the data member name (in this example, *State* corresponds to the Region table column). The *Table* attribute specifies that the class is an entity representing data of a database table; its *Name* property can specify a table name that is different from the entity name. It is common to use the singular form for the name of the class (a single row) and the plural form for the name of the table (a set of rows).

You need a Customers table to build a LINQ to SQL query over Customers data. The *Table<T>* generic class is the right way to create such a type:

```
Table<Customer> Customers = ...;
// ...
var query =
    from    c in Customers
    // ...
```

> **Note**   To build a LINQ query on *Customers*, you need a class implementing *IEnumerable<T>*, using *Customer* as *T*. However, LINQ to SQL needs to implement extension methods in a different way than the SQL to Objects implementation that we used in the Chapter 4, "LINQ Syntax Fundamentals." For this reason, you need to use an object implementing *IQueryable<T>* to build LINQ to SQL queries. The *Table<T>* class implements *IQueryable<T>*. To include the LINQ to SQL extension, the statement *using System.Data.Linq;* must be part of the source code.

The *Customers* table object has to be instantiated. To do that, we need an instance of a *Data-Context* class, which defines the bridge between the LINQ world and the external relational database. The nearest concept to *DataContext* that comes to mind is a database connection—in fact, a mandatory parameter needed to create a *DataContext* instance is the connection string or the *Connection* object. Its *GetTable* method returns a corresponding *Table<T>* for the specified type:

```
DataContext db = new DataContext("Database=Northwind");
Table<Customer> Customers = db.GetTable<Customer>();
```

Listing 5-2 shows the resulting code when you put all the pieces together.

Listing 5-2   Simple LINQ to SQL query

```
DataContext db = new DataContext( ConnectionString );
Table<Customer> Customers = db.GetTable<Customer>();

var query =
    from    c in Customers
    where   c.Country == "USA"
            && c.State == "WA"
    select  new {c.CustomerID, c.CompanyName, c.City };

foreach( var row in query ) {
    Console.WriteLine( row );
}
```

The query variable is initialized with a query expression that forms an expression tree. As we noted in Chapter 2, "C# Language Features," an expression tree maintains a representation of the expression in memory instead of pointing to a method through a delegate. When the *foreach* loop enumerates data selected by the query, the expression tree is used to generate the corresponding SQL query, using all metadata and information we have in the entity classes and in the referenced *DataContext* instance.

> **Note**   The *deferred execution* method used by LINQ to SQL converts the expression tree into an SQL query that is valid in the underlying relational database. The LINQ query is functionally equivalent to a string containing an SQL command, with at least two important differences. First, it is tied to the object model and not to the database structure. Second, its representation is semantically meaningful without requiring an SQL parser and without being tied to a specific SQL dialect. The expression tree can also be manipulated in memory before its use.

The data returned from the SQL query accessing *row* and placed into the *foreach* loop is then used to fill the projected anonymous type following the *select* keyword. In this sample, the *Customer* class is never instantiated, and it is used only by LINQ to analyze its metadata.

We can explore the generated SQL query by using the *GetQueryText* method of the *Data-Context* class:

```
Console.WriteLine( db.GetQueryText( query ) );
```

The previous simple LINQ to SQL query generates the following *GetQueryText* output:

```
SELECT [t0].[CustomerID], [t0].[CompanyName], [t0].[City]
FROM   [Customers] AS [t0]
WHERE  ([t0].[Country] = @p0) AND ([t0].[Region] = @p1)
```

An alternative way to get a trace of all SQL statements sent to the database is to assign a value to the *Log* property of *DataContext*:

```
db.Log = Console.Out;
```

In the next section, you will see in more detail how to generate entity classes for LINQ to SQL.

Data Modeling

The set of entity classes that LINQ to SQL requires is a thin abstraction layer over the relational model. Each entity class defines an accessible table of data, which can be queried and modified. Entity instances that are modified can apply their changes on data contained in the relational database. You will see the options for data updates in the "Data Update" section of this chapter. In this section, you will learn how to build a data model for LINQ to SQL.

DataContext

The *DataContext* class handles the communication between LINQ and external relational data sources. Each instance has a single *Connection* to a relational database. Its type is *IDb-Connection*; therefore, it is not specific to a particular database product.

Important   The architecture of LINQ to SQL supports many data providers so that it can map to different underlying relational databases. At the time of this writing, beta versions of LINQ support only Microsoft SQL Server for LINQ to SQL, but anyone can implement providers of his own.

DataContext uses metadata information to map the physical structure of relational data, on which the SQL code generation is based. *DataContext* can also be used to call a stored procedure and persist data changes in entity class instances in the relational database.

Classes that specialize access for a particular database can be derived from *DataContext*. Such classes offer an easier way to access relational data, including members that represent available tables. You can define the existing tables simply by declaring them, without a specific initialization, as in the following code:

```
public class SampleDb : DataContext {
    public SampleDb(IDbConnection connection)
            : base( connection ) {}
    public SampleDb(string fileOrServerOrConnection)
            : base( fileOrServerOrConnection ) {}
    public SampleDb(IDbConnection connection, MappingSource mapping)
            : base( connection, mapping ) {}

    public Table<Customer> Customers;
}
```

Note   Table members are initialized automatically by the *DataContext* base constructor, which examines the type at execution time through Reflection, finds those members, and initializes them.

Entity Classes

An entity class has two roles. The first is to provide metadata to LINQ queries; for this purpose, an entity class is not instantiated. The second is to provide storage for data read from the relational data source, as well as to track possible updates and support their submission back to the relational data source.

An entity class is any reference type definition decorated with the *Table* attribute. A struct (value type) cannot be used for this. The *Table* attribute can have a *Name* parameter that defines the name of the corresponding table in the database. If *Name* is omitted, the name of the class is used as the default:

```
[Table(Name="Products")]
public class Product { ... }
```

> **Note**   Although the term commonly used is *table*, nothing prevents you from using an updatable view in place of a table name in the *Name* parameter. Using a non-updatable view will work too, at least until you try to update data without using that entity class.

Inside an entity class, there can be any number and type of members. Only data members or properties decorated with the *Column* attribute are significant in defining the mapping between the entity class and the corresponding table in the database:

```
[Column] public int ProductID;
```

An entity class should have a unique key. This key is necessary to support unique identity (more on this later), to identify corresponding rows in database tables, and to generate SQL statements that update data. If you do not have a primary key, instances of the entity class can be created but are not modifiable. The Boolean *IsPrimaryKey* property of the *Column* attribute, set to *true*, states that the column belongs to the primary key of the table. If the primary key used is a composite key, all the columns that form the primary key will have *IsPrimaryKey=true* in their parameters:

```
[Column(IsPrimaryKey=true)] public int ProductID;
```

By default, a column is mapped using the same name of the member to which the *Column* attribute is applied. You can use a different name, specifying a value for the *Name* parameter. For example, the following *Price* member corresponds to the *UnitPrice* field in the database table:

```
[Column(Name="UnitPrice")] public decimal Price;
```

If you want to filter data access through member property accessors, you have to specify the underlying storage member with the *Storage* parameter. If you specify a *Storage* parameter, LINQ to SQL bypasses the public property accessor and interacts directly with the underlying value. Understanding this is particularly important if you want to track only the modifications made by your code and not the read/write operations made by the LINQ framework. In the following code, the *ProductName* property is accessed for each read/write operation made by your code; a direct read/write operation on the *_ProductName* data member is made when a LINQ operation is executed:

```
[Column(Storage="_ProductName")]
public string ProductName {
    get { return this._ProductName; }
    set { this.OnPropertyChanging("ProductName");
        this._ProductName = value;
        this.OnPropertyChanged("ProductName");
    }
}
```

The correspondence between relational type and .NET type is made assuming a default relational type corresponding to the used .NET type. Whenever you need to define a different type, you can use the *DBType* parameter, specifying a valid type by using a valid SQL syntax for the relational data source. This property is used only if you want to create a database schema starting from entity class definitions:

```
[Column(DBType="NVARCHAR(20)")] public string QuantityPerUnit;
```

If a column value is auto-generated by the database (which is a service offered by the IDEN-TITY keyword in SQL Server), you might want to synchronize the entity class member with the generated value whenever you insert an entity instance into the database. To get this behavior, you need to set the *IsDBGenerated* parameter to *true*, and you also need to adapt the *DBType* accordingly—for example, by adding the *IDENTITY* modifier for SQL Server tables:

```
[Column(DBType="INT NOT NULL IDENTITY",
 IsPrimaryKey=true, IsDBGenerated=true)]
public int ProductID;
```

Other parameters that are relevant in updating data are *IsVersion* and *UpdateCheck*. You will see a deeper explanation of *IsDBGenerated*, *IsVersion*, and *UpdateCheck* later in the "Data Update" section.

Entity Inheritance

Sometime a single table contains many types of entities. For example, imagine a list of contacts—some of them can be customers, others can be suppliers, and others can be company employees. From a data point of view, each entity can have some specific fields. (For example, a customer can have a discount field, which is not relevant for employees and suppliers.) From a business logic point of view, each entity can implement different business rules. The best way to model this kind of data in an object-oriented environment is by leveraging inheritance to create a hierarchy of specialized classes. LINQ to SQL allows a set of classes derived from the same base class to map the same relational table.

The *InheritanceMapping* attribute decorates the base class of a hierarchy, indicating the corresponding derived classes that are based on the value of a special *discriminator column*. The *Code* parameter defines a possible value, and the *Type* parameter defines the corresponding derived type. The discriminator column is defined by the *IsDiscriminator* argument being set to *true* in the *Column* attribute specification. Listing 5-3 provides an example of a hierarchy based on the Contacts table of the Northwind sample database.

Listing 5-3   Hierarchy of classes based on contacts

```
[Table(Name="Contacts")]
[InheritanceMapping(Code = "Customer", Type = typeof(CustomerContact))]
[InheritanceMapping(Code = "Supplier", Type = typeof(SupplierContact))]
[InheritanceMapping(Code = "Shipper", Type = typeof(ShipperContact))]
[InheritanceMapping(Code = "Employee", Type = typeof(Contact), IsDefault = true)]
```

```
public class Contact {
    [Column(IsPrimaryKey=true)] public int ContactID;
    [Column(Name="ContactName")] public string Name;
    [Column] public string Phone;
    [Column(IsDiscriminator = true)] public string ContactType;
}

public class CompanyContact : Contact {
    [Column(Name="CompanyName")] public string Company;
}
public class CustomerContact : CompanyContact {
}

public class SupplierContact : CompanyContact {
}

public class ShipperContact : CompanyContact {
    public string Shipper {
        get { return Company; }
        set { Company = value; }
    }
}
```

Contact is the base class of the hierarchy. If the contact is a *Customer*, a *Supplier*, or a *Shipper*, the corresponding classes derive from an intermediate *CompanyContact*, which defines the *Company* field corresponding to the CompanyName column in the source table. The *Company-Contact* intermediate class is necessary because you cannot reference the same column (CompanyName) in more than one field, even if this happens in different classes in the same hierarchy. The *ShipperContact* class defines a *Shipper* property that exposes the same value of *Company*, with a different semantic meaning.

> **Note** This approach requires you to flatten the union of all possible data columns for the whole hierarchy into a single table. If you have a normalized database, you might have data for different entities separated in different tables. You can define a view to use LINQ to SQL to support entity hierarchy, but to update data you must make the view updatable.

The level of abstraction offered by having different entity classes in the same hierarchy is well described by the sample queries shown in Listing 5-4. The *queryTyped* query uses the *OfType* operator, while *queryFiltered* relies on a standard *where* condition to filter out contacts that are not customers.

Listing 5-4 Queries using a hierarchy of entity classes

```
var queryTyped =
    from    c in contacts.OfType<CustomerContact>()
    select  c;

var queryFiltered =
    from    c in contacts
```

```
        where   c is CustomerContact
        select  c;

    foreach( var row in queryTyped ) {
        Console.WriteLine( row.Company );
    }

    // We need an explicit cast to access the CostumerContact members
    foreach( CustomerContact row in queryFiltered ) {
        Console.WriteLine( row.Company );
    }
```

The SQL queries produced by these LINQ queries are functionally identical to the following one. (The actual query is different because of generalization coding.)

```
SELECT [t0].[ContactType], [t0].[CompanyName] AS [Company],
       [t0].[ContactID], [t0].[ContactName] AS [Name],
       [t0].[Phone]
FROM   [Contacts] AS [t0]
WHERE  [t0].[ContactType] = 'Customer'
```

The difference between *queryTyped* and *queryFiltered* queries lies in the returned type. A *queryTyped* query returns a sequence of *CustomerContact* instances, while *queryFiltered* returns a sequence of the base class *Contact*. With *queryFiltered*, you need to explicitly cast the result into a *CustomerContact* type if you want to access the *Company* property.

Unique Object Identity

An instance of an entity class stores an in-memory representation of table row data. If you try to instantiate two different entities containing the same row, you obtain a reference to the same in-memory object. In other words, object identity (same references) maintains data identity (same table row) using the entity unique key. The LINQ to SQL engine ensures that the same object reference is used when an entity instantiated from a query result is already in memory. This check does not happen if you create an instance of an entity by yourself. In Listing 5-5, you can see that *c1* and *c2* reference the same *Contact* instance, even if they originate from two different queries, while *c3* is a different object, even if its content is equivalent to the others.

Note If you want to force reloading data from the database, you must use the *Refresh* method of the *DataContext* class. We will say more about this later in the "Concurrent Operations" section.

Listing 5-5 Object identity

```
var queryTyped =
    from   c in contacts.OfType<CustomerContact>()
    orderby c.ContactID
    select  c;
```

```
var queryFiltered =
    from   c in contacts
    where  c is CustomerContact
    orderby c.ContactID
    select c;

Contact c1 = null;
Contact c2 = null;
foreach( var row in queryTyped.Take(1) ) {
    c1 = row;
}
foreach( var row in queryFiltered.Take(1) ) {
    c2 = row;
}
Contact c3 = new Contact();
c3.ContactID = c1.ContactID;
c3.ContactType = c1.ContactType;
c3.Name = c1.Name;
c3.Phone = c1.Phone;
Debug.Assert( c1 == c2 ); // same instance
Debug.Assert( c1 != c3 ); // different objects
```

Entity Constraints

The entity classes cannot represent all possible check constraints of a relational table. No attributes are available to specify the same alternate keys (unique constraint), triggers, and check expressions that can be defined in a relational database. This fact is relevant when you start to manipulate data using entity classes, because you cannot guarantee that an updated value will be accepted by the underlying database. (For example, it could have a duplicated unique key.) However, because you can load into entity instances only parts (rows) of the whole table, these kinds of checks are not possible without accessing the relational database, anyway.

There is partial support for describing a primary key, unique constraint, and other indexes only through XML external metadata specification. You will see this discussed later in the "External Mapping" section. This support is useful only to generate a database starting from LINQ to SQL metadata.

More complete support is available for maintaining valid relationships between entities, just like the support offered by foreign keys in a standard relational environment.

Associations Between Entities

Relationships between entities in a relational database are modeled on the concept of foreign keys referring to primary keys of a table. Class entities can use the same concept through the *Association* attribute, which can describe both sides of a *one-to-many* relationship described by a foreign key.

EntityRef   Let us start with the concept of *lookup*, which is the typical operation used to get the customer related to one order. Lookup can be seen as the direct translation into the entity model of the foreign key relationship existing between the CustomerID column of the Orders table and the primary key of the Customers table. In our entity model, the *Order* entity class will have a *Customer* property (of type *Customer*), that shows the customer data. This property is decorated with the *Association* attribute and stores its information in an *EntityRef<Customer>* member (named *_Customer*), which enables the deferred loading of references that you will see shortly. Listing 5-6 shows the definition of this association.

Listing 5-6   *Association EntityRef*

```
[Table(Name="Orders")]
public class Order {
    [Column(IsPrimaryKey=true)] public int OrderID;
    [Column] private string CustomerID;

    [Association(Storage="_Customer", ThisKey="CustomerID")]
    public Customer Customer {
        get { return this._Customer.Entity; }
        set { this._Customer.Entity = value; }
    }

    private EntityRef<Customer> _Customer;
}
```

As you can see, the CustomerID column must be defined in *Order* because otherwise it would not be possible to obtain the related *Customer*. The *ThisKey* argument or the *Association* attribute indicates the "foreign key" column (which would be a comma-separated list if more columns were involved for a composite key) that is used to define the relationship between entities. If you want to hide this detail in the entity properties, you can declare that column as private, just as in the *Order* class shown earlier.

Using the *Order* class in a LINQ query, you can specify a *Customer* property in a filter without the need to write a join between *Customer* and *Order* entities. In the following query, the *Country* member of the related *Customer* is used to filter orders that come from customers of a particular *Country*:

```
Table<Order> Orders = db.GetTable<Order>();
var query =
    from   o in Orders
    where  o.Customer.Country == "USA"
    select o.OrderID;
```

The previous query is translated into an SQL JOIN like the following one:

```
SELECT    [t0].[OrderID]
FROM      [Orders] AS [t0]
LEFT JOIN [Customers] AS [t1]
      ON [t1].[CustomerID] = [t0].[CustomerID]
WHERE     [t1].[Country] = "USA"
```

Until now, we have used entity relationships only for their metadata-building LINQ queries. When an instance of an entity class is created, a reference to another entity (such as the previous *Customer* property) works with a technique called *deferred loading*. The related *Customer* entity is not instantiated and loaded into memory from the database until it is accessed either in read or write mode.

> **More Info**   *EntityRef<T>* is a wrapper class that is instantiated with the container object to give a valid reference for any access to the referenced entity. Each read/write operation is filtered by a property *getter* and *setter*, which execute a query to load data from the database the first time this entity is accessed.

In other words, to generate an SQL query to populate the *Customer* related entity when the *Country* property is accessed, you would use the following code:

```
var query =
    from    o in Orders
    where   o.OrderID == 10528
    select o;

foreach( var row in query ) {
    Console.WriteLine( row.Customer.Country );
}
```

The process of accessing the *Customer* property involves checking to determine whether the related *Customer* entity is already in memory. If it is, that entity is accessed; otherwise, the following SQL query is executed and the corresponding *Customer* entity is loaded in memory and then accessed:

```
SELECT [t0].[Country], [t0].[CustomerID], [t0].[CompanyName]
FROM    [Customers] AS [t0]
WHERE   [t0].[CustomerID] = "GREAL"
```

The GREAL string is the *CustomerID* value for order 10528. As you can see, the SELECT statement queries all columns declared in the *Customer* entity, even if they are not used in the expression that accessed the *Customer* entity. (In this case, the executed code never referenced the *CompanyName* member.)

EntitySet   The other side of an association is a table that is referenced from another table through its primary key. Although this is an implicit consequence of the foreign key constraint in a relational model, you need to explicitly define this association in the entity model. If the Customers table is referenced from the Orders table, you can define an *Orders* property in the *Customer* class that represents the set of *Order* entities related to a given *Customer*. The relationship is implemented by an instance of *EntitySet<Order>*, which is a wrapper class over the sequence of related orders. You might want to directly expose this *EntitySet<T>* type, as in the code shown in Listing 5-7. In that code, the *OtherKey* argument of the *Association* attribute specifies the name of the member on the related type (*Order*) that defines the association between *Customer* and the set of *Order* entities.

Listing 5-7   *Association EntitySet* (visible)

```
[Table(Name="Customers")]
public class Customer {
    [Column(IsPrimaryKey=true)] public string CustomerID;
    [Column] public string CompanyName;
    [Column] public string Country;

    [Association(OtherKey="CustomerID")]
    public EntitySet<Order> Orders;
}
```

You might also decide to hide this implementation detail, making only an *ICollection<Order>* visible outside of the *Customer* class, as in the declaration shown in Listing 5-8. In this case, the *Storage* argument of the *Association* attribute specifies the *EntitySet<T>* physical storage.

Listing 5-8   *Association EntitySet* (hidden)

```
public class Customer {
    [Column(IsPrimaryKey=true)] public string CustomerID;
    [Column] public string CompanyName;
    [Column] public string Country;

    private EntitySet<Order> _Orders;

    [Association(OtherKey="CustomerID", Storage="_Orders")]
    public ICollection<Order> Orders {
        get { return this._Orders; }
        set { this._Orders.Assign(value); }
    }
}
```

With both models of association declaration, you can use the *Customer* class in a LINQ query, accessing the related *Order* entities without the need to write a join. You simply specify the *Orders* property. The next query returns the names of customers who placed more than 20 orders:

```
Table<Customer> Customers = db.GetTable<Customer>();
var query =
    from   c in Customers
    where  c.Orders.Count > 20
    select c.CompanyName;
```

The previous LINQ query is translated into an SQL query like the following one:

```
SELECT [t0].[CompanyName]
FROM [Customers] AS [t0]
WHERE ( SELECT COUNT(*)
        FROM [Orders] AS [t1]
        WHERE [t1].[CustomerID] = [t0].[CustomerID]
      ) > 20
```

In this case, no instances of the *Order* entity are created. The *Orders* property serves only as a metadata source to generate the desired SQL query. If you return a *Customer* entity from a LINQ query, you can access the *Orders* of a customer on demand:

```
var query =
    from    c in Customers
    where   c.Orders.Count > 20
    select c;

foreach( var row in query ) {
    Console.WriteLine( row.CompanyName );
    foreach( var order in row.Orders ) {
        Console.WriteLine( order.OrderID );
    }
}
```

In the previous code, you are using deferred loading. Each time you access the *Orders* property of a customer for the first time (as indicated by the highlighted code in the preceding code sample), a query like the following one (which uses *@p0* as the parameter to filter *CustomerID*) is sent to the database:

```
SELECT [t0].[OrderID], [t0].[CustomerID]
FROM    [Orders] AS [t0]
WHERE   [t0].[CustomerID] = @p0
```

If you want to load all orders for all customers into memory using only one query to the database, you need to request *immediate loading* instead of deferred loading. To do that, you have two options. The first approach, which is demonstrated in Listing 5-9, is to force the inclusion of an *EntitySet* using a *DataShape* instance and the call of its *LoadWith<T>* method.

Listing 5-9   Use of *DataShape* and *LoadWith<T>*

```
DataContext db = new DataContext( ConnectionString );
Table<Customer> Customers = db.GetTable<Customer>();

DataShape ds = new DataShape();
ds.LoadWith<Customer>( c => c.Orders );
db.Shape = ds;
var query =
    from    c in Customers
    where   c.Orders.Count > 20
    select c;
```

The second option is to return a new entity that explicitly includes the *Orders* property for the *Customer*:

```
var query =
    from    c in Customers
    where   c.Orders.Count > 20
    select new { c.CompanyName, c.Orders };
```

These LINQ queries send an SQL query to the database to get all customers who placed more than 20 orders, including the whole order list for each customer. That SQL query might be similar to the one shown in the following code:

```
SELECT [t2].[CompanyName], [t3].[OrderID], [t3].[CustomerID], (
    SELECT COUNT(*)
    FROM [Orders] AS [t4]
    WHERE [t4].[CustomerID] = [t2].[CustomerID]
    ) AS [count]
FROM (
    SELECT [t0].[CustomerID], [t0].[CompanyName]
    FROM [Customers] AS [t0]
    WHERE (
        SELECT COUNT(*)
        FROM [Orders] AS [t1]
        WHERE [t1].[CustomerID] = [t0].[CustomerID]
        ) > 20
    ) AS [t2]
LEFT OUTER JOIN [Orders] AS [t3] ON [t3].[CustomerID] = [t2].[CustomerID]
ORDER BY [t2].[CustomerID], [t3].[OrderID]
```

> **Note**   You can observe that there is a single SQL statement here and the LINQ to SQL engine parses the result, extracting different entities (Customers and Orders). Keeping the result ordered by *CustomerID*, the engine can build in-memory entities and relationships in a faster way.

You can filter the subquery produced by relationship navigation. Suppose you want to see only customers who placed at least five orders in 1997, and you want to load and see only these orders. You can use the *AssociateWith<T>* method of the *DataShape* class to do that, as demonstrated in Listing 5-10.

Listing 5-10   Use of *DataShape* and *AssociateWith<T>*

```
DataShape ds = new DataShape();
ds.AssociateWith<Customer>(
    c => c.Orders.Where(
        o => o.OrderDate.Value.Year == 1997 ) );
db.Shape = ds;
var query =
    from   c in Customers
    where  c.Orders.Count > 5
    select c;
```

You will appreciate that the C# filter condition (*o.OrderDate.Value.Year == 1997*) is translated into the following SQL expression:

```
(DATEPART(Year, [t2].[OrderDate]) = 1997)
```

Using *AssociateWith<T>* alone does not apply the immediate loading behavior. If you want both immediate loading and filtering through a relationship, you have to call both the *Load-With<T>* and *AssociateWith<T>* methods. The order of these calls is not relevant. For example, you can write the following code:

```
DataShape ds = new DataShape();
ds.AssociateWith<Customer>(
    c => c.Orders.Where(
        o => o.OrderDate.Value.Year == 1997 ) );
ds.LoadWith<Customer>( c => c.Orders );
db.Shape = ds;
```

Loading all data into memory using a single query might be a better approach if you are sure you will access all data that is loaded, because you will spend less time in round-trip latency. However, this technique will consume more memory and bandwidth when the typical access to a graph of entities is random. Think about these details when you decide how to query your data model.

Other *Association* Attributes   The *Association* attribute can also have other parameters. *Name* corresponds to the foreign key constraint name, *Unique* defines a real one-to-one relationship, and *OtherKey* can specify the comma-separated value of members that forms the primary key of the related entity.

Graph Consistency   Relationships are bidirectional between entities—when an update is made on one side, the other side should be kept synchronized. LINQ to SQL does not automatically manage this kind of synchronization, which has to be done by the class entity implementation. LINQ to SQL offers an implementation pattern that is also used by code-generation tools such as SQLMetal, a tool that is part of the Microsoft .NET 3.5 Software Development Kit (SDK), which will be described later in this chapter. This pattern is based on the *EntitySet<T>* class on one side and on the complex *setter* accessor on the other side. The product documentation offers a detailed explanation of how to implement this pattern if you do not want to rely on tools-generated code.

Change Notification   You will see in the "Data Update" section that LINQ to SQL is able to track changes in entities, submitting equivalent changes to the database. This process is implemented by default through an algorithm that compares an object's content with its original values, requiring a copy of each tracked object. The memory consumption can be high, but it can be optimized if entities participate in the change tracking service by announcing when an object has been changed.

The implementation requires an entity to expose all its data through properties, and each property *setter* needs to call the *PropertyChanging* method of *DataContext*. Entities that implement this pattern should also implement the *System.Data.Linq.INotifyPropertyChanging* interface. Further details are available in the product documentation. Tools-generated code for entities (such as that emitted by SQLMetal) already implements this pattern.

> **Note**   The *System.Data.Linq.INotifyPropertyChanging* interface should not be confused with the *System.ComponentModel.INotifyPropertyChanged* interface that is used in frameworks such as Windows Forms and Windows Presentation Foundation (WPF). These interfaces can work in conjunction with each other when performing data binding in a User Interface layer.

Relational Model vs. Hierarchical Model

The entity model used by LINQ to SQL defines a set of objects that maps the database tables into objects that can be used and manipulated by LINQ queries. The resulting model makes a paradigm shift that has been revealed in describing associations between entities. We moved from a relational model (tables in a database) to a hierarchical or graph model (objects in memory).

A hierarchical/graph model is the natural way to manipulate objects in a program written in C# or Microsoft Visual Basic. When you try to consider how to translate an existing SQL query into a LINQ query, this is the major conceptual obstacle you encounter. In LINQ, you can write a query using joins between separate entities, just as you do in SQL. However, you can also write a query leveraging the existing relationships between entities, as we did with *EntitySet* and *EntityRef* associations.

> **Important**   Remember that SQL does not make use of relationships between entities when querying data. Those relationships exist only to define the data integrity conditions. LINQ does not have the concept of *referential integrity*, but it makes use of relationships to define possible navigation paths into the data.

Data Querying

A LINQ to SQL query is sent to the database only when the program needs to read data. For example, the following *foreach* loop iterates rows returned from a table:

```
var query =
    from    c in Customers
    where   c.Country == "USA"
    select  c.CompanyName;

  foreach( var company in query ) {
     Console.WriteLine( company );
}
```

The code generated by the *foreach* statement is equivalent to the code shown next. The exact moment the query is executed corresponds to the call of *GetEnumerator*:

```
// GetEnumerator sends the query to the database
IEnumerator<string> enumerator = query.GetEnumerator();
while (enumerator.MoveNext()) {
    Console.WriteLine( enumerator.Current );
}
```

Writing more *foreach* loops of the same query generates as many calls to *GetEnumerator*, and thus an equal number of repeated executions of the same query. If you want to iterate the same data many times, you might prefer to cache data in memory. Using *ToList* or *ToArray*, you convert the results of a query into a *List* or an *Array*, respectively. When you call these methods, the SQL query is sent to the database:

```
// ToList() sends the query to the database
var companyNames = query.ToList();
```

You might want to send the query to the database several times when you manipulate the LINQ query between data iterations. For example, you might have an interactive user interface that allows the user to add a new filter condition for each iteration of data. In Listing 5-11, the *DisplayTop* method shows only the first few rows of the result; query manipulation between *DisplayTop* calls simulates a user interaction that ends in a new filter condition each time.

Listing 5-11   Query manipulation

```
static void QueryManipulation() {
    DataContext db = new DataContext( ConnectionString );
    Table<Customer> Customers = db.GetTable<Customer>();
    db.Log = Console.Out;

    // All Customers
    var query =
        from   c in Customers
        select new {c.CompanyName, c.State, c.Country };

    DisplayTop( query, 10 );

    // User interaction add a filter
    // to the previous query
    // Customers from USA
    query =
        from   c in query
        where  c.Country == "USA"
        select c;

    DisplayTop( query, 10 );

    // User interaction add another
    // filter to the previous query
    // Customers from WA, USA
    query =
        from   c in query
        where  c.State == "WA"
        select c;

    DisplayTop( query, 10 );
}
```

```
static void DisplayTop<T>( IQueryable<T> query, int rows ) {
    foreach( var row in query.Take(rows)) {
        Console.WriteLine( row );
    }
}
```

 Important   In the previous example, we used *IQueryable<T>* as the *DisplayTop* parameter. If you pass *IEnumerable<T>* instead, the results would appear identical, but the query sent to the database would not contain the *TOP (rows)* clause to filter data directly on the database. When using *IEnumerable<T>*, you use a different set of extension methods to resolve the *Take* operator without generating a new expression tree.

A common query used for accessing a database is the read of a single row from a table, defining a condition that is guaranteed to be unique, such as a record key. Here is a typical query:

```
var query =
    from    c in db.Customers
    where   c.CustomerID == "ANATR"
    select  c;

var enumerator = query.GetEnumerator();
if (enumerator.MoveNext()) {
    var customer = enumerator.Current;
    Console.WriteLine( "{0} {1}", customer.CustomerID, customer.CompanyName );
}
```

In this case, it might be shorter and more explicit to state your intention by using the *Single* operator. The previous query can be written in this more compact way:

```
var customer = db.Customers.Single( c => c.CustomerID == "ANATR" );
Console.WriteLine( "{0} {1}", customer.CustomerID, customer.CompanyName );
```

Projections

The transformation from an expression tree to an SQL query requires the complete understanding of the query operations sent to the LINQ to SQL engine. This transformation affects the use of object initializers. You can use projections through the *select* keyword, as in the following example:

```
var query =
    from    c in Customers
    where   c.Country == "USA"
    select  new {c.CustomerID, Name = c.CompanyName.ToUpper()} into r
    orderby r.Name
    select  r;
```

The whole LINQ query is translated into this SQL statement:

```sql
SELECT [t1].[CustomerID], [t1].[value] AS [Name]
FROM ( SELECT [t0].[CustomerID],
               UPPER([t0].[CompanyName]) AS [value],
               [t0].[Country]
        FROM [Customers] AS [t0]
     ) AS [t1]
WHERE     [t1].[Country] = "USA"
ORDER BY [t1].[value]
```

As you can see, the *ToUpper* method has been translated into an UPPER T-SQL function call. To do that, the LINQ to SQL engine needs a deep knowledge of the meaning of any operation in the expression tree. Consider this query:

```csharp
var queryBad =
    from    c in Customers
    where   c.Country == "USA"
    select  new CustomerData( c.CustomerID, c.CompanyName.ToUpper()) into r
    orderby r.Name
    select  r;
```

In this case, we call a constructor of the *CustomerData* type that can do anything a piece of Intermediate Language (IL) code can do. In other words, there is no semantic value in calling a constructor other than the initial assignment of the instance created. The consequence is that LINQ to SQL cannot correctly translate this syntax into an equivalent SQL code, and it throws an exception if you try to execute the query. However, you can safely use a parameterized constructor in the final projection of a query, as in the following sample:

```csharp
var queryParamConstructor =
    from    c in Customers
    where   c.Country == "USA"
    orderby c.CompanyName
    select  new CustomerData( c.CustomerID, c.CompanyName.ToUpper() );
```

If you only need to initialize an object, use the object initializers instead of a parameterized constructor call, as in following query:

```csharp
var queryGood =
    from    c in Customers
    where   c.Country == "USA"
    select  new CustomerData { CustomerID = c.CustomerID,
                               Name = c.CompanyName.ToUpper() } into r
    orderby r.Name
    select  r;
```

Important   Always use object initializers to encode projections in LINQ to SQL. Use parameterized constructors only in the final projection of a query.

Stored Procedures

Accessing data through stored procedures and user-defined functions requires the definition of corresponding methods decorated with attributes. This enables you to write LINQ queries in a strongly typed form. From the LINQ point of view, there is no difference if a stored procedure or user-defined function is written in T-SQL or SQLCLR.

Consider the *Customers by City* stored procedure:

```
CREATE PROCEDURE [dbo].[Customers By City]( @param1 NVARCHAR(20) )
AS BEGIN
    SET NOCOUNT ON;
    SELECT CustomerID, ContactName, CompanyName, City
    FROM    Customers AS c
    WHERE   c.City = @param1
END
```

You can define a method decorated with a *StoredProcedure* attribute that calls the stored procedure through the *ExecuteMethodCall<T>* method of the *DataContext* class. In Listing 5-12, we define *CustomersByCity* as a member of a class derived from *DataContext*.

Listing 5-12   Stored procedure declaration

```
class SampleDb : DataContext {
    // ...
    [StoredProcedure( Name = "dbo.[Customers By City]" )]
    public IEnumerable<CustomerInfo> CustomersByCity( string param1 ) {
        return (IEnumerable<CustomerInfo>)
            this.ExecuteMethodCall<CustomerInfo>(
                this,
                ((MethodInfo) (MethodInfo.GetCurrentMethod())),
                param1 );
    }
}
```

The returned type implements *IEnumerable<CustomerInfo>* and can be enumerated in a *foreach* statement like this one:

```
SampleDb db = new SampleDb( ConnectionString );
foreach( var row in db.CustomersByCity( "Seattle" )) {
    Console.WriteLine( "{0} {1}", row.CustomerID, row.CompanyName );
}
```

You will find many more details on stored procedure declarations in the product documentation. You can have output parameters, integer results, and multiple resultsets. You always need to know the metadata of all possible returned resultsets. Whenever you have multiple resultsets from a stored procedure, you will use the *IMultipleResults* return type, calling one *GetResult<T>* method for each resultset sequentially and specifying the right *T* type for the expected result. Consider the following stored procedure that returns two resultsets with different structures:

```
CREATE PROCEDURE TwoCustomerGroups
AS BEGIN
    SELECT  CustomerID, ContactName, CompanyName, City
    FROM    Customers AS c
    WHERE   c.City = 'London'

    SELECT  CustomerID, CompanyName, City
    FROM    Customers AS c
    WHERE   c.City = 'Torino'
END
```

The declaration of the LINQ counterpart should be like the one shown in Listing 5-13.

Listing 5-13   Stored procedure with multiple results

```
class SampleDb : DataContext {
    // ...
    [StoredProcedure(Name="TwoCustomerGroups")]
    public IMultipleResults TwoCustomerGroups() {
        return (IMultipleResults)
            this.ExecuteMethodCallWithMultipleResults(
                this,
                (MethodInfo) (MethodInfo.GetCurrentMethod()) );
    }
}
```

Each resultset has a different type. When calling each *GetResult<T>*, you need to specify the right type, which needs at least a public member with the same name of each returned column. If you specify a type with more public members than available columns, these "missing" members will have a default value. In the next sample, the first resultset must match the *CustomerInfo* type, while the second resultset must correspond to the *CustomerShortInfo* type:

```
IMultipleResults results = db.TwoCustomerGroups();
foreach( var row in results.GetResult<CustomerInfo>()) {
    // Access to CustomerInfo instance
}
foreach( var row in results.GetResult<CustomerShortInfo>()) {
    // Access to CustomerShortInfo instance
}
```

The declaration for *CustomerInfo* and *CustomerShortInfo* does not require any attribute. You can also use inheritance if the same structure is present in different resultsets, but remember that in this case the use is driven by *GetResult* usage and not by the *InheritanceMapping* attribute that you have seen in entity class declaration:

```
public class CustomerShortInfo {
    public string CustomerID;
    public string CompanyName;
```

```
        public string City;
}

public class CustomerInfo : CustomerShortInfo{
    public string ContactName;
}
```

> **Important**   The fact that you can do something does not imply that it is the right thing to do in any case. The use of inheritance to differentiate the result type of a stored procedure has a demonstrative purpose—to illustrate how the mapping works. You can also use a single type containing all possible columns returned from all resultsets. It is your responsibility to choose the right way.

User-Defined Functions

A user-defined function (UDF) needs the same kind of declaration you have just seen for stored procedures. A UDF can be used inside a LINQ query; thus, it must be considered from the LINQ to SQL engine in the SQL statement construction. Remember that there is no difference if a UDF is written in T-SQL or SQLCLR.

Listing 5-14 provides an example of a LINQ declaration of the scalar-valued UDF *MinUnit-PriceByCategory* that is defined in the sample Northwind database.

Listing 5-14   Scalar-valued user-defined function

```
class SampleDb : DataContext {
    // ...
    [Function(Name="dbo.MinUnitPriceByCategory")]
    public decimal MinUnitPriceByCategory( int categoryID ) {
        IExecuteResults mc =
            this.ExecuteMethodCall(
                this,
                (MethodInfo) (MethodInfo.GetCurrentMethod()),
                categoryID );
        return (decimal)mc.ReturnValue;
    }
}
```

The call of a UDF as an isolated expression generates a single SQL query invocation. You can also use a UDF in a LINQ query like the following one:

```
var query =
    from   c in Categories
    select new { c.CategoryID,
                 c.CategoryName,
                 MinPrice = db.MinUnitPriceByCategory( c.CategoryID )};
```

The generated SQL query looks like this:

```
SELECT  [t0].[CategoryID],
        [t0].[CategoryName],
        dbo.MinUnitPriceByCategory([t0].[CategoryID]) AS [value]
FROM    [Categories] AS [t0]
```

A table-valued UDF has a different declaration that must match the returned type, as demonstrated in Listing 5-15.

Listing 5-15   Table-valued user-defined function

```
class SampleDb : DataContext {
    // ...
    [Function(Name="dbo.CustomersByCountry")]
    public IQueryable<Customer> CustomersByCountry( string country ) {
        return (IQueryable<Customer>)
            this.ExecuteMethodCall<Customer>(
                this,
                (MethodInfo) MethodInfo.GetCurrentMethod(),
                country );
    }
}
```

A table-valued UDF can be used like any other table in a LINQ query. For example, you can join customers returned by the previous UDF with the orders made by them, as in the following query:

```
Table<Order> Orders = db.GetTable<Order>();
var queryCustomers =
    from   c in db.CustomersByCountry( "USA" )
    join   o in Orders
           on c.CustomerID equals o.CustomerID
           into orders
    select new { c.CustomerID, c.CompanyName, orders };
```

The generated SQL query will be similar to this one:

```
SELECT  [t0].[CustomerID], [t0].[CompanyName],
        [t0].[City], [t0].[Region], [t0].[Country]
FROM    dbo.CustomersByCountry('USA') AS [t0]
```

Compiled Queries

If you need to repeat the same query many times, eventually with different argument values, you might be worried about the multiple query construction. Several databases, such as SQL Server, try to auto-parameterize received SQL queries to optimize the compilation of the query execution plan. However, the program that sends a parameterized query to SQL Server will get better performance, because SQL Server does not spend time to analyze it if the query is similar to another one already processed. LINQ already does a fine job of query optimization, but each time that the same query tree is evaluated, the LINQ to SQL engine parses the query tree to build the equivalent SQL code. You can optimize this behavior by using the *CompiledQuery* class.

> **More Info**   LINQ providers are in charge of creating optimized queries. For example, the built-in SQL Server provider sends parameterized queries to the database. Every time you see a constant value in the SQL code presented in this chapter, keep in mind that the real SQL query sent to the database has a parameter for each constant in the query. That constant can be the result of an expression that is independent from the query execution. This kind of expression is resolved by the host language (C# in this case). When you use the *CompiledQuery* class, the parsing of the query tree and the creation of the equivalent SQL code is the operation that is not repeated every time LINQ has to process the same query.

To compile a query, you can use the *CompiledQuery.Compile* static method. This approach passes the LINQ query as a parameter in the form of a lambda expression, and then obtains a delegate with arguments corresponding to both the *DataContext* on which you want to operate and the parameters of the query. Listing 5-16 illustrates compiled query declaration and use.

Listing 5-16   Compiled query in a local scope

```
static void CompiledQueriesLocal() {
    DataContext db = new DataContext( ConnectionString );
    Table<Customer> Customers = db.GetTable<Customer>();

    var query =
        CompiledQuery.Compile(
            ( DataContext context, string filterCountry ) =>
                from c in Customers
                where c.Country == filterCountry
                select new { c.CustomerID, c.CompanyName, c.City } );

    foreach (var row in query( db, "USA" )) {
        Console.WriteLine( row );
    }

    foreach (var row in query( db, "Italy" )) {
        Console.WriteLine( row );
    }
}
```

As you can see in the preceding example, the *Compile* method requires a lambda expression whose first argument is a *DataContext* instance. That argument defines the connection over which the query will be executed. Assigning the *CompiledQuery.Compile* result to a local variable is easy (because you declare that variable with *var*) but probably not very frequent. Chances are that you need to store the delegate returned from *CompiledQuery.Compile* in an instance or a static member to easily reuse it several times. To do that, you need to know the right declaration syntax.

A compiled query is stored in a *Func* delegate, where the first argument must be an instance of *DataContext* (or a derived class) and the last argument must be the type returned from the query. You can define other arguments in the middle that will be arguments of the compiled query and will need to be specified for each compiled query invocation. Listing 5-17 shows the syntax you can use in this scenario to create the compiled query and then use it.

Listing 5-17   Compiled query assigned to a static member

```
public static Func< nwind.Northwind, string, IQueryable<nwind.Customer>>
    CustomerByCountry =
        CompiledQuery.Compile(
            ( nwind.Northwind db, string filterCountry ) =>
                from c in db.Customers
                where c.Country == filterCountry
                select c );

static void CompiledQueriesStatic() {
    nwind.Northwind db = new nwind.Northwind( ConnectionString );

    foreach (var row in CustomerByCountry( db, "USA" )) {
        Console.WriteLine( row.CustomerID );
    }

    foreach (var row in CustomerByCountry( db, "Italy" )) {
        Console.WriteLine( row.CustomerID );
    }
}
```

Different Approaches to Querying Data

When using LINQ to SQL entities, you have two approaches to querying the same data. The classical way to navigate a relational schema is to write associative queries, just as you can do in SQL. The alternative way offered by LINQ to SQL is through graph traversal. Given the same result, we might obtain different SQL queries and a different level of performance.

Consider this SQL query that calculates the total quantity of orders for a product (in this case, Chocolade, which is a localized name in the Northwind database):

```
SELECT    SUM( od.Quantity ) AS TotalQuantity
FROM      [Products] p
LEFT JOIN [Order Details] od
     ON   od.[ProductID] = p.[ProductID]
WHERE     p.ProductName = 'Chocolade'
GROUP BY  p.ProductName
```

The natural conversion into a LINQ query is shown in Listing 5-18. The *Single* operator gets the first row and puts it into *quantityJoin*, which is used to display the result.

Listing 5-18   Query with *Join*

```
var queryJoin =
    from  p in db.Products
    join  o in db.Order_Details
          on p.ProductID equals o.ProductID
          into OrdersProduct
    where p.ProductName == "Chocolade"
    select OrdersProduct.Sum( o => o.Quantity );
var quantityJoin = queryJoin.Single();
Console.WriteLine( quantityJoin );
```

As you can see, the associative query in LINQ can explicitly require the join between *Products* and *Order_Details* through *ProductID* equivalency. By leveraging entities, you can implicitly use the relationship between *Products* and *Order_Details* defined in the *Product* class, as shown in Listing 5-19.

Listing 5-19   Query using *Association*

```
var queryAssociation =
    from  p in db.Products
    where p.ProductName == "Chocolade"
    select p.Order_Details.Sum( o => o.Quantity );
var quantityAssociation = queryAssociation.Single();
Console.WriteLine( quantityAssociation );
```

The single SQL queries produced by both of these LINQ queries are identical. The LINQ query with *join* is more explicit about the access to data, while the query that uses the association between *Product* and *Order_Details* is more implicit in this regard. Using implicit associations results in shorter queries that are less error-prone (because you cannot be wrong about the join condition). At first, you might find that a shorter query is not easier to read. However, this perception might arise because you are accustomed to seeing lengthier queries, and your comfort level with shorter ones could change over time.

Looking further, you can observe that reading a single product does not require a query expression. You can apply the *Single* operator directly on the *Products* table, as shown in Listing 5-20.

Listing 5-20   Access through *Entity*

```
var chocolade = db.Products.Single( p => p.ProductName == "Chocolade" );
var quantityValue = chocolade.Order_Details.Sum( o => o.Quantity );
Console.WriteLine( quantityValue );
```

This is a two-step operation that sends two SQL queries to the database. The first one retrieves the *Product* entity, and the second one accesses the Order Details table to calculate the total quantity for the required product. At first glance, this kind of access is shorter to write compared to a query, but its performance is worse. This conclusion is true if you consider the single operation isolated from any other aspect. It might be false in a real-world scenario.

The unique identity management of LINQ to SQL grants that a single instance of an entity exists in memory. If you know that a *Product* entity is already in memory for Chocolade when you need to calculate the total quantity of orders, or that the same *Product* entity will be used later for other purposes, this double access can be balanced by fewer instances of accessing the whole program. The previous queries did not create *Product* instances because only the total for the product was required as output. From this point of view, if we already had a *Product* instance for Chocolade in memory, the performance of queries would be worse because they make a useless join with *Product* just to transform the product name (Chocolade) into its corresponding *ProductID*.

A final thought on the number of generated queries: You might think that we generated two queries when accessing data through the *Product* entity because we had two distinct statements—one to assign the *chocolade* variable, and the other to assign a value to *quantityEntity*. This assumption is not completely true. Even if you write a single statement, the use of a *Product* entity (the results from the *Single* operator call) generates a separate query. Listing 5-21 produces the same results (in terms of memory objects and SQL queries) as Listing 5-20.

Listing 5-21   Access through *Entity* with a single statement

```
var quantityChocolade = db.Products.Single( p => p.ProductName == "Chang" )
                          .Order_Details.Sum( o => o.Quantity );
Console.WriteLine( quantityChocolade );
```

Finding a better way to access data really depends on the whole set of operations performed by a program. If you extensively use entities in your code to store data in memory, access to data through graph traversal based on entity access might offer better performance. On the other hand, if you always transform query results in anonymous types and never manipulate entities in memory, you might prefer an approach based on LINQ queries. As always, the right answer is, "It depends."

Direct Queries

Sometime you might need access to some database SQL features that are not available with LINQ. For example, imagine that you want to use Common Table Expressions (CTE) or the PIVOT command with SQL Server. LINQ does not have an explicit constructor to do that, even if (in the future) its SQL Server provider could use these features to optimize some queries. Listing 5-22 shows how you can use the *ExecuteQuery<T>* method of the *DataContext* class to send a query directly to the database. The *T* in *ExecuteQuery<T>* is an entity class that represents a returned row.

Listing 5-22   Direct query

```
var query = db.ExecuteQuery<EmployeeInfo>( @"
    WITH EmployeeHierarchy (EmployeeID, LastName, FirstName,
        ReportsTo, HierarchyLevel) AS
    ( SELECT EmployeeID,LastName, FirstName,
            ReportsTo, 1 as HierarchyLevel
        FROM    Employees
        WHERE   ReportsTo IS NULL

        UNION ALL

        SELECT     e.EmployeeID, e.LastName, e.FirstName,
                   e.ReportsTo,eh.HierarchyLevel + 1 AS HierarchyLevel
        FROM       Employees e
        INNER JOIN EmployeeHierarchy eh
              ON   e.ReportsTo = eh.EmployeeID
    )
    SELECT *
    FROM EmployeeHierarchy
    ORDER BY HierarchyLevel, LastName, FirstName" );

foreach (var row in query) {
    Console.WriteLine( row );
}
```

Warning   Columns in the resulting rows that do not match entity attributes are ignored. Entity members that do not have corresponding columns are initialized with the default value. If the *EmployeeInfo* class would contain a mismatched column name, that member would be not assigned without an error. Be careful and check name correspondence when some column or member values are not filled in the result.

Read-Only *DataContext* Access

If you need to access data only in a read-only way, you might want to improve performance by disabling a *DataContext* service that supports data modification:

```
DataContext db = new DataContext( ConnectionString );
db.ObjectTracking = false;
var query = ...
```

The *ObjectTracking* property controls the change tracking service that we will describe in the next section.

Data Update

All entity instances are tracked by the *identity management service* of LINQ to SQL to keep a unique instance of a row of data. This service is guaranteed only for objects created or handled by *DataContext*. (This has implications that you will see shortly.) Keeping a single instance of a row of data allows the manipulation of in-memory objects without concern for potential data inconsistencies or duplication in memory. We will analyze how to deal with concurrent operations later.

> **Important** Remember that a class entity must have at least a column with the *IsPrimaryKey=true* setting in the *Column* attribute; otherwise, it cannot be tracked by the identity management service, and data manipulation is not allowed.

Entity Updates

Changing data members and properties of an entity instance is an operation tracked by the *change tracking service* of LINQ to SQL. This service retains the original value of a modified entity. With this information, the service generates a corresponding list of SQL statements that make the same changes on the database. You can see these SQL statements by calling the *GetChangeText* method on *DataContext*:

```
var customer = db.Customers.Single( c => c.CustomerID == "FRANS" );
customer.ContactName = "Marco Russo";
Console.WriteLine( db.GetChangeText() );
```

The output from the previous code is similar to that shown here:

```
UPDATE [Customers]
SET    [ContactName] = "Marco Russo"
FROM   [Customers]
WHERE  ...
```

We will discuss the *WHERE* condition later. Remember that SQL statements in the list are not sent to the database until the call to the *SubmitChanges* method is made.

If you want to add a record to a table or remove a record from a table, creating or deleting an object in memory is not enough. The *DataContext* instance must be notified also. This can be done directly by calling *Add* or *Remove* on the corresponding *Table* collection (these methods operate on the in-memory copy of the data; a subsequent *SubmitChanges* call will forward the SQL commands to the database):

```
var newCustomer = new Customer {
                    CustomerID = "DLEAP",
                    CompanyName = "DevLeap",
                    Country = "Italy" };
db.Customers.Add( newCustomer );

var oldCustomer = db.Customers.Single( c => c.CustomerID == "FRANS" );
db.Customers.Remove( oldCustomer );
```

Looking at the generated SQL statements, you will see that a single INSERT is generated to add a new customer, while the deletion of a customer might generate many UPDATE statements before the DELETE one. This is because of the need to "break" the relationship between a customer and its orders. Related orders are not deleted, but simply "disconnected" from the customer that was tied to them.

```
INSERT INTO [Customers](CustomerID, CompanyName, ...)
VALUES("DEVLEAP", "DevLeap", ...)

UPDATE [Orders]
SET    [CustomerID] = NULL
FROM   [Orders]
WHERE  ([OrderID] = @p1) AND ...
-- Other UPDATE statements here, one for each Order of the removed customer
DELETE FROM [Customers] WHERE [CustomerID] = "FRANS"
```

> **Note**   Calling *Add* or *Remove* several times for the same object (entities have a unique identity) will not generate the same SQL statement multiple times.

Another way to notify the *DataContext* of a new entity is to attach the new entity to an existing object already tracked by *DataContext*:

```
var newCustomer = new Customer {
                    CustomerID = "DLEAP",
                    CompanyName = "DevLeap",
                    Country = "Italy" };
var order = db.Orders.Single( o => o.OrderID == 10248 );
order.Customer = newCustomer;
```

The examples just shown introduced the need to understand how relationships between entities work when updates are applied to the database. Relationships are bidirectional between entities, and when an update is made on one side, the other side should be kept synchronized. This has to be done by the class entity implementation. Entity classes generated by code-generation tools (such as SQLMetal) usually offer this level of service.

The previous operation inserted a customer tied to order 10248. If you explore the *new-Customer* entity after the *order.Customer* assignment, you will see that its *Orders* properties contain order 10248. Executing the following code will display one row containing the order 10248:

```
foreach( var o in newCustomer.Orders ) {
    Console.WriteLine( "{0}-{1}", o.CustomerID, o.OrderID );
}
```

You can work in the opposite way, assigning an order to the *Orders* properties of a customer. Consequently, the *Customer* property of the moved order will be updated.

```
var oldCustomer = db.Customers.Single( c => c.CustomerID == "VINET" );
var newCustomer = new Customer {
                    CustomerID = "DLEAP",
```

```
                          CompanyName = "DevLeap",
                          Country = "Italy" };
db.Customers.Add( newCustomer );
var order = oldCustomer.Orders.Single( o => o.OrderID == 10248 );
oldCustomer.Orders.Remove( order );
newCustomer.Orders.Add( order );
```

You have seen that there are two ways to add a record to a table (one direct and one indirect). However, if you need to remove a row, you always have to do this in a direct way, calling the *Remove* method on the corresponding *Table* collection. When you remove an object, related entities are unbound (that is, the foreign key is set to NULL), but this might throw an exception if constraints do not allow NULL values. If you also want to remove the "child" objects of a removed object, you have to call the *Remove* method on them. You can do that by leveraging the *RemoveAll* method:

```
var order = db.Orders.Single( o => o.OrderID == 10248 );
db.Order_Details.RemoveAll( order.Order_Details );
db.Orders.Remove( order );
```

This update at the moment of calling *SubmitChanges* will generate SQL statements that respect the referential integrity constraints shown in the following statements:

```
DELETE FROM [Order Details] WHERE ([OrderID] = 10248) AND ([ProductID] = 11)
DELETE FROM [Order Details] WHERE ([OrderID] = 10248) AND ([ProductID] = 42)
DELETE FROM [Order Details] WHERE ([OrderID] = 10248) AND ([ProductID] = 72)
DELETE FROM [Orders] WHERE [OrderID] = 10248
```

After a call to *SubmitChanges*, all tracked changes history is thrown away.

> **Important** As we have already seen, you can disable the change tracking service for a *DataContext* by specifying *false* on its *ObjectTracking* property. Whenever you need to get data only in a read-only way—for example, to display a report or a Web page in a noninteractive mode—this setting will improve overall performance.

Database Updates

With LINQ to SQL, many SQL queries are sent to the database in a transparent and implicit way. On the other hand, all SQL commands that modify the state of the database are sent only when you decide to do that, calling *SubmitChanges* on the *DataContext* object (which is eventually derived), as shown in Listing 5-23.

Listing 5-23 Submit changes to the database

```
Northwind db = new Northwind( Program.ConnectionString );
var customer = db.Customers.Single( c => c.CustomerID == "FRANS" );
customer.ContactName = "Marco Russo";
db.SubmitChanges();
```

Concurrent Operations

Operating with in-memory entities in LINQ is a form of disconnected operation on data. In these cases, you always have to deal with concurrent operations made by other users or connections between the read of data and its successive updates. Usually, you operate with optimistic concurrency. In the case of a conflict, a *ChangeConflictException* error is thrown by default. This exception contains a *Conflicts* collection that explains the reasons for the error. (There can be several conflicts on different tables in a single *SubmitChanges* call.) Listing 5-24 provides a demonstration.

Listing 5-24   Retry loop for a concurrency conflict

```
Northwind db2 = new Northwind( Program.ConnectionString );
for( int retry = 0; retry < 4; retry++ ) {
    var customer2 = db2.Customers.Single( c => c.CustomerID == "FRANS" );
    // Another connection updates database table here
    customer2.ContactName = "Paolo Pialorsi";
    try {
        db2.SubmitChanges(); // May throw exception
        break;               // Exit the "for" loop if submit succeed
    }
    catch (ChangeConflictException ex) {
        Console.WriteLine( ex.Message );
        db2.Refresh( customer2, RefreshMode.KeepChanges );
    }
}
```

Important   After a conflict, you might decide to re-read all the data or rely on the *Refresh* method, as demonstrated in the previous code sample. The *RefreshMode.KeepChanges* argument keeps the data found in the concurrent update if it was unchanged in the updated entity. Other *RefreshMode* values are *KeepCurrentValues* and *OverwriteCurrentValues*, which specify different behaviors. See the product documentation for a detailed explanation.

SubmitChanges can have a parameter specifying whether you want to stop at the first conflict or try all updates regardless of the conflict. The default is to stop at the first conflict:

```
db.SubmitChanges(ConflictMode.FailOnFirstConflict);
db.SubmitChanges(ConflictMode.ContinueOnConflict);
```

You can control how the concurrency conflict is determined through entity class definition. Each *Column* attribute can have an *UpdateCheck* argument that can have one of the following three values:

- **Always**   Always use this column (which is the default) for conflict detection.
- **Never**   Never use this column for conflict detection.
- **WhenChanged**   Use this column only when the member has been changed by the application.

Other options in column definitions are represented by two Boolean flags: *IsDBGenerated* identifies that the value is auto-generated by the database, and *IsVersion* identifies a database timestamp or a version number. If a column has *IsVersion* set to *true*, the concurrency conflict is identified and only the entity unique key and its timestamp/version column are compared.

> **Note** Using *IsVersion* simplifies the query sent to the database to check concurrency conflict—updates and deletes can have a long WHERE condition if an *IsVersion* column is not specified.
>
> *IsDBGenerated* and *IsVersion* require a SELECT to be submitted after the UPDATE or INSERT operation. The tradeoff between having an *IsVersion* column or not depends on the number and complexity of table columns.

Transactions

A *SubmitChanges* call automatically starts a database explicit transaction, using *IDbConnection* *.BeginTransaction* and applying all changes made in memory to the database inside the same transaction. Using the *TransactionScope* class contained in the *System.Transactions* library since .NET 2.0, you can add any standard command to the database or change any other transactional resource in the same transaction, which eventually will be transparently promoted to a distributed transaction. Listing 5-25 is an example of a transaction controlled in this way.

Listing 5-25 Transaction controlled by *TransactionScope*

```
using(TransactionScope ts = new TransactionScope()) {
    Product prod = db.Products.Single(p => p.ProductID == 42);

    if (prod.UnitsInStock > 0) {
        prod.UnitsInStock--;
    }

    db.SubmitChanges();
    ts.Complete();
}
```

In the case of an exception, the database transaction is canceled. If you have an existing ADO.NET application that does not use *System.Transactions*, you can control database transactions by accessing the *Transaction* property of *DataContext*.

Stored Procedures

You can override the default insert, update, and delete SQL statements generated by LINQ to SQL when submitting changes. To do that, you can define one or more methods with specific signatures and pattern names. This is the syntax to use—note that you need to replace the name of the modified type to *TYPE*:

```
public void UpdateTYPE(TYPE original, TYPE current) { ... }
public void InsertTYPE(TYPE inserted) { ... }
public void DeleteTYPE(TYPE deleted) { ... }
```

Important   The name of the method is important. The LINQ to SQL engine looks for a method with a matching signature and that has a name that starts with the word corresponding to the operation you override (*Update*, *Insert*, or *Delete*) followed by the name of the modified type.

Usually, this particular override is used to call stored procedures instead of sending SQL statements to execute data manipulation on the database. These methods have to be defined on the *DataContext* derived class. Because a derived class is already generated by some tool (such as SQLMetal or the LINQ to SQL designer in Microsoft Visual Studio), you can add your methods by using the *partial* class syntax, as shown in Listing 5-26.

Listing 5-26   Stored procedure to override an update

```
public partial class Northwind : DataContext {
    public void UpdateProduct(Product original, Product current) {
        // Execute the stored procedure for UnitsInStock update
        if (original.UnitsInStock != current.UnitsInStock) {
            int rowCount = this.ExecuteCommand(
                        "exec UpdateProductStock " +
                        "@id={0}, @originalUnits={1}, @decrement={2}",
                        original.ProductID,
                        original.UnitsInStock,
                        (original.UnitsInStock - current.UnitsInStock) );
            if (rowCount < 1) {
                throw new OptimisticConcurrencyException();
            }
        }
    }
}
```

Important   Conflict detection is your responsibility if you decide to override insert, update, and delete methods.

Binding Metadata

The mapping between LINQ to SQL entities and database structures has to be described through metadata information. Until now, you have seen attributes on entity definition fulfilling this rule. There is an alternative way to do this (using external XML mapping file), and there are tools and methods that automate the generation of entity classes starting from a database and vice versa.

Creating a Database from Entities

An application that auto-installs itself on a machine might be interested in creating a database that can persist its objects graph. This is a typical situation—you need to handle simple configurations that are represented by a graph of objects.

If you have a class derived from *DataContext* that contains entity definitions decorated with *Table* and *Column* attributes, you can create the corresponding database by calling the *Create-Database* method. This method sends the necessary CREATE DATABASE statement as well as the subsequent CREATE TABLE and ALTER TABLE statements:

```
const string ConnectionString =
    "Database=Test_Northwind;Trusted_Connection=yes";
public static void Create() {
    Northwind db = new Northwind( ConnectionString );
    db.CreateDatabase();
}
```

You can also drop a database and check for its existence. The name of the database is inferred from the connection string. You can duplicate a database schema into several databases simply by changing the connection string:

```
if (db.DatabaseExists()) {
    db.DeleteDatabase();    // Send a DROP DATABASE
}
db.CreateDatabase();
```

Creating Entities from a Database

If you already have an existing physical data layer, you might want to create a set of entity classes for an existing database. You can use two available tools: SQLMetal and the LINQ to SQL designer integrated in Visual Studio.

SQLMetal is a command-line tool. It generates a source file containing entity class declarations based on metadata read from the specified database. This process can be split into two steps: First, an XML file describing the database structure is created. That XML file can be edited by adding or removing desired entities, constraints, or both. At the end, the XML file is used to generate source code files for entity classes. The following commands create the XML file from database metadata and the source code from the XML file, respectively:

```
SqlMetal /server:localhost /database:Northwind /pluralize /xml:Northwind.xml
SqlMetal /namespace:northwind /code:Northwind.cs Northwind.xml
```

See the product documentation for details about SQLMetal and the related XML file. This same XML file can be used as a basis for the LINQ external mapping feature.

The LINQ to SQL designer integrated in Visual Studio allows the creation of LINQ entity classes in a more interactive way—you have a graphical editor that allows the design of a graphical schema of entities. To open the designer, use the Project / Add New Item command in Visual Studio 2005 and choose the Linq to SQL File template.

External Mapping

An XML file similar to the one created by the SQLMetal utility can be used as a mapping file to decorate entity classes instead of using attributes. The additions to the automatically generated file are a *Type* element and a *Member* attribute that bind the entity classes and columns to their respective mapping information. An XML mapping file will appear that looks like the following code sample:

```
<Database Name="Northwind">
   <Table Name="Products">
      <Type Name=" Product">
         <Column Name="ProductID" Member="ProductID"
                 Storage="_ProductID" DbType="Int NOT NULL IDENTITY"
                 IsPrimaryKey="True" IsDbGenerated="True" />
```

The XML file can be loaded using an *XmlMappingSource* instance generated by calling its *FromXml* static method. The following example shows how to use such syntax:

```
string path = "Northwind.xml";
XmlMappingSource prodMapping =
      XmlMappingSource.FromXml(File.ReadAllText(path));
Northwind db = new Northwind(
      @"Database=Test_Northwind;Trusted_Connection=yes",
      prodMapping
   );
```

One possible use of this technique is a scenario in which different databases must be mapped to a specific data model. Differences in databases might be table and field names (for example, localized versions of the database). In general, consider this option when you need to realize "light" decoupling of mapping between entity classes and the physical data structure of the database.

Differences Between .NET and SQL Type Systems

The product documentation illustrates all types of system differences between the .NET Framework and LINQ to SQL. Many operators require a specific conversion, such as cast operations and the *ToString* method that are converted in *CAST* or *CONVERT* operators in SQL translation. There could be significant differences if your code is sensitive to rounding differences. (*Math.Round* and *ROUND* have different logic. See the *MidpointRounding* enumeration used to control the behavior.) There are also minor differences in date and time manipulation. Above all, you need to remember that SQL Server supports *DATETIME* but not *DATE*. See the documentation for further details.

LINQ to DataSet

The .NET native *System.Data.DataSet* is an in-memory representation of a set of data. It is useful to get a disconnected copy of data that comes from an external data source. Regardless of the data source, the internal representation of a *DataSet* follows the relational model, including tables, constraints, and relationships among the tables. In other words, you can consider the *DataSet* as a sort of in-memory relational database. This makes it a good target for a LINQ implementation.

Using LINQ to Load a *DataSet*

A *DataSet* can be loaded by querying a relational database. One possible way to do this is through a *DataAdapter*, as shown in Listing 5-27.

Listing 5-27   Loading *DataSet* using a *DataAdapter*

```
DataSet ds = new DataSet("CustomerOrders");
SqlDataAdapter da = new SqlDataAdapter( QueryOrders, ConnectionString );
da.SelectCommand.Parameters.AddWithValue( "@CustomerID", "QUICK" );
da.TableMappings.Add( "Table", "Orders" );
da.TableMappings.Add( "Table1", "OrderDetails" );
da.Fill( ds );

const string ConnectionString = "Database=Northwind;Trusted_Connection=yes";
const string QueryOrders = @"
SET @CustomerID = 'QUICK'
SELECT  OrderID, OrderDate, Freight, ShipName,
        ShipAddress, ShipCity, ShipCountry
FROM    Orders
WHERE   CustomerID = @CustomerID

SELECT     od.OrderID, od.UnitPrice, od.Quantity, od.Discount,
           p.[ProductName]
FROM       [Order Details] od
INNER JOIN Orders o
       ON  o.[OrderID] = od.[OrderID]
LEFT JOIN  Products p
       ON  p.[ProductID] = od.[ProductID]
WHERE      o.CustomerID = @CustomerID";
```

The previous code combines two *DataTable* instances into one *DataSet*, which corresponds to the orders placed by a specific customer.

Using LINQ to Query a *DataSet*

A *DataTable* can be queried with LINQ, just as any other *IEnumerable<T>* list.

> **Note**   *DataTable* does not implement *IEnumerable<T>*. You have to call *AsEnumerable*, which is an extension method for *DataTable*, to obtain a wrapper that implements that interface.

The list is made of *DataRow* objects; thus, you must access *DataRow* member properties to get a field value. This arrangement allows the call of any *DataRow* member instead of using a query expression over a *DataTable*. You can use the *Field<T>* accessor method instead of using a direct cast on the result of the standard *DataRow* accessor (such as *o["OrderDate"]*). The query shown in Listing 5-28 gets the orders that show a date of 1998 or later.

Listing 5-28   Querying a *DataTable* with LINQ

```
DataSet ds = LoadDataSetUsingDataAdapter();
DataTable orders = ds.Tables["Orders"];
DataTable orderDetails = ds.Tables["OrderDetails"];

var query =
    from   o in orders.AsEnumerable()
    where  o.Field<DateTime>( "OrderDate" ).Year >= 1998
    orderby o.Field<DateTime>( "OrderDate" ) descending
    select  o;
```

Note   *AsEnumerable* and *Field<T>* are two custom extension methods for *DataTable* and *DataRow* types. They are defined in *System.Data.DataTableExtensions* and *System.Data.DataRow-Extensions*, respectively.

When you have several *DataTable* objects in a *DataSet*, you might want to use some type of join. The query shown in Listing 5-29 calculates the total order amount for each order from 1998 to the present.

Listing 5-29   Joining two *DataTable* objects with LINQ

```
DataSet ds = LoadDataSetUsingDataAdapter();
DataTable orders = ds.Tables["Orders"];
DataTable orderDetails = ds.Tables["OrderDetails"];

var query =
    from   o in orders.AsEnumerable()
    join   od in orderDetails.AsEnumerable()
    on o.Field<int>( "OrderID" ) equals od.Field<int>( "OrderID" )
    into orderLines
    where  o.Field<DateTime>( "OrderDate" ).Year >= 1998
    orderby o.Field<DateTime>( "OrderDate" ) descending
    select  new { OrderID = o.Field<int>( "OrderID" ),
                  OrderDate = o.Field<DateTime>( "OrderDate" ),
                  Amount = orderLines.Sum(
                               od => od.Field<decimal>( "UnitPrice" )
                                   * od.Field<short>( "Quantity" ) ) };
```

In the previous examples, you specified the relationship between *orders* and *orderDetails* through the *join* syntax. If the *DataSet* contains information about existing relationships between entities, a LINQ query can take advantage of this. In Listing 5-30, we use *GetChild-Rows* to get the lines for the order details instead of explicitly joining the two tables.

Listing 5-30   Leveraging *DataSet* relationships in LINQ queries

```
DataSet ds = LoadDataSetUsingDataAdapter();
DataTable orders = ds.Tables["Orders"];
DataTable orderDetails = ds.Tables["OrderDetails"];
```

```
ds.Relations.Add( "OrderDetails",
                orders.Columns["OrderID"],
                orderDetails.Columns["OrderID"]);

var query =
    from    o in orders.AsEnumerable()
    where   o.Field<DateTime>( "OrderDate" ).Year >= 1998
    orderby o.Field<DateTime>( "OrderDate" ) descending
    select  new { OrderID = o.Field<int>( "OrderID" ),
                OrderDate = o.Field<DateTime>( "OrderDate" ),
                Amount = o.GetChildRows( "OrderDetails" ).Sum(
                            od => od.Field<decimal>( "UnitPrice" )
                                * od.Field<short>( "Quantity" ) ) };
```

Using LINQ to Query a Typed *DataSet*

A typed *DataSet* can be queried with a simpler syntax because it is not necessary to use the *Field<T>* accessor and the *AsEnumerable* method.

> **Note**   If you create the typed *DataSet* with Visual Studio, your typed *DataTable* classes will be derived from the *TypedTableBase<T>* class, which implements the *IEnumerable<T>* interface. For this reason, it is not required to call *AsEnumerable* to get a wrapper.

The previous query, which we also used to leverage the existing *DataSet* relationships, can be written as shown in Listing 5-31, which uses a typed *DataSet*.

Listing 5-31   Querying a typed *DataSet* with LINQ

```
var query =
    from    o in ds.Orders
    where   o.OrderDate.Year >= 1998
    orderby o.OrderDate descending
    select  new { o.OrderID, o.OrderDate,
                Amount = o.GetOrder_DetailsRows().Sum(
                            od => od.UnitPrice * od.Quantity ) };
```

As you can see, the query syntax is much simpler and similar to the one we used earlier to query other type of entities. However, you must use a predefined schema (the typed *DataSet*) to query *DataSet* in such a way, and this prevents the use of this syntax with *DataSet* containing a flexible schema defined at execution time. This does not mean that you should use an untyped *DataSet*; it only emphasizes that untyped *DataSet*s can be queried only with the *Field<T>* accessor.

Accessing Untyped *DataSet* Data

Accessing data in an untyped *DataSet* requires the use of the *Field<T>* and *SetField<T>* accessors to get and set field values, respectively. These accessors are important because a null value in a *DataSet* is represented by the *IsNull* method returning *true*. You should check this condition each time you access a column just to avoid potential cast errors. The use of these accessors is allowed in any *DataTable* or *DataRow* access, even outside a query expression, as you can see in Listing 5-32.

Listing 5-32   Querying an untyped *DataSet* with LINQ

```
foreach( DataRow r in orderDetails.Rows ) {
    if (r.Field<decimal>( "UnitPrice" ) < 10 ){
        r.SetField<decimal>( "UnitPrice", 10 );
    }
}
```

LINQ to Entities

By now, we have seen how to leverage LINQ queries to select data over SQL databases and *DataSet* instances, using a data-centric approach. Every single query we ran was against a particular data table, with a one-to-one mapping between data tables and query results. However, the real world of enterprise application development requires abstraction from a physical data persistence layer to guarantee maintainability and platform independency.

Whenever we work with an Entity Data Model (EDM), we create an abstraction, modeling entities at a conceptual level rather than at the data level. LINQ to Entities allows querying a list of entities abstracted from the physical data layer, using LINQ syntax. We define *entities* as instances of entity types (such as *Order*, *Customer*, *Product*, and so on), which are structured and built starting from any kind of persistence layer but independent of it. Entities are grouped into *EntitySet* objects and can be related to each other through relationships, which are instances of relationship types (such as *CustomerOrders*, *OrderProducts*, and so on).

With LINQ to Entities, we can leverage object inheritance and data complexity. For instance, we can have a complex *Customer* type that includes its *Orders* as a sequence property, inheriting its base structure from the *Contact* type. From an entity point of view, we do not care how the *Contact*, *Customer*, and *Orders* of the *Customer* are brought to us; we care about them only when they are in memory. On the other hand, under the cover, we need a program to query a particular database to extract the content of these entities. Whatever makes the magic is defined by the mapping between .NET classes and the database structure. This mapping is made of a set of files and can be defined using a tool, called with an EDM schema as input, that generates the .NET classes that map to the EDM structure. This tool maps the conceptual layer (entities) with the database physical schema (persistence layer), making the inner workings transparent. We can imagine having a *Customer* entity, defined starting from a subset of the classic Northwind sample application, like the one defined in Listing 5-33.

Listing 5-33 A handmade *Customer* entity

```
public partial class Customer {

    public string CustomerID {
        get { return this._CustomerID; }
        set { this._CustomerID = value; }
    }
    private string _CustomerID = string.Empty;

    public string CompanyName {
        get { return this._CompanyName; }
        set { this._CompanyName = value; }
    }
    private string _CompanyName = string.Empty;

    public string Country {
        get { return this._ Country; }
        set { this._ Country = value; }
    }
    private string _ Country = string.Empty;
}
```

We defined this entity by hand, and you probably know the effort required to keep each instance of *Customer* synchronized with a physical data layer, including eventually handling relationships with instances of *SalesOrders*. To solve this problem, you can use one of the many Object Relational Mapping (ORM) frameworks built on top of .NET, or you can simply base your solution on LINQ to Entities and ADO.NET Entity Framework. If you use LINQ to Entities, you should define any of your entities by using a designer for Visual Studio, or define them manually with a text or XML editor. Whatever technique you use, you must define a set of XML files that describes each *Entity*, *EntitySet*, and *Association* and that maps each of them to corresponding tables and views on a particular data layer. The result of this mapping will be a set of auto-generated classes that define entities such as the *Customer* shown in Listing 5-33, but with metadata information to influence the behavior of their instances. Listing 5-34 shows how this is done.

Listing 5-34 An ADO.NET Entity Framework auto-generated *Customer* entity

```
[System.Data.Objects.DataClasses.EntityTypeAttribute(
  SchemaName = "NorthwindLib", TypeName = "Customer" )]
public partial class Customer :
global::System.Data.Objects.DataClasses.Entity {

  // ...

  [System.Data.Objects.DataClasses.EntityKeyPropertyAttribute()]
  [System.Data.Objects.DataClasses.NullableAttribute( false )]
  public string CustomerID {
    get { return this._CustomerID; }
    set {
      this.ReportPropertyChanging( "CustomerID",
                this._CustomerID );
      this._CustomerID = global::System.Data.Objects.DataClasses.StructuralObject.Set
```

```
ValidValue( value, false, 5, true );
      this.ReportPropertyChanged( "CustomerID", this._CustomerID );
      }
  }
  private string _CustomerID = string.Empty;

  [System.Data.Objects.DataClasses.EdmScalarPropertyAttribute()]
  [System.Data.Objects.DataClasses.NullableAttribute( false )]
  public string CompanyName {
    get { return this._CompanyName; }
    set {
      this.ReportPropertyChanging( "CompanyName",
                  this._CompanyName );
      this._CompanyName = global::System.Data.Objects.DataClasses.StructuralObject.Set
ValidValue( value, false, 40, true );
      this.ReportPropertyChanged( "CompanyName", this._CompanyName );
      }
  }
  private string _CompanyName = string.Empty;

  [System.Data.Objects.DataClasses.EdmScalarPropertyAttribute()]
  [System.Data.Objects.DataClasses.NullableAttribute(true)]
  public string Country {
    get { return this._Country; }
    set {
      this.ReportPropertyChanging("Country", this._Country);
      this._Country =
global::System.Data.Objects.DataClasses.StructuralObject.SetValidValue(
  value, true, 15, true);
      this.ReportPropertyChanged("Country", this._Country);
      }
  }
  private string _Country;
}
```

This second *Customer* class, shown in Listing 5-34, is broadly decorated with attributes of the *System.Data.Objects.DataClasses* namespace. These attributes provide information about the entity model, regardless of its database mapping. You can see that they describe relationships between the class properties and the schema model, not the physical database model. Listing 5-35 shows a sample query to select all the instances of Italian customers.

Listing 5-35   A query to select all the Italian customers

```
using (Northwind db = new Northwind( NWIND_CONNECTION_STRING ) ) {

  ObjectQuery<Customer> customers = db.CreateQuery<Customer>(
    "SELECT VALUE c FROM Customers AS c WHERE c.Country = 'Italy'" );

  foreach(Customer c in customers) {
    Console.WriteLine( c );
  }
}
```

As you can see, the query uses an SQL-like syntax that works with typed entities (that is, instances of our *Customer* type) rather than with tables. A lot of the plumbing code—usually defined to work with databases, invoke specific SQL statements, iterate over records, and so forth—has been moved under the cover. Starting from the previous query, we can see that LINQ works with deferred queries, evaluated when we effectively access them, which are converted to the right extension method for the sequences we are querying. Consider Listing 5-36, which shows the LINQ query against the previously seen sequence of *Customers* entities.

Listing 5-36   A LINQ query over a sequence of *Customers* entities

```
using (Northwind db = new Northwind( NWIND_CONNECTION_STRING ) ) {

  var customers =
    from   c in db.Customers
    where  c.Country == "Italy"
    select c;

  foreach(Customer c in customers) {
    Console.WriteLine( c );
  }
}
```

The result of this query, when it is evaluated, will be the one shown in Listing 5-36. The query expression deferred evaluation will produce it. This approach can be very interesting whenever we define the business layer and the components that need to handle business entities, and handle them independently from the persistence layer and without concern for the real source of entity data sources.

With these concepts, you can make a case for using the capabilities of LINQ to Entities in everyday programming. More details on LINQ to Entities and ADO.NET Entity Framework are provided in the Appendix, "ADO.NET Entity Framework."

Summary

In this chapter, we discussed the LINQ to ADO.NET implementations. LINQ to SQL allows querying a relational structure for converting LINQ queries into native SQL queries and accessing UDF and stored procedure if required. LINQ to DataSet interacts with typed and untyped *DataSet* structures. Finally, LINQ to Entities enables LINQ queries over entities defined in a logical model using the ADO.NET Entity Framework. All the LINQ implementations extend the existing base LINQ features that we saw in Chapter 4.

Chapter 6
LINQ to XML

Since it became available on February 10, 1998, Extensible Markup Language (XML) has been broadly supported and used. Today every development framework supports XML and its related specifications, such as the following:

- **XML Schema Definition (XSD)**   To define the structure of XML documents

- **Extensible Stylesheet Language for Transformations (XSLT)**   To transform XML documents from one schema to another

- **XPath and XQuery**   To search and traverse XML contents

- **Document Object Model (DOM)**   To manage in-memory representations of documents

- **Simple Object Access Protocol (SOAP) services**   To realize platform interoperability using XML messages

Despite its widespread use, XML is still often a hostile technology for many developers because of its rigorous syntax. LINQ to XML provides a new unified API, called the LINQ to XML API, to define and manage XML contents using Microsoft .NET code. The LINQ to XML API is fully integrated with the .NET type system and syntax. LINQ to XML uses LINQ extension methods to read, create, search, query, and generally manage XML contents within application code using .NET code and a language-agnostic API, the same as with entities, database records, and collections of items in general.

Introducing LINQ to XML

LINQ to XML provides the power of the DOM and the expressiveness of XPath and XQuery through LINQ extension methods to manage and query in-memory XML nodes. It uses the latest enhancements of .NET languages, such as anonymous methods, generics, nullable types, and so forth. Consider the following introductory sample XML document:

```xml
<?xml version="1.0" encoding="UTF-16" standalone="yes"?>
<customer id="C01>
  <firstName>Paolo</firstName>
  <lastName>Pialorsi</lastName>
  <addresses>
    <address type="email">paolo@devleap.it</address>
    <address type="url">http://www.devleap.it/</address>
    <address type="home">Brescia - Italy</address>
  </addresses>
</customer>
```

Listing 6-1 shows how you can build such a document with LINQ to XML syntax using C#.

Listing 6-1   A sample of XML functional construction

```
XDocument customer =
    new XDocument(
        new XDeclaration("1.0", "UTF-16", "yes"),
        new XElement("customer",
            new XAttribute("id", "C01"),
            new XElement("firstName", "Paolo"),
            new XElement("lastName", "Pialorsi"),
            new XElement("addresses",
                new XElement("address",
                    new XAttribute("type", "email"),
                        "paolo@devleap.it"),
                new XElement("address",
                    new XAttribute("type", "url"),
                        "http://www.devleap.it/"),
                new XElement("address",
                    new XAttribute("type", "home"),
                        "Brescia - Italy"))));
```

The preceding example is called "functional construction," and it reveals how it is simple and intuitive to define an XML nodes hierarchy with the LINQ to XML API. As you can see, the code layout describes the final hierarchical structure using nested constructors. A standard DOM approach requires you to declare and collect many objects, while this new syntax uses a single "hierarchical" statement to achieve this goal, allowing the developer to focus on the final output XML structure rather than on DOM rules.

As you saw in Chapter 3, "Visual Basic 9.0 Language Features," Visual Basic 9.0 language enhancements introduce a new feature called *XML literals* that makes it easier to write and read XML contents. In fact, the previous example, when written in Microsoft Visual Basic 9.0, looks like the excerpt shown in Listing 6-2.

Listing 6-2   A sample of Visual Basic 9.0 XML literals

```
Dim customerXml As XDocument = _
  <?xml version="1.0" encoding="UTF-16" standalone="yes"?>
    <customer id="C01">
      <firstName>Paolo</firstName>
      <lastName>Pialorsi</lastName>
      <addresses>
        <address type="email">paolo@devleap.it</address>
        <address type="url">http://www.devleap.it/</address>
        <address type="home">Brescia - Italy</address>
      </addresses>
    </customer>
```

The power and expressiveness of this syntax is truly evident. We write pure XML code, even if it is inside a Visual Basic 9.0 piece of code. Also, querying XML with LINQ to XML is really simple. In the following sample code, we enumerate all the *address* tags of a given customer, using C#:

```
foreach(XElement a in customer.Descendants("addresses").Elements()) {
    Console.WriteLine(a);
}
```

Using Visual Basic 9.0, this query can be written using a more intuitive syntax, like the following one:

```
Dim address As XElement
For Each address In xCustomer.<customer>.<addresses>.<address>
    Console.WriteLine(address.Value)
Next
```

We will come back to this fancy syntax later, but now just notice that once again we are using an XML-like syntax within Visual Basic 9.0 code. From the next section to the end of this chapter, we will cover all the features of LINQ to XML.

LINQ to XML API

The LINQ to XML API is independent from LINQ to XML queries, and it allows developers to build and manage XML contents regardless of whether they will query them with LINQ and extension methods. You can use this API as a stand-alone utility or in conjunction with LINQ queries. This new API is built with World Wide Web Consortium (W3C) XML Infoset instances in mind, rather than just XML 1.0 documents. Therefore, the in-memory tree is the objective of this API, not the bare XML text file.

Note   W3C defines *XML Infoset* as a set of information items that describes the structure of any well-formed XML document. You can think of an XML Infoset as the in-memory node graph description, corresponding to an XML document, aside from the physical nature of the document itself. For further details on XML Infoset, read the W3C Recommendation: *http://www.w3.org/TR/xml-infoset/*.

The goal of the LINQ to XML API is to provide an object-oriented approach for XML construction and management, avoiding or solving many common issues related to XML manipulation through W3C DOM. With LINQ to XML, the approach to XML is no longer document centric, as it is in W3C DOM. Using LINQ to XML, elements can be created and can exist detached from any document, namespace usage has been simplified, and traversing the in-memory tree is like scanning any other object graph. To make all of this possible, the API is based on a set of classes, all with names prefixed by an X (and which we will often refer to as *X* classes* in this the chapter), that correspond to the main common nodes of an XML document. In Figure 6-1, you can see the object model hierarchy.

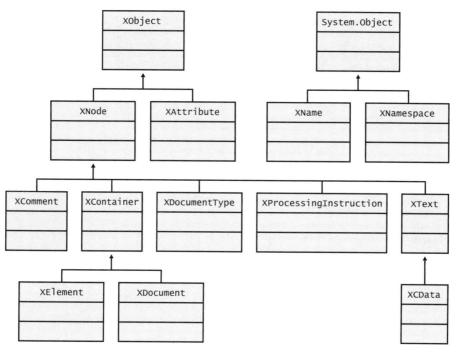

Figure 6-1   The object model hierarchy of main X* classes

To start using this API, you must reference the *System.Xml.Linq* assembly and use its classes. The following sections describe the main types defined in *System.Xml.Linq*.

XElement

This is one of the main classes of the LINQ to XML API. As you can see from Figure 6-1, it has the same hierarchical level as the *XDocument* class and is derived from the base *XNode* class, through *XContainer*. As its name suggests, it describes an XML element and can be used as the container of any XML fragment parented to a tag. It provides many constructors and static methods, some of which are very useful. For instance, we can load the content of an *XElement* from an existing *XmlReader* instance to reuse existing code based on *System.Xml* classes by using the static *Load* method of *XElement*. Constructors such as the following create XML node graphs using functional construction:

```
public XElement (XName name);
public XElement (XElement other);
public XElement (XName name, Object content);
public XElement (XName name, params Object[] content);
```

The *params Object[]* optional list of parameters of one constructor represents a list of child nodes, attributes, or both of the elements we are defining. For instance, an *XElement* named *customer*, with a child element named *firstName*, can be defined by using the code in Listing 6-3.

Listing 6-3   A sample *XElement* constructed using the LINQ to XML API

```
XElement tag = new XElement("customer",
    new XElement("firstName", "Paolo"));
```

Using a standard DOM approach, we should have to define an *XmlDocument* instance, explicitly create the elements, and append each child node to its parent. Take a look at the code block in Listing 6-4 to compare a DOM approach with the new functional construction we have just used.

Listing 6-4   Definition of an XML element using DOM

```
XmlDocument doc = new XmlDocument();
XmlElement customerElement = doc.CreateElement("customer");
XmlElement firstNameElement = doc.CreateElement("firstName");
firstNameElement.InnerText = "Paolo";
customerElement.AppendChild(firstNameElement);
doc.AppendChild(customerElement);
```

As you can see, the DOM approach is verbose and difficult to understand. Probably the easiest way to define this customer element is to use Visual Basic 9.0 XML literals, as demonstrated in Listing 6-5.

Listing 6-5   Definition of an XML element using Visual Basic 9.0 XML literals

```
Dim customerName As String = "Paolo"
Dim tag As XElement = _
  <customer>
    <firstName><%= customerName %></firstName>
  </customer>
```

As you saw in Chapter 3, this syntax will be translated by the Visual Basic 9.0 compiler into the equivalent functional construction.

XElement instances can also be saved into a *String*, an *XmlWriter*, or a *TextWriter*. Every *XElement* allows the reading of its content with direct casting, using a custom implementation of the

Explicit operator, defined to obtain a typed version of the *Value* of the element. Compared to a classic *System.Xml.XmlElement*, this is a great improvement because we can manage XML nodes typed from a .NET point of view with a value-centric approach. To better understand this concept, consider the sample code in Listing 6-6.

Listing 6-6   Sample of explicit type casting using *XElement* content

```
XElement order = new XElement("order",
    new XElement("quantity", 10),
    new XElement("price", 50),
    new XAttribute("idProduct", "P01"));

Decimal orderTotalAmount =
    (Decimal)order.Element("quantity") *
    (Decimal)order.Element("price");
Console.WriteLine("Order total amount: {0}", orderTotalAmount);
```

Here we use an *XElement* that describes an order. Imagine that we received this instance of the order from an order management system rather than constructing it explicitly by code. As you can see, we extract the elements named *quantity* and *price* and we convert them to a *Decimal* type. The conversion will return the inner *Value* of each element node, trying to cast it to *Decimal*. To handle the case of invalid content, we need to catch a *FormatException*, because the various *Explicit* operator overloads internally use *XmlConvert* from *System.Xml* or *Parse* methods of .NET types.

Finally, note that the *XElement* constructor automatically handles XML encoding of text. Consider Listing 6-7.

Listing 6-7   Sample of explicit escaping of XML text

```
XElement notes = new XElement("notes",
    "Some special characters like & > < <div/> etc.");
```

The result is encoded automatically using *XmlConvert* and looks like the following:

```
<notes>Some special characters like &amp; &gt; &lt; &lt;div/&gt; etc.</notes>
```

Also, node names are checked against XML naming rules and invalid names are rejected, throwing a *System.Xml.XmlException*. (For further details, see XSD types *Name* and *NMToken* on the W3C Web site at: *http://www.w3.org*.) This behavior is different from that of old *XmlWriter*, where names were automatically encoded. Sincerely, we think that it is better to make developers aware of syntactic rules rather than always hide them under the cover. However, if you want to define "irregular" node names with LINQ to XML, you can just use the *XmlConvert* class, invoking its methods, *EncodeName* or *EncodeNmToken*, respectively.

XDocument

The *XDocument* class represents an XML Infoset document instance. We can create document instances starting from a *params Object[]* list of objects of the following types: *XElement*, *XDeclaration*, *XProcessingInstruction*, *XDocumentType*, and *XComment*.

Surprisingly, *XDocument* does not have a constructor with a parameter of type *XmlReader*, *Stream*, or whatever describes a source file or Uniform Resource Identifier (URI). In fact, *XDocument*, like *XElement*, provides a set of static *Load* methods that can work with *String*, *XmlReader/XmlWriter*, and *TextReader* or *TextWriter*. To persist the XML Infoset *XDocument* instances, you need to provide a set of *Save* methods. Generally, an *XDocument* instance is useful whenever you need to create processing instructions or document type declarations on top of the XML document; otherwise, *XElement* is a better choice and is easier to use.

Important   As we have already seen, Visual Basic 9.0 XML literals are parsed by the Visual Basic 9.0 compiler to generate standard LINQ to XML API syntax. During this parsing phase, the compiler supports a subset of constructors provided by the various LINQ to XML types. For instance, whenever you need to create an *XDocument* using Visual Basic 9.0 XML literals, the only constructor supported is the one that requires a first argument of type *XDeclaration* (for example, a processing instruction) on top of the document. Any other XML literal missing the trailing *XDeclaration* will be assumed to be an *XElement* instance.

XAttribute

This class represents an XML attribute instance and can be added to any *XContainer* by using its constructor and LINQ to XML functional construction. Notice that the *XAttribute* class is independent from *XNode* and, consequently, from *XElement* and *XDocument*. It has only the base *XObject* class in common with all other X* classes. Like the *XElement* class, it provides a rich set of conversion operators so that it can provide its content already typed from a .NET point of view. From a practical point of view, working with attributes is quite similar to working with elements. However, from an internal point of view, attributes are handled as a name/ value pair mapped to the container element. Each *XAttribute* provides a couple of properties, called *NextAttribute* and *PreviousAttribute*, that are useful for browsing the sequence of attributes of an element.

XNode

XNode is the base class for many of the X* classes, and it implements the entire tree-node management infrastructure, providing methods to add, move, remove, and replace nodes within the XML Infoset. For instance, the *AddAfterSelf* and *AddBeforeSelf* methods are useful for inserting one or more nodes after or before the current one. Listing 6-8 provides an example of these methods—specifically, it shows how to use these methods to insert a couple of addresses into the previously seen customer, just after the first address.

Listing 6-8 Sample usage of the *AddAfterSelf* method of *XNode*

```
XElement customer = XElement.Load(@"..\..\customer.xml");
XElement firstAddress =
(customer.Descendants("addresses").Elements("address")).First();

firstAddress.AddAfterSelf(
    new XElement("address",
        new XAttribute("type", "IT-blog"),
            "http://blogs.devleap.com/"),
    new XElement("address",
        new XAttribute("type", "US-blog"),
            "http://weblogs.asp.net/PaoloPia/"));
```

As you can see, we can add a set of nodes because these methods provide a couple of overloads, which are shown here:

```
public void AddAfterSelf(Object content);
public void AddBeforeSelf(Object content);
public void AddAfterSelf(params Object[] content);
public void AddBeforeSelf(params Object[] content);
```

The first two overloads in the preceding list require a single parameter of type *Object*, while the second two overloads accept a *params Object[]* variable list of parameters. You might be wondering why these methods, like many of the previously seen constructors, accept the type *Object* instead of *XNode* or any other X* class instance. The answer is quite simple but very interesting: Whenever we provide an object to methods and constructors of X* classes, the API checks to determine whether they implement *IEnumerable* to recursively handle their contents; if they do not, the API converts them to a *String*, calling their *ToString()* implementation. NULL parameters are just ignored.

We can write LINQ to XML syntax to load a set of nodes, as in the following code block, based on functional construction and using C# merged with LINQ queries. In Listing 6-9, we use the well-known customers sequence—which we used in Chapter 4, "LINQ Syntax Fundamentals"—to build an XML document based on those customers.

Listing 6-9 A LINQ to XML sentence merged with LINQ queries

```
XElement xmlCustomers = new XElement("customers",
    from   c in customers
    where  c.Country == Countries.Italy
    select new XElement("customer",
                new XAttribute("name", c.Name),
                new XAttribute("city", c.City),
                new XAttribute("country", c.Country)));
```

The result looks like the following XML document:

```xml
<?xml version="1.0" encoding="utf-8"?>
<customers>
  <customer name="Paolo" city="Brescia" country="Italy" />
  <customer name="Marco" city="Torino" country="Italy" />
</customers>
```

The same result can be achieved by using Visual Basic 9.0 XML literals with the code shown in Listing 6-10.

Listing 6-10   A LINQ to XML sentence merged with LINQ queries, using Visual Basic 9.0 XML literals

```vb
Dim xmlCustomers As XElement = _
  <customers>
    <%= From c In customers _
        Where (c.Country = Countries.Italy) _
        Select _
        <customer>
          <firstName><%= c.FirstName %></firstName>
        </customer> %>
  </customers>
```

Another interesting method provided by *XNode* is *DeepEqual*. It is a static method, useful to fully compare a couple of XML nodes for equality, as the name suggests. It works by comparing nodes using an internal abstract instance method still called *DeepEqual*. In this way, every type inherited from *XNode* implements its own *DeepEqual* behavior. For example, *XElement* compares element names, element content, and element attributes. The *XNodeEqualityComparer* class that we will use later in this chapter, within LINQ to XML queries, is based on *DeepEqual*.

XName and *XNamespace*

When defining XML contents and node graphs, usually you must also map nodes to their XML namespace. In Listing 6-11, you can see how to define nodes with an XML namespace by using a classic DOM approach.

Listing 6-11   XML namespace handling using classic DOM syntax

```csharp
XmlDocument document = new XmlDocument();

XmlElement customer = document.CreateElement("c", "customer",
    "http://schemas.devleap.com/Customer");
document.AppendChild(customer);

XmlElement firstName = document.CreateElement("c", "firstName",
    "http://schemas.devleap.com/Customer");
customer.AppendChild(firstName);
```

As you can see, we use an overload of the *CreateElement* method, which requires three parameters: a namespace prefix, a tag local name, and the full namespace URI. The same can be done for XML attributes, using *CreateAttribute* of *XmlDocument* or *SetAttribute* of *XmlElement*. To tell the truth, this way of working is not all that difficult to understand and implement. Nevertheless, developers often create confusion when using this approach and complain that XML namespaces are difficult to manage. The real issue probably derives from namespace prefixes, which are just aliases to the real XML namespaces. Theoretically, prefixes are used to simplify namespace references; in reality, they might cause confusion. To address feedback from developers, the LINQ to XML API was designed to provide an easier way of working with XML namespaces, avoiding any explicit use of prefixes. Every node name is an instance of the *XName* class, which can be defined by a *String* or by a pairing of an *XNamespace* and a *String*. In Listing 6-12, you can see how to define XML content by using a single default XML namespace.

Listing 6-12   LINQ to XML namespace declaration

```
XNamespace ns = "http://schemas.devleap.com/Customer";
XElement customer = new XElement(ns + "customer",
    new XAttribute("id", "C01"),
    new XElement(ns + "firstName", "Paolo"),
    new XElement(ns + "lastName", "Pialorsi"));
```

As you can see, the *XNamespace* definition looks like a *String*, but it is not. Internally, every *XNamespace* has a more complex behavior. Here is the output of the preceding code:

```
<?xml version="1.0" encoding="utf-8"?>
<customer id="C01" xmlns="http://schemas.devleap.com/Customer">
  <firstName>Paolo</firstName>
  <lastName>Pialorsi</lastName>
</customer>
```

Using Visual Basic 9.0 syntax, we can define the namespace directly inside the XML content, as Listing 6-13 shows.

Listing 6-13   Visual Basic 9.0 XML literals used to declare XML content with a default XML namespace

```
Dim customer As XDocument = _
    <?xml version="1.0" encoding="utf-8"?>
    <customer id="C01" xmlns="http://schemas.devleap.com/Customer">
      <firstName>Paolo</firstName>
      <lastName>Pialorsi</lastName>
    </customer>
```

Now consider Listing 6-14, where we use a couple of XML namespaces.

Listing 6-14   Multiple XML namespaces within a single *XElement* declaration

```
XNamespace nsCustomer = "http://schemas.devleap.com/Customer";
XNamespace nsAddress = "http://schemas.devleap.com/Address";

XElement customer = new XElement(nsCustomer + "customer",
    new XAttribute("id", "C01"),
    new XElement(nsCustomer + "firstName", "Paolo"),
    new XElement(nsCustomer + "lastName", "Pialorsi"),
    new XElement(nsAddress + "addresses",
        new XElement(nsAddress + "address",
            new XAttribute("type", "email"),
                "paolo@devleap.it"),
        new XElement(nsAddress + "address",
            new XAttribute("type", "home"),
                "Brescia - Italy")));
```

Again, the output is a document with all qualified XML nodes:

```
<?xml version="1.0" encoding="utf-8"?>
<customer id="C01" xmlns="http://schemas.devleap.com/Customer">
  <firstName>Paolo</firstName>
  <lastName>Pialorsi</lastName>
  <addresses xmlns="http://schemas.devleap.com/Address">
    <address type="email">paolo@devleap.it</address>
    <address type="home">Brescia - Italy</address>
  </addresses>
</customer>
```

At this point, we have seen that *XNamespace* is quite simple to use and that the LINQ to XML API automatically handles namespace declaration, avoiding the explicit use of prefixes. You are probably curious about what happens when we define an *XName* as a concatenation of an *XNamespace* instance and a *String* to represent the local name of the node. Each *XName* instance can be represented as a *String*, using its *ToString* method:

```
Console.WriteLine(customer.Name.ToString());
```

Here is the result of the preceding line of code:

```
{http://schemas.devleap.com/Customer}customer
```

Let's try to use this "resolved" text instead of the concatenation (*XNamespace* instance plus local name) used previously:

```
XElement testCustomer = new XElement("{http://schemas.devleap.com/Customer}customer");
Console.WriteLine(testCustomer.Name);
```

In the *System.Xml.Linq* API, the resolved text "{namespace}local-name" is called the "expanded name" and is semantically equivalent to defining the *XNamespace* separately. The concatenation of an *XNamespace* and a *String* produces a new *XName* equivalent to the expanded name.

Now we are missing only XML namespace prefixes. We have seen that this new API handles namespace declaration by itself. However, sometimes we might need to influence how to serialize nodes and represent namespaces by overriding the default behavior of LINQ to XML. To achieve this goal, we can explicitly define the prefixes to use for namespaces by using *xmlns* attributes within our elements, as we do in the example in Listing 6-15.

Listing 6-15   LINQ to XML declaration of an XML namespace with a custom prefix

```
XNamespace ns = "http://schemas.devleap.com/Customer";
XElement customer = new XElement(ns + "customer",
    new XAttribute(XNamespace.Xmlns + "c", ns),
    new XAttribute("id", "C01"),
    new XElement(ns + "firstName", "Paolo"),
    new XElement(ns + "lastName", "Pialorsi"));
```

The output looks like the following:

```
<?xml version="1.0" encoding="utf-8"?>
<c:customer xmlns:c="http://schemas.devleap.com/Customer" id="C01">
  <c:firstName>Paolo</c:firstName>
  <c:lastName>Pialorsi</c:lastName>
</c:customer>
```

As you can see, we defined "c" as the prefix of nodes associated with the *XNamespace* instance named *ns*.

One more time, the corresponding and easiest Visual Basic 9.0 syntax is shown in Listing 6-16.

Listing 6-16   Visual Basic 9.0 XML literals used to declare an XML namespace with a custom prefix

```
Dim customer As XDocument = _
<?xml version="1.0" encoding="utf-8"?>
<c:customer xmlns:c="http://schemas.devleap.com/Customer" id="C01">
  <c:firstName>Paolo</c:firstName>
  <c:lastName>Pialorsi</c:lastName>
</c:customer>
```

You might think that, starting from LINQ to XML, namespaces are simpler to handle and prefixes are transparently taken out of your control. On the other hand, you might now have the impression that if you need to influence prefixes, you need to do a little more work, at least using C# 3.0. In fact, Visual Basic 9.0 XML literals also simplify namespace declaration, leveraging a feature called *global XML namespaces*. This new feature allows you to globally declare an XML namespace URI with its corresponding prefix within a Visual Basic 9.0 code file so that you can reuse it many times in code. In Listing 6-17, you can see an example.

Listing 6-17   Visual Basic 9.0 XML literals and global XML namespaces

```vbnet
Imports System.Xml.Linq
Imports System.Linq
Imports <xmlns:c="http://schemas.devleap.com/Customer">

Public Class Program
  Private Shared Sub Listing6_17()

    Dim xmlCustomers As XDocument = _
      <?xml version="1.0" encoding="utf-8"?>
      <c:customers>
          <c:customer name="Paolo" city="Brescia" country="Italy"/>
          <c:customer name="Marco" city="Torino" country="Italy"/>
          <c:customer name="James" city="Dallas" country="USA"/>
          <c:customer name="Frank" city="Seattle" country="USA"/>
      </c:customers>

  End Sub
End Class
```

The key point of this sample is the *Imports* statement, which declares the global namespace prefix *c* for namespace *http://schemas.devleap.com/Customer*. This particular kind of *Imports* syntax can be used only to declare an XML namespace with its prefix. It is not allowed to declare a default XML namespace without a prefix.

Let's look at a final example, shown in Listing 6-18, using C# 3.0 to define a default namespace and a custom prefixed one.

Listing 6-18   C# 3.0 syntax used to define a default namespace and a custom prefix for one

```csharp
XNamespace nsCustomer = "http://schemas.devleap.com/Customer";
XNamespace nsAddress = "http://schemas.devleap.com/Address";
XElement customer = new XElement(nsCustomer + "customer",
    new XAttribute("id", "C01"),
    new XElement(nsCustomer + "firstName", "Paolo"),
    new XElement(nsCustomer + "lastName", "Pialorsi"),
    new XElement(nsAddress + "address", "Brescia - Italy",
        new XAttribute(XNamespace.Xmlns + "a", nsAddress)));
```

The code in Listing 6-18 produces an XML fragment like the following one:

```xml
<?xml version="1.0" encoding="utf-8"?>
<customer id="C01">
  <firstName>Paolo</firstName>
  <lastName>Pialorsi</lastName>
  <a:address xmlns:a="http://schemas.devleap.com/Address">Brescia - Italy</a:address>
</customer>
```

To query the previous XML content for the purpose of extracting the *lastName* node, we can just write a line of code like the following one:

```csharp
Console.WriteLine(customer.Elements(nsCustomer + "lastName"));
```

Using Visual Basic 9.0 and global XML namespaces, we can use code like this:

```
Console.WriteLine(customer.<c:lastName>);
```

Later in this chapter, we will examine in detail how to query XML contents using LINQ to XML queries with both C# 3.0 and Visual Basic 9.0 syntax.

Other X* Classes

This new API has other available classes that define processing instructions (*XProcessingInstruction*), document types (*XDocumentType*), comments (*XComment*), and text nodes (*XText*). They are all derived from *XNode* and are typically used to build *XDocument* instances.

XObject and Annotations

XObject represents the base class of the whole LINQ to XML API, and it mainly provides methods and properties to work with annotations on nodes. Annotations are a new mechanism that maps metadata to XML nodes. For instance, we can add custom user information to our nodes as shown in Listing 6-19.

Listing 6-19   Annotations applied to an *XElement* instance

```
XElement customer = XElement.Load(@"..\..\customer.xml");

CustomerAnnotation annotation = new CustomerAnnotation();
annotation.Notes = "This is a good customer!";
customer.AddAnnotation(annotation);
```

CustomerAnnotation is a custom type and can be any .NET type. We can then retrieve annotations from XML nodes by using one of the two generic methods, *Annotation<T>* and *Annotations<T>*. These generic methods search for an annotation of type *T* or one that is derived from *T* in the current node, and if one exists, *Annotation<T>* and *Annotations<T>* return the first one or the full set of them, respectively.

```
annotation = customer.Annotation<CustomerAnnotation>();
```

Because *XObject* is the base class of every kind of X* class that is used to describe an XML node, annotations can be added to any node. Usually, annotations are used to keep state information, such as the mapping to source entities or documents used to build XML, while the code handles real XML content.

Reading, Traversing, and Modifying XML

You have seen how to create and annotate XML content using the LINQ to XML API. Whenever we have XML available in memory, we can also navigate and eventually modify it. To navigate XML content, we can use methods and properties of X* classes, or we can also rely on LINQ queries over an X* object. In this section, we will see the former way of working, and in the next section we will see the latter.

Every *XNode* provides some methods and properties to navigate its hierarchy. For instance, we can use *IsAfter* or *IsBefore* methods to compare ordinal positioning of nodes in the document. These methods internally use the *CompareDocumentOrder* static method of the *XNode* class and return a numeric index, of type *Integer*, that represents the "distance" of two *XNode* instances in the containing *XDocument*. It is also used by *XNodeDocumentOrderComparer*, and it is useful when ordering nodes in LINQ to XML queries. Every *XNode* also provides a couple of properties, called *NextNode* and *PreviousNode*, that map to the next and previous nodes in the graph, as their names indicate. Pay attention to the relative cost of these properties. *NextNode* returns a reference to an internal field and is relatively cheap; *PreviousNode* requires a partial scan of the tree branch containing the current node and is a little bit more expensive. *XContainer* also provides *LastNode* and *FirstNode* properties. Finally, every *XObject* offers a *Parent* property that represents the parent node in the graph.

Whenever you find a node traversing the document using one of these techniques and you want to modify it, you can use methods such as *Remove* or *ReplaceWith*, which are available for any *XNode*, to remove the node itself from the graph or to replace it with a new fragment. There are also *RemoveAttributes*, *ReplaceAttributes*, and *ReplaceAll* for objects of type *XElement*, which work with their respective attributes or with the full set of child nodes. Finally, *XElement* also offers *SetAttributeValue*, *SetElementValue*, and *SetValue* to change the value of an attribute, a child element, or the entire current element, respectively.

In Listing 6-20, you can see how to replace one tag with another.

Listing 6-20 Example of tag replacement using the *XElement ReplaceWith* method

```
XElement customer = new XElement("customer",
    new XAttribute("id", "C01"),
    new XElement("firstName", "Paolo"),
    new XElement("lastName", "Pialorsi"));

// Do something in the meantime ...

customer.LastNode.ReplaceWith(
    new XElement("nickName", "PaoloPia"));
```

The preceding code block changes this XML:

```
<?xml version="1.0" encoding="utf-8"?>
<customer id="C01">
  <firstName>Paolo</firstName>
  <lastName>Pialorsi</lastName>
</customer>
```

into this XML:

```xml
<?xml version="1.0" encoding="utf-8"?>
<customer id="C01">
  <firstName>Paolo</firstName>
  <nickName>PaoloPia</nickName>
</customer>
```

Listing 6-21 shows you how to change attribute and element values.

Listing 6-21 Example of attribute and child element management using *XElement* methods

```
customer.SetAttributeValue("id", "C02");
customer.SetElementValue("notes", "Notes about this customer");
```

By calling these methods, the API creates attributes or elements that do not yet exist or changes the values of ones that already exist. When the value provided to these methods is NULL and the nodes already exist, they are removed.

While traversing the XML, keep in mind that the navigation technique you use influences the result. The methods and properties shown until now work directly in memory and determine their results at the time that you invoke them. If you ask to remove or replace a node, the action is taken instantly within the in-memory structure. In the case of queries over XML, based on the LINQ to XML query engine, modification methods are applied to query expression results that will be evaluated only when they are effectively used, like the ones you saw in Chapter 4.

LINQ to XML Queries

Now consider XML nodes from a different point of view: every node set can be thought of as a sequence of nodes and queried by using LINQ queries, just as with any other sequence of type *IEnumerable<T>*. Starting from this postulate, we argue that every concept we have already seen applied to other sequences in the fields of LINQ queries (such as LINQ to Objects, LINQ to Entities, and so forth) can also be leveraged with XML nodes, because LINQ to XML exposes every collection of nodes as an *IEnumerable<T>* instance.

For example, we can use the standard query extension methods, already described in Chapter 4, to query XML nodes, too. There are also custom extension methods, specifically defined to be applied to sequences of *IEnumerable<X*>*, declared in the *System.Xml.Linq.Extensions* class. In this section, we will cover all these methods.

Attribute, Attributes

Each instance of *XElement* supports a set of methods to access its attributes, as shown here:

```
public XAttribute Attribute(XName name);
public IEnumerable<XAttribute> Attributes();
public IEnumerable<XAttribute> Attributes(XName name);
```

As you can see, the first method returns a single *XAttribute* instance that is retrieved by name if it exists. If it does not exist, the method returns NULL. The second method returns a sequence of attributes of type *IEnumerable<XAttribute>*, which are useful for LINQ queries, containing all the attributes of an *XElement* instance. The last method shown returns a sequence of type *IEnumerable<XAttribute>* that contains zero or one items. Attributes of one element are a collection of unique named nodes; therefore, an element with multiple occurrences of the same attribute name cannot exist.

Element, Elements

Every *XContainer* instance provides methods to select single elements by name or to select sequences of elements that are eventually filtered by their name (of type *XName*). Here are their signatures:

```
public XElement Element(XName name);
public IEnumerable<XElement> Elements();
public IEnumerable<XElement> Elements(XName name);
```

The *Element* method iterates over the child nodes of the current *XContainer* and returns the first *XElement*, whose name corresponds to the argument of type *XName* provided. Because of the argument type (*XName*), you have to provide a valid node name, with its XML namespace URI in a case in which you are looking for a qualified element, as shown in Listing 6-22.

Listing 6-22   A sample LINQ to XML query based on the *Element* extension method

```
XNamespace ns = "http://schemas.devleap.com/Customers";
XElement xmlCustomers = new XElement(ns + "customers",
    from  c in customers
    where c.Country == Countries.Italy
    select new XElement(ns + "customer",
            new XAttribute("name", c.Name),
            new XAttribute("city", c.City),
            new XAttribute("country", c.Country)));
XElement element = xmlCustomers.Element(ns + "customer");
```

To get all the customers, we can use the *Elements* method, as shown in Listing 6-23.

Listing 6-23   Another sample LINQ to XML query based on the *Elements* extension method

```
var elements = xmlCustomers.Elements();
foreach (XElement e in elements) {
    Console.WriteLine(e);
}
```

Here is the result:

```
<customer name="Paolo" city="Brescia" country="Italy" />
<customer name="Marco" city="Torino" country="Italy" />
```

The last overload of the *Elements* method just allows filtering child elements by name. There is no way, using the *Element* or *Elements* method, to get a single *XElement* child of the current *XContainer* without providing a filtering name, given that there are more than one child elements. However, you can leverage the *First* extension method of LINQ to Objects to achieve this goal. Here is an example:

```
XElement firstElement = xmlCustomers.Elements().First();
```

Let's try to leverage what we have just learned with LINQ queries. Imagine that you need to transform a source document into a new schema. Listing 6-24 shows the source document.

Listing 6-24   Source XML with a list of customers

```
<?xml version="1.0" encoding="utf-8"?>
<customers>
  <customer name="Paolo" city="Brescia" country="Italy" />
  <customer name="Marco" city="Torino" country="Italy" />
  <customer name="James" city="Dallas" country="USA" />
  <customer name="Frank" city="Seattle" country="USA" />
</customers>
```

And Listing 6-25 shows the desired output, where we changed the namespace of elements and filtered *customer* elements on a *country* value basis.

Listing 6-25   Destination XML with a list of customers transformed

```
<?xml version="1.0" encoding="utf-8"?>
<c:customers xmlns:c="http://schemas.devleap.com/Customers">
  <c:customer>
    <c:name>Paolo</c:name>
    <c:city>Brescia</c:city>
  </c:customer>
  <c:customer>
    <c:name>Marco</c:name>
    <c:city>Torino</c:city>
  </c:customer>
</c:customers>
```

We could use XSLT code to transform the source into the output. Listing 6-26 provides really simple XSLT to do that.

Listing 6-26   XSLT to transform XML from Listing 6-24 to Listing 6-25

```
<?xml version="1.0" encoding="UTF-8" ?>
<xsl:stylesheet version="1.0"
  xmlns:xsl="http://www.w3.org/1999/XSL/Transform"
  xmlns:c="http://schemas.devleap.com/Customers">
  <xsl:template match="customers">
    <c:customers>
      <xsl:for-each select="customer[@country = 'Italy']">
```

```
          <c:customer>
            <c:name><xsl:value-of select="@name"/></c:name>
            <c:city><xsl:value-of select="@city"/></c:city>
          </c:customer>
        </xsl:for-each>
      </c:customers>
    </xsl:template>
</xsl:stylesheet>
```

Nevertheless, if we are already in .NET code, we can avoid exiting from our code context and instead use a simple LINQ query like the one in Listing 6-27.

Listing 6-27   A functional construction used to transform XML from Listing 6-24 to Listing 6-25

```
XNamespace ns = "http://schemas.devleap.com/Customers";
XElement destinationXmlCustomers =
    new XElement(ns + "customers",
        new XAttribute(XNamespace.Xmlns + "c", ns),
        from   c in sourceXmlCustomers.Elements("customer")
        where  c.Attribute("country").Value == "Italy"
        select new XElement(ns + "customer",
                 new XElement(ns + "name", c.Attribute("name")),
                 new XElement(ns + "city", c.Attribute("city"))));
```

We personally like and appreciate XSLT features and their strong syntax, but using them requires learning another query language. We know and clearly understand that many developers are not familiar with XSLT syntax and probably will prefer the LINQ solution, which is easier for a .NET developer to write and also typed and checked from a compiler point of view. Finally, you can consider the Visual Basic 9.0 version of this code, shown in Listing 6-28.

Listing 6-28   A Visual Basic 9.0 XML literal used to transform XML from Listing 6-24 to Listing 6-25

```
Dim destinationXmlCustomers = _
    <c:customers xmlns:c="http://schemas.devleap.com/Customers">
        <%= From c In sourceXmlCustomers.<customers>.<customer> _
            Where (c.@country = "Italy") _
            Select _
            <c:customer xmlns:c="http://schemas.devleap.com/Customers">
                <c:name><%= c.@name %></c:name>
                <c:city><%= c.@city %></c:city>
            </c:customer> %>
    </c:customers>
```

This approach is probably the one that is the quickest to write and easiest to understand because you can directly think about the output XML. We can make it even easier by using global XML namespaces. It is important to notice the syntax used to select elements and attributes from the source XML document. We use a special Visual Basic 9.0 syntax that you already saw in Chapter 3. The syntax recalls XPath node selection. As you can see, we select all the element nodes named *customer*, which are children of the *customers* element within the *sourceXmlCustomer*, by using the following syntax:

```
sourceXmlCustomers.<customers>.<customer>
```

The Visual Basic 9.0 compiler, as with XML literals, converts the syntax into a standard LINQ to XML invocation of *Elements* methods. In the same way, the syntax used to select attributes named *name* and *city* (*c.@name* and *c.@city*) recalls XPath attribute selection rules and is converted into calls of the *Attribute* method of the *XElement* type.

Sometimes XML schemas support optional elements or optional attributes. When we define transformations using LINQ to XML, we work at a higher level and use object instances rather than nodes. In cases where we define an *XElement*—using functional construction—and assign it a NULL value, the result is an empty closed element, like the one shown in the following example:

```
// Where c.City == null
XElement city = new XElement("customer",
    new XAttribute("id", c.IdCustomer),
    new XElement("city", c.City));
```

The result is an empty tag: *<city />*, as shown here:

```
<customer id="10"><city /></customer>
```

In cases where we need to omit the element declaration when it is empty (NULL), we can use the conditional operator, as shown in the following sample:

```
// Where c.City == null
XElement city = new XElement("customer",
    new XAttribute("id", c.IdCustomer),
    c.City != null ? new XElement("city", c.City), null);
```

Whenever we add NULL content to an *XContainer*, it is skipped without throwing any kind of exception.

XNode Selection Methods

The *XNode* class provides some methods that are useful for selecting elements and nodes related to the current node itself. For instance, the *ElementsBeforeSelf* and *ElementsAfterSelf* methods both return a sequence of type *IEnumerable<XElement>* that contains the elements before or after the current node, respectively. They both provide an overload with a parameter of type *XName* to filter elements by name.

In addition, *NodesBeforeSelf* and *NodesAfterSelf* methods return a sequence of type *IEnumerable<XNode>* that contains all the nodes, regardless of their node type, before or after the current one.

Similarities Between XPath Axes and Extension Methods

Extension methods are defined in the *System.Xml.Linq.Extensions* class that recall XPath Axes functions. The first two methods that we will consider are *Ancestors* and *Descendants*, which return an *IEnumerable<XElement>* sequence of elements for a particular *XNode* instance. *Descendants* returns all the elements after the current node in the document graph, regardless of their depth in the graph. *Ancestors* is somehow complementary to *Descendants* and returns all the elements before the current node in the document graph. Both are shown here:

```
public static IEnumerable<XElement> Ancestors<T>(
  this IEnumerable<T> source)
    where T: XNode;
public static IEnumerable<XElement> Ancestors<T>(
  this IEnumerable<T> source, XName name)
    where T: XNode;
public static IEnumerable<XElement> Descendants<T>(
  this IEnumerable<T> source)
    where T: XContainer;
public static IEnumerable<XElement> Descendants<T>(
  this IEnumerable<T> source, XName name)
    where T: XContainer;
```

These methods are useful for querying an XML source to find a particular element after or before the current one, regardless of its position in the graph. Consider the XML document in Listing 6-29.

Listing 6-29   An XML instance to search with LINQ to XML

```
<?xml version="1.0" encoding="ibm850"?>
<customers>
  <customer>
    <name>Paolo</name>
    <city>Brescia</city>
    <country>Italy</country>
  </customer>
  <customer>
    <name>Marco</name>
    <city>Torino</city>
    <country>Italy</country>
  </customer>
</customers>
```

The following line of code returns 8 as the number of descendant elements of an XML document like the one in Listing 6-29:

```
Console.WriteLine(xmlCustomers.Descendants().Count());
```

The descendant elements are as follows: two *<customer />* elements, two *<name />* elements, two *<city />* elements, and two *<country />* elements.

Two other extension methods that work like the previous ones are *AncestorsAndSelf* and *DescendantAndSelf*. They both act like the previously seen methods but also return the current element. As it happens with XPath Axes, we can retrieve all the elements of an XML source just by specifying the union of the results of *Ancestors* and *DescendantsAndSelf* or *AncestorsAndSelf* and *Descendants*.

If you need to select all the descendant nodes rather than only the elements, you can use methods such as *DescendantNodes* of *XContainer* or *DescendantNodesAndSelf* of *XElement*, which return all descendant nodes regardless of their node types, eventually with the node itself for the *DescendantNodesAndSelf* method. There is also a *Nodes* extension method, which returns all child nodes of one *XContainer*, again regardless of their node types.

InDocumentOrder

One last extension method that needs to be explained is the *InDocumentOrder* method. It orders an *IEnumerable<XNode>* sequence of nodes related to the same *XDocument* using the previously seen *XNodeDocumentOrderComparer* class, which bases its behavior on the *CompareDocumentOrder* method. This extension method is very useful whenever you want to select nodes ordered on the basis of their order of occurrence in a document.

In the following example, you can see how to use it:

```
foreach (XNode a in xmlCustomers.DescendantsAndSelf().InDocumentOrder()) {
    Console.WriteLine(a);
}
```

The result of this sample code is the full list of nodes declared within our *xmlCustomers* document, ordered by declaration.

Deferred Query Evaluation

Under the cover, all the extension methods described in the previous section work with deferred query evaluation, like every other LINQ query. The consequence of this is that every time we use them, the result can change if the source XML on which they are applied has been changed. Consider the example in Listing 6-30, where we output to the console window all the *city* nodes of the customers located in Italy.

Listing 6-30   A LINQ to XML query to extract all city nodes from a customers list

```
XElement xmlCustomers = new XElement("customers",
    from   c in customers
    where  c.Country == Countries.Italy
    select new XElement("customer",
               new XElement("name", c.Name),
               new XElement("city", c.City),
               new XElement("country", c.Country)));
```

```
var cities = xmlCustomers.DescendantsAndSelf("city");

Console.WriteLine("\nBefore XML source modification");
foreach (var city in cities) {
    Console.WriteLine(city);
}
```

The result of the query is the following:

```
Before XML source modification
<city>Brescia</city>
<city>Torino</city>
```

Now let's try to change the content of the *xmlCustomers* object. We will add customers that are not located in Italy and then repeat the iteration over the *cities* variable, representing the LINQ query over *XElements* with the XML name of *city*. The code is shown in Listing 6-31.

Listing 6-31   A LINQ to XML query to extract all city nodes from a customers list after adding some customers

```
xmlCustomers.Add(
    from   c in customers
    where  c.Country != Countries.Italy
    select new XElement("customer",
                new XElement("name", c.Name),
                new XElement("city", c.City),
                new XElement("country", c.Country)));

Console.WriteLine("\nAfter XML source modification");
foreach (var name in names) {
    Console.WriteLine(name);
}
```

This time the result also includes the new cities, which are outside of Italy:

```
After XML source modification
<city>Brescia</city>
<city>Torino</city>
<city>Dallas</city>
<city>Seattle</city>
```

To get a static result, we can invoke one of the methods we saw in Chapter 4: *ToList*, *ToArray*, *ToDictionary*, or *ToLookup*.

Using LINQ Queries over XML

We have already seen that many of the LINQ to XML methods navigate XML content and return instances of type *IEnumerable<XNode>* or *IEnumerable<XElement>*. Because LINQ queries can be applied to sequences of *IEnumerable<T>*, we can also use them to query XML content. In some of the previous examples, we used LINQ queries to create new XML content or to transform XML graphs.

Now consider a different situation: you want to create sequences of items (objects, entities, or whatever) whose value is taken from XML content. We can use LINQ queries over XML nodes through LINQ to XML syntax.

Listing 6-32 is an example of a LINQ query applied to the well-known XML list of customers. It filters the list of *customer* elements to extract the *name* element and the *city* attribute of each customer located in Italy, ordering the result by the *name* element value.

Listing 6-32   Using LINQ to XML and LINQ queries to query XML content

```
var customersFromXml =
    from    c in xmlCustomers.Elements("customer")
    where   (String)c.Attribute("country") == "Italy"
    orderby (String)c.Element("name")
    select  new {
                Name = (String)c.Element("name"),
                City = (String)c.Attribute("city") };

foreach (var customer in customersFromXml) {
    Console.WriteLine(customer);
}
```

The result is shown in the following output block:

```
{ Name = Marco, City = Torino }
{ Name = Paolo, City = Brescia }
```

This result is interesting, even if it is not all that exciting. To make these opportunities more challenging, suppose you have the same XML list of customers and a sequence of orders defined using the following LINQ query:

```
var orders =
    from    c in customers
    from    o in c.Orders
    select new {c.Name, o.IdProduct, o.Quantity};
```

You can imagine that the orders were loaded via LINQ to Entities from a Microsoft SQL Server database. We can write a complex query that joins XML nodes with entities to extract a sequence of new objects, as shown in Listing 6-33.

Listing 6-33   A LINQ query that merges LINQ to XML and LINQ to Objects

```
var ordersWithCustomersFromXml =
    from    c in xmlCustomers.Elements("customer")
    join    o in orders
    on      (String)c.Element("name") equals o.Name
    orderby (String)c.Element("name")
```

```
        select  new {
                    Name = (String)c.Element("name"),
                    City = (String)c.Attribute("city"),
                    IdProduct = o.IdProduct,
                    Quantity = o.Quantity };
```

This is a new and really powerful feature of LINQ and LINQ to XML, because we can define queries over mixed contents using a unique language and programming environment.

If you do not like the repetition of explicit casting of XML nodes inside the LINQ query, remember that we can use the *let* clause to define a more maintainable alias, as shown in Listing 6-34.

Listing 6-34   A LINQ query that merges LINQ to XML and LINQ to Objects, simplified by using the *let* clause

```
var ordersWithCustomersFromXml =
    from    c in xmlCustomers.Elements("customer")
    let     xName = (String)c.Element("name")
    let     xCity = (String)c.Attribute("city")
    join    o in orders
    on      xName equals o.Name
    orderby xName
    select  new {
                    Name = xName,
                    City = xCity,
                    IdProduct = o.IdProduct,
                    Quantity = o.Quantity };
```

Both of the previous examples return a sequence that, when printed to the Console window, looks like the following:

```
{ Name = Frank, City = Seattle, IdProduct = 5, Quantity = 20 }
{ Name = James, City = Dallas, IdProduct = 3, Quantity = 20 }
{ Name = Marco, City = Torino, IdProduct = 1, Quantity = 10 }
{ Name = Marco, City = Torino, IdProduct = 3, Quantity = 20 }
{ Name = Paolo, City = Brescia, IdProduct = 1, Quantity = 3 }
{ Name = Paolo, City = Brescia, IdProduct = 2, Quantity = 5 }
```

Using a LINQ query, we can also create a new XML graph, merging XML nodes and entities.

Support for XSD and Validation of Typed Nodes

In many of the previous examples, we used explicit casting and accessed nodes through their names as quoted strings. All those casts and quotes are not type safe and cannot be checked at compile time. However, XML document structure is often defined using an XML Schema Definition (XSD). There is a LINQ to XSD project that allows access to XML nodes using a typed and self-describing approach, and it is supported by Microsoft IntelliSense. For instance, the last query you saw in the previous section would be written like the one in Listing 6-35.

Listing 6-35   A LINQ query over XML, based on an XSD typed approach

```
var ordersWithCustomersFromXml =
    from    c in xmlCustomers.customerCollection
    join    o in orders
    on      c.Name equals o.Name
    orderby c.Name
    select  new {
                Name = c.Name,
                City = c.City,
                IdProduct = o.IdProduct,
                Quantity = o.Quantity };
```

As you can see, when using this approach the XML nodes graphs look like any other object graphs—regardless of whether they are made of elements, attributes, or nodes instead of objects. Keep in mind that the LINQ to XSD project is still under construction at the time of writing this book.

XML schema support is also offered through some extension methods defined in the *System.Xml.Schema.Extensions* class of the *System.Xml.Linq* assembly. There are just a couple of methods with a few overloads. Those methods are *GetSchemaInfo*, which extends any *XElement* or *XAttribute* instance, and *Validate*, which extends *XDocument*, *XElement*, and *XAttribute*. The first method (*GetSchemaInfo*) returns an annotation of type *System.Xml.Schema.IXmlSchemaInfo* taken from the current node, if present. It retrieves a schema definition mapped to the current node by using LINQ to XML annotations. The *Validate* method, as you can figure out from its name, validates the source XML node using an *XmlSchemaSet* containing the schemas to use. Consider the XML schema shown in Listing 6-36.

Listing 6-36   An XML Schema Definition for our sample list of customers

```
<?xml version="1.0" encoding="utf-8" ?>
<xsd:schema id="Customer"
    targetNamespace="http://schemas.devleap.com/Customer"
    elementFormDefault="qualified"
    xmlns="http://schemas.devleap.com/Customer"
    xmlns:xsd="http://www.w3.org/2001/XMLSchema">
  <xsd:element name="customers">
    <xsd:complexType>
      <xsd:sequence>
        <xsd:element name="customer" minOccurs="0" maxOccurs="unbounded">
          <xsd:complexType>
            <xsd:attribute name="name" type="xsd:string" use="required" />
            <xsd:attribute name="city" type="xsd:string" use="required" />
            <xsd:attribute name="country">
              <xsd:simpleType>
                <xsd:restriction base="xsd:string">
                  <xsd:enumeration value="Italy" />
```

```
                <xsd:enumeration value="USA" />
            </xsd:restriction>
          </xsd:simpleType>
        </xsd:attribute>
      </xsd:complexType>
    </xsd:element>
  </xsd:sequence>
</xsd:complexType>
</xsd:element>
</xsd:schema>
```

You can define an XML graph with this structure, using LINQ to XML as usual, and map the nodes to the previous schema using an *XNamespace* instance. An example is shown in Listing 6-37.

Listing 6-37   An XML document with the schema of Listing 6-36, built using the LINQ to XML API

```
XNamespace ns = "http://schemas.devleap.com/Customer";
XDocument xmlCustomers = new XDocument(
    new XElement(ns + "customers",
        from   c in customers
        select new XElement(ns + "customer",
                   new XAttribute("city", c.City),
                   new XAttribute("name", c.Name),
                   new XAttribute("country", c.Country)))));
```

At this point, you have the *xmlCustomers* variable that represents an XML Infoset instance related to the schema of Listing 6-36 using its corresponding XML namespace.

In Listing 6-38, you can see how to validate this *XDocument* using the *Validate* extension method.

Listing 6-38   XML validation using the *Validate* extension method

```
static void validateXDocument() {

    // ...

    XmlSchemaSet schemas = new XmlSchemaSet();
    schemas.Add(XmlSchema.Read(new StreamReader(@"..\..\customer.xsd"), null));

    xmlCustomers.Validate(schemas, xmlCustomers_validation);
}

static void xmlCustomers_validation(Object source, ValidationEventArgs args) {
    // In case of validation messages
    Console.WriteLine(args.Message);
}
```

The *Validate* method internally uses all the standard and common classes and tools of the *System.Xml.Schema* namespace.

Support for XPath and *System.Xml.XPath*

One last group of extension methods offered by LINQ to XML is related to *System.Xml.XPath* integration. The *System.Xml.XPath.Extensions* class provides a few extension methods useful for managing *XNode* contents via XPath. The first method is *CreateNavigator*, which returns an *XPathNavigator*:

```
public static XPathNavigator CreateNavigator(this XNode node);
public static XPathNavigator CreateNavigator(this XNode node, XmlNameTable nameTable);
```

Internally, it creates an instance of an *XNodeNavigator* class, which is derived from *XPathNavigator* and is specifically defined to navigate X* class graphs. The main goal of this method is to make possible the transformation of an *XNode* using standard *System.Xml.Xsl* classes. *XslCompiledTransform* can work with *XPathNavigator* derived classes as input. Listing 6-39 provides sample code that transforms our customers list using the XSLT we defined in Listing 6-26.

Listing 6-39 XSLT transformation using *XslCompiledTransform* and the *CreateNavigator* extension method

```
XslCompiledTransform xslt = new XslCompiledTransform();
xslt.Load(@"..\..\customerFromSourceToDestination.xslt");
xslt.Transform(sourceXmlCustomers.CreateNavigator(), null, Console.Out);
```

Another interesting method is *XPathEvaluate*, which evaluates an XPath rule against the current *XNode*, returning its value by using the internal class *XPathEvaluator*. The code in Listing 6-40 selects all attributes of name "*name*" of all the customers located in Italy.

Listing 6-40 Sample usage of the *XPathEvaluate* extension method

```
XElement xmlCustomers = new XElement("customers",
    from   c in customers
    select new XElement("customer",
                new XAttribute("name", c.Name),
                new XAttribute("city", c.City),
                new XAttribute("country", c.Country)));

var result = (IEnumerable<Object>)xmlCustomers.XPathEvaluate(
    "/customer[@country = 'Italy']/@name");

foreach (var item in result) {
    Console.WriteLine(item);
}
```

Consider that, in the current beta version of LINQ to XML, the *XPathEvaluateMethod* cannot determine the result of the XPath query. Therefore, it always returns a value of type *Object*. It is our responsibility to know and correctly cast the result type. The last two methods to take care of are *XPathSelectElement* and *XPathSelectElements*. The former returns the first element corresponding to the XPath expression provided as an argument, and the latter returns the full list of elements matching the expression. Internally, they both use the *XPathEvaluator* class. The following example selects all the *customer* elements of customers located in Italy:

```
var result = xmlCustomers.XPathSelectElements(
  "/customer[@country = 'Italy']");
```

This method is sometimes useful for defining LINQ queries that work on a subset of nodes of the source XML graph—in case we need to filter *customer* elements by the *country* attribute value. An example is shown in Listing 6-41.

Listing 6-41   Sample LINQ query over the result of the *XPathSelectElements* extension method

```
var ordersOfItalianCustomersFromXml =
    from    c in xmlCustomers.XPathSelectElements(
                    "/customer[@country = 'Italy']")
    let     xName = (String)c.Element("name")
    let     xCity = (String)c.Attribute("city")
    join    o in orders
    on      xName equals o.Name
    orderby xName
    select  new {
                Name = xName,
                City = xCity,
                IdProduct = o.IdProduct,
                Quantity = o.Quantity };
```

Remember that XPath rules are checked at run time, not at compile time. Therefore, be careful when defining them within LINQ queries. Consider also that like many other LINQ extension methods, the XPath methods we have just evaluated also support deferred query evaluation. Once again, keep in mind that every time we use queries defined using these methods, the result is refreshed by rescanning the source XML graph, unless you copy it yourself by using any of the extension methods provided by LINQ queries for doing that (such as *ToList*, *ToArray*, *ToDictionary*, or *ToLookup*).

Summary

In this chapter, you saw how to define XML content using the LINQ to XML API—by means of both functional construction and Visual Basic 9.0 XML literals. You also saw how to query, traverse, and transform XML nodes graphs using LINQ to XML query extensions. Finally, you evaluated the support offered by *System.Xml.Linq* to XPath, XSD, and XSLT.

ADO.NET Entity Framework

In this appendix, we will evaluate the new data access framework—ADO.NET Entity Framework—provided by Microsoft ADO.NET Orcas. In particular, we will focus our attention on the capability to manage and query entities, which is something we can do with a standard common relational data source, but with a deep abstraction from the physical data layer.

ADO.NET Standard Approach

Consider a common example of an order management application based on the Microsoft SQL Server 2005 Northwind sample database. In Figure A-1, you can see a subset of the database schema for the order management side.

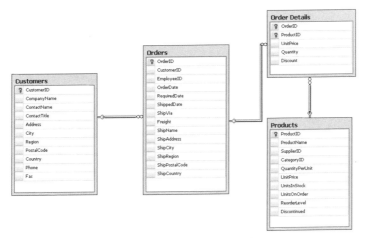

Figure A-1   The Northwind orders database schema

If you want to query the data from a standard .NET application using ADO.NET 2.0, you can choose a connected or disconnected approach, using a *SqlCommand* with a *SqlDataReader* in the former case or a *SqlDataAdapter* and a *DataSet* instance in the latter. Imagine that you are developing an online e-commerce Web application and you decide to use a connected approach. You will probably need to query the list of orders placed and submit new orders. Each order made is a main order row (in the Orders table) mapped to a set of order items (in the Order Details table).

In the following example, you can see a simplified query to extract all the orders placed by each customer:

```
SELECT c.CustomerID, c.CompanyName, c.ContactName,
       o.OrderID, o.OrderDate
FROM Customers AS c
INNER JOIN Orders AS o
    ON c.CustomerID = o.CustomerID
```

Here are two simplified parametric queries to insert orders and order items:

```
-- Order insert statement
INSERT INTO [Northwind].[dbo].[Orders]
  ([CustomerID] ,[EmployeeID], [OrderDate] ,[RequiredDate])
VALUES
  (@CustomerID, @EmployeeID, @OrderDate, @RequiredDate)
-- Order Detail insert statement
INSERT INTO [Northwind].[dbo].[Order Details]
  ([OrderID], [ProductID], [UnitPrice], [Quantity], [Discount])
VALUES
  (@OrderID, @ProductID, @UnitPrice, @Quantity, @Discount)
```

In Listing A-1, you can see how to invoke the first selection query—for instance, to bind the result to an ASP.NET 2.0 *GridView*.

Listing A-1   A classic ADO.NET 2.0 query using a *SqlDataReader*

```
SqlConnection cn = new SqlConnection(NWindConnectionString);
SqlCommand cmd = new SqlCommand("SELECT c.CustomerID, c.CompanyName, " +
"c.ContactName, o.OrderID, o.OrderDate FROM Customers AS c INNER JOIN " +
"Orders AS o ON c.CustomerID = o.CustomerID", cn );

using (cn) {
    cn.Open();

    using (SqlDataReader dr = cmd.ExecuteReader(
                           CommandBehavior.CloseConnection)) {
        gridCustomersOrders.DataSource = dr;
        gridCustomersOrders.DataBind();
    }
}
```

This book is not the right place to discuss whether it is better to use a *DbDataReader* or a *DataSet* to achieve the best balance between performance and scalability. For this reason, we will skip these kinds of considerations. However, we do want to highlight some possible issues with this approach to querying.

First, we are querying the database persistence layer directly from our application code (the ASPX page, in this example), and we are tied to a particular kind of database engine (Microsoft SQL Server 2005). You probably know that ADO.NET 2.0 code can leverage *DbProviderFactories* to be more independent from the physical database. This flexibility is enormously helpful in our efforts to write more flexible code and to reuse our applications against different database persistence layers. On the other hand, even when using *DbProviderFactories*, we are working with code that mixes typed .NET syntax and untyped SQL code, as shown in Listing A-2.

Listing A-2   A classic ADO.NET 2.0 query using *DbProviderFactories*

```
DbProviderFactory dbFactory =
    DbProviderFactories.GetFactory(NWindProviderName);
DbConnection cn = dbFactory.CreateConnection();
cn.ConnectionString = NWindConnectionString;
DbCommand cmd = cn.CreateCommand();
cmd.CommandText = "SELECT c.CustomerID, c.CompanyName, c.ContactName, " +
    "o.OrderID, o.OrderDate FROM Customers AS c INNER JOIN Orders AS o " +
    "ON c.CustomerID = o.CustomerID";

using (cn) {
    cn.Open();

    using (SqlDataReader dr = cmd.ExecuteReader(
                            CommandBehavior.CloseConnection)) {
        gridCustomersOrders.DataSource = dr;
        gridCustomersOrders.DataBind();
    }
}
```

The first issue we are facing is the lack of strongly typed code and the need to merge different kinds of code and syntaxes (C#, SQL, and so on). Consider also that each order is made of a main header row and a set of items. With regard to the physical database, these records are retrieved from different database tables (Orders and Order Details). When querying orders, we can just execute a multiple-resultset query. However, if the application requirements involve common needs such as paging, sorting, and custom ordering in querying items, we will probably need to write queries that are not trivial (even if any good database developer should be able to do that). Finally, another problem in this code is that we are too close to the database within our application code. As you probably know, modern applications are often logically and physically divided into layers, as shown in Figure A-2.

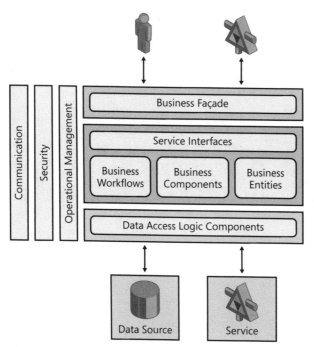

Figure A-2   A modern application with a distributed architecture

At a minimum, applications consist of the following layers:

- An abstract data access layer, which can make the real physical persistence layer transparent to the entire application.

- One or more physical data access layers to map the application to a real persistence layer. Consider that modern applications can have a remote data source, achieved through Simple Object Access Protocol (SOAP) services, and not only and always a relational database.

- A business layer in which we can place validation rules, business logic, transaction management (which is eventually distributed), security checks and authorization policies, business processes, and workflows.

- One or more presentation layers that interact only with the underlying business layer and that usually have no intelligence or logic. This arrangement is necessary to make the higher-level application core business engine independent from the presentation layer.

There are more issues and needs to manage within Service Oriented Architectures (SOA). Nevertheless, even with SOA we will probably have at least all of those basic layers plus some others so that we can abstract the service façade from the physical back end.

In such architectures, we usually cannot transfer data between layers using *DbDataReader* instances because we do not want to keep database connections open for a long time and because the physical layers could be deployed on different machines (servers). Therefore, it is not convenient to marshal or serialize *DbDataReader* instances over the wire. You could use a *DataSet* or a typed *DataSet* to avoid these issues. However, what happens when your physical data layer consists of more than a database or an XML file? And what other issues will you encounter when you have different physical persistence layers that eventually describe the same conceptual information (such as Orders and Order Details) with different database structures? For instance, you could have a SQL Server 2000 database that describes, with a normalized relational data structure, custom options (color, size, and so on) of each order detail, while you might also have an XML field with SQL Server 2005 to be more versatile. Modern architectures, for these and many other reasons, tend to use custom entities to describe at a conceptual level what you need to manage. The physical layer is just another detail from this point of view, and the overall application architecture should be independent from it.

We have discussed some common issues related to data retrieval for orders already placed. Now consider the other goal of our application: placing orders. We need a data structure to store orders while customers are placing them—the common and classic shopping basket. When the customer confirms his shopping basket, we need to save the header row and each child order detail within the persistence layer using an ACID (Atomicity, Consistency, Isolation, Durability) transaction. Once again, we could use a *DataSet* to solve this problem, updating the database with a *DbDataAdapter*. However, keep in mind the same considerations we made regarding data retrieval. As an alternative, we could use custom entities to describe our concept of an order. These orders would be made of various pieces of information, some of which might have multiple occurrences.

Abstracting from the Physical Layer

In Figure A-3, we can see a short conceptual definition (illustrated with a Visual Studio 2005 class diagram) of some of our entities, which can be convenient if we decide to provide a conceptual definition of our application domain.

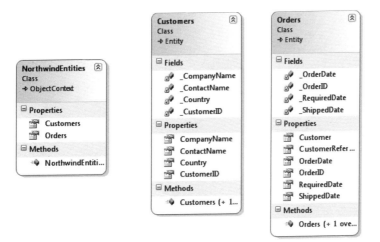

Figure A-3   The Visual Studio 2005 class diagram of our order system from a conceptual point of view

In Listing A-3, you can see a C# representation of this conceptual description.

Listing A-3   A sample object-oriented definition of our conceptual entities

```csharp
namespace NorthwindModel {
    public partial class NorthwindEntities {
        public List<Customer> Customers {
            // ...          }

        public List<Order> Orders {
            // ...          }
    }

    public partial class Customer {

        public string CustomerID {
            get { return this._CustomerID; }
            set { this._CustomerID = value; }
        }
        private string _CustomerID = string.Empty;

        public string CompanyName {
            get { return this._CompanyName; }
            set { this._CompanyName = value; }
        }
        private string _CompanyName = string.Empty;

        public string ContactName {
            get { return this._ContactName; }
            set { this._ContactName = value; }
        }
        private string _ContactName;

        public string Country {
            get { return this._Country; }
            set { this._Country = value; }
        }
        private string _Country;

        public List<Order> Orders
        {
            get {
                // ...
            }
        }
    }

    public partial class Order {

        public int OrderID {
            get { return this._OrderID; }
            set { this._OrderID = value; }
        }
        private int _OrderID;
```

```
        public DateTime? OrderDate {
            get { return this._OrderDate; }
            set { this._OrderDate = value; }
        }
        private DateTime? _OrderDate;

        public DateTime? RequiredDate {
            get { return this._RequiredDate; }
            set { this._RequiredDate = value; }
        }
        private DateTime? _RequiredDate;

        public DateTime? ShippedDate {
            get { return this._ShippedDate; }
            set { this._ShippedDate = value; }
        }
        private DateTime? _ShippedDate;

        public Customer Customer {
            get {
                // ...                }
            set {
                // ...
            }
        }
    }
}
```

The real problem is to load and manage entities like the ones we have just defined (which involves reading their contents from a database) in a way that is independent from the nature and structure of the database itself. Using standard programming languages, we have to define, write, test, and maintain a lot of plumbing to achieve this goal.

We also have to deal with several issues. For instance, whenever we load a parent entity (such as a *Customer*), is it best to also load its children (*Orders* for *Customer* instances, *Order Details* for *Orders*)? Or is it better to load children only when we really need to access them? The answer is probably, "It depends." This is because when we access a *Customer*, we do not automatically also want her *Orders*. On the other hand, many times when accessing one *Order* we also need to enumerate its *Details*. Every time we need a *Customer*, is it better to execute a single query and load it from the database, or is it easier and faster to reuse an in-memory instance of that particular *Customer*? If we reuse object instances, do we need to worry about concurrency issues? We could go on for hours with questions like these. Unfortunately, there are not absolute solutions for every problem and application. There are just a few patterns and rules that suggest the most common and reasonable solutions. The best solution might be a data access technique that allows us to decide on a case-by-case basis.

Entity Data Modeling

The first feature of ADO.NET Orcas that we will examine is the capability to model entities from a conceptual level of abstraction. This approach leverages a set of XML schemas (which are useful for defining entities) and maps them to the physical persistence layer. These XML files will be parsed by a tool to generate the corresponding .NET implementation code. Whenever we do that, we speak about Entity Data Modeling (EDM).

The first XML metadata file we will examine is the Conceptual Schema Definition Language (CSDL) file, which defines the entity side of our application framework. A file of this type describes each *EntityType* (a specific entity), *EntitySet* (group of entities), and *Association* (relationship between entities).

In Listing A-4, you can see an excerpt of our Northwind CSDL metadata file, describing the *Customer* and *Order* entities.

Listing A-4   The *Customer* and *Order EntityType* definition within Northwind.CSDL

```xml
<?xml version="1.0" encoding="utf-8"?>
<Schema Namespace="NorthwindModel" Alias="Self"
  xmlns="http://schemas.microsoft.com/ado/2006/04/edm">
  <EntityContainer Name="NorthwindEntities">
    <EntitySet Name="Customers" EntityType="NorthwindModel.Customer" />
    <EntitySet Name="Orders" EntityType="NorthwindModel.Order" />
    <AssociationSet Name="Relationship_Orders_Customers"
      Association="NorthwindModel.Relationship_Orders_Customers">
      <End Role="Customer" EntitySet="Customers" />
      <End Role="Order" EntitySet="Orders" />
    </AssociationSet>
  </EntityContainer>
  <EntityType Name="Customer" Key="CustomerID">
    <Property Name="CustomerID" Type="String"
      Nullable="false" MaxLength="4000" FixedLength="true" />
    <Property Name="CompanyName" Type="String"
      Nullable="false" MaxLength="4000" />
    <Property Name="ContactName" Type="String" MaxLength="4000" />
    <Property Name="Country" Type="String" />
    <NavigationProperty Name="Orders"
      Relationship="NorthwindModel.Relationship_Orders_Customers"
      FromRole="Customer" ToRole="Order" />
  </EntityType>
  <EntityType Name="Order" Key="OrderID">
    <Property Name="OrderID" Type="Int32" Nullable="false" />
    <Property Name="OrderDate" Type="DateTime" />
    <Property Name="RequiredDate" Type="DateTime" />
    <Property Name="ShippedDate" Type="DateTime" />
    <NavigationProperty Name="Customer"
      Relationship="NorthwindModel.Relationship_Orders_Customers"
      FromRole="Order" ToRole="Customer" />
  </EntityType>
```

```
  <Association Name="Relationship_Orders_Customers">
    <End Role="Customer" Type="NorthwindModel.Customer"
      Multiplicity="0..1" />
    <End Role="Order" Type="NorthwindModel.Order"
      Multiplicity="*" />
  </Association>
</Schema>
```

This file defines an *EntityContainer*, named *NorthwindEntities*, which contains a couple of *EntitySet*s, called *Customers* and *Orders*. *Customers* is a list of entities of type *Customer*, and *Orders* is a set of *Order* instances. There is also a relationship, called *Relationship_Orders_Customers*, that describes how to traverse the object graph of *Customer* and *Order* instances, using the definition of an *Association* between them.

As you can see, this code fragment describes only entities, without any kind of reference to the database, and all the *Customer* and *Order* properties are defined using only .NET types. The schema also describes validation rules and constraints that will also be made available in our code, as specific validation code.

A second XML metadata file to consider is the Storage Schema Definition Language (SSDL) file, which describes the physical data layer. Listing A-5 provides an example.

Listing A-5   The physical data layer *Customer* and *Order* definition within Northwind.SSDL

```
<?xml version="1.0" encoding="utf-8"?>
<Schema Namespace="Northwind" Alias="Self"
  xmlns="http://schemas.microsoft.com/ado/2006/04/edm/ssdl">
  <EntityContainer Name="dbo">
    <EntitySet Name="Customers" EntityType="Northwind.Customer"
      Schema="dbo" Table="Customers" />
    <EntitySet Name="Orders" EntityType="Northwind.Order"
      Schema="dbo" Table="Orders" />
    <AssociationSet Name="FK_Orders_Customers"
      Association="Northwind.FK_Orders_Customers">
      <End Role="Customer" EntitySet="Customers" />
      <End Role="Order" EntitySet="Orders" />
    </AssociationSet>
  </EntityContainer>
  <EntityType Name="Customer" Key="CustomerID">
    <Property Name="CustomerID" Type="nchar" Nullable="false" />
    <Property Name="CompanyName" Type="nvarchar" Nullable="false" />
    <Property Name="ContactName" Type="nvarchar" />
    <Property Name="Country" Type="nvarchar" />
  </EntityType>
  <EntityType Name="Order" Key="OrderID">
    <Property Name="OrderID" Type="int" Nullable="false"
      StoreGeneratedPattern="identity" />
    <Property Name="CustomerID" Type="nchar" />
    <Property Name="OrderDate" Type="datetime" />
    <Property Name="RequiredDate" Type="datetime" />
    <Property Name="ShippedDate" Type="datetime" />
  </EntityType>
```

```
    <Association Name="FK_Orders_Customers">
      <End Role="Customer" Type="Northwind.Customer" Multiplicity="0..1" />
      <End Role="Order" Type="Northwind.Order" Multiplicity="*" />
      <ReferentialConstraint
        FromRole="Customer" ToRole="Order"
        FromProperty="CustomerID" ToProperty="CustomerID" />
    </Association>
  </Schema>
```

Unlike the CSDL file, this XML document has explicit references to the physical data structure—such as primary keys, nullability rules, identities, foreign key constraints, and data types related to the SQL Server side. In this example, the two CSDL and SSDL files are quite similar, because we are defining a very simple situation. In real-world applications, these files will probably hold more complex and less symmetric code.

The last metadata file to consider is the Mapping Schema Language (MSL) file, which simply maps the two previous metadata definition files. In Listing A-6, you can see a sample mapping file.

Listing A-6   CSDL and SSDL mapping described by Northwind.MSL

```
<?xml version="1.0" encoding="utf-8"?>
<Mapping cs:Space="C-S"
  xmlns:cs="urn:schemas-microsoft-com:windows:storage:mapping:CS"
  xmlns="urn:schemas-microsoft-com:windows:storage:mapping:CS">
  <cs:EntityContainerMapping
    cs:StorageEntityContainer="dbo"
    cs:CdmEntityContainer="NorthwindEntities">
  <cs:EntitySetMapping cs:Name="Customers"
    cs:TableName="Customers" cs:TypeName="NorthwindModel.Customer">
    <cs:ScalarProperty cs:Name="CustomerID" cs:ColumnName="CustomerID" />
    <cs:ScalarProperty cs:Name="CompanyName" cs:ColumnName="CompanyName" />
    <cs:ScalarProperty cs:Name="ContactName" cs:ColumnName="ContactName" />
    <cs:ScalarProperty cs:Name="Country" cs:ColumnName="Country" />
  </cs:EntitySetMapping>
  <cs:EntitySetMapping cs:Name="Orders"
    cs:TableName="Orders" cs:TypeName="NorthwindModel.Order">
    <cs:ScalarProperty cs:Name="OrderID" cs:ColumnName="OrderID" />
    <cs:ScalarProperty cs:Name="OrderDate" cs:ColumnName="OrderDate" />
    <cs:ScalarProperty cs:Name="RequiredDate"
      cs:ColumnName="RequiredDate" />
    <cs:ScalarProperty cs:Name="ShippedDate" cs:ColumnName="ShippedDate" />
  </cs:EntitySetMapping>
  <cs:AssociationSetMapping cs:Name="Relationship_Orders_Customers"
    cs:TypeName="NorthwindModel.Relationship_Orders_Customers"
    cs:TableName="Orders">
    <cs:EndProperty cs:Name="Customer">
      <cs:ScalarProperty cs:Name="CustomerID" cs:ColumnName="CustomerID" />
    </cs:EndProperty>
```

```
    <cs:EndProperty cs:Name="Order">
      <cs:ScalarProperty cs:Name="OrderID" cs:ColumnName="OrderID" />
    </cs:EndProperty>
    <cs:Condition cs:ColumnName="CustomerID" cs:IsNull="false" />
  </cs:AssociationSetMapping>
 </cs:EntityContainerMapping>
</Mapping>
```

You can see that this last file explicitly maps metadata between the conceptual model (*CdmEntityContainer*) and the physical storage (*StorageEntityContainer*), defining the containing table (TableName) and column (ColumnName) for each scalar property (*Name*) of each entity (*TypeName*).

These files can be defined by hand, as we did in our examples, just by using XML Schema IntelliSense. Or they can be generated by using the Visual Studio Orcas file template named "ADO.NET Entity Data Model," which starts a simple wizard that produces the files based on user input. Regardless of how the metadata files are produced, after they are defined within a Visual Studio Orcas project they are automatically parsed to dynamically create their corresponding .NET code. The result is a code file that contains definitions of all the *EntityType*, *EntitySet*, and *Association* types defined within the CSDL file. While CSDL is converted in code, SSDL and MSL remain in XML so that they can change the physical layer without changing the conceptual model.

Querying Entities with ADO.NET

You have seen how to model your data layer at the right level of abstraction, using the ADO.NET metadata files and the EDM schema tools.

ADO.NET Orcas also provides a set of classes that allows you to work with the entities produced by the metadata files parsing result. Starting from the already defined and broadly adopted architecture of ADO.NET, this last version provides a new ADO.NET Managed Provider to manage entities instead of records.

> **Note** An ADO.NET Managed Provider is a set of classes defined to manage a particular kind of data source. There are providers for SQL Server, Oracle, ODBC, OLE DB, and so on. All of them implement common interfaces defined by ADO.NET. Every developer can use them from an abstract point of view—accessing their members through common interfaces instead of using explicit type casting. The *DbProviderFactories* engine that we have previously seen is mainly based on this concept.

This new managed provider, defined within the *System.Data.EntityClient* namespace of *System.Data.Entity* assembly, offers an *EntityConnection* class that inherits from *System.Data.Common.DbConnection*, like any other ADO.NET connection does (for example, *SqlConnection*, *OleDbConnection*, and so on). *EntityConnection* accepts a particular connection string that requires not only a database connection, but also a path to the set of XML metadata files (CSDL, SSDL, and MSL) and the type of the provider to use for the physical data layer. Here is a sample connection, defined in an *App.Config* file, for an *EntityConnection* instance:

```
<connectionStrings>
  <add name="Northwind"
    connectionString="metadata=.\Northwind.csdl|.\Northwind.ssdl|.\Northwind.msl;
      provider=System.Data.SqlClient;provider connection string=&quote;Data Source=.;
      Initial Catalog=Northwind;Integrated Security=True;
      multipleactiveresultsets=true &quote;"
      providerName="System.Data.EntityClient"/>
</connectionStrings>
```

Pay attention to the *MultipleActiveResultsets* feature configured in the connection string. This feature is very useful whenever you need to dynamically load entities while traversing the objects graph. With that setting, the *EntityClient* provider can leverage multiple parallel queries to achieve this result.

EntityConnection can be used by an *EntityCommand* instance to select a set of entities instead of a set of records. In Listing A-7, you can see an example of a query that retrieves the full list of Northwind customer entities.

Listing A-7 A sample query against a set of entities, using *EntityCommand* and *EntityConnection*

```
using (EntityConnection cn = new EntityConnection(NwindConnectionString)) {
    EntityCommand cmd = new EntityCommand(
        "SELECT c FROM NorthwindEntities.Customers AS c", cn);

    cn.Open();
    using (DbDataReader dr =
                cmd.ExecuteReader(CommandBehavior.SequentialAccess)) {
        while (dr.Read()) {
            Console.WriteLine(((DbDataRecord)dr.GetValue(0))[0]);
        }
    }
}
```

The query provided as an argument to the *EntityCommand* constructor is interesting. It looks like a classic SQL query, but it is not. In reality, it is a query against the *EntitySets* of the conceptual model. *NorthwindEntities* is the *EntityContainer*, and *Customers* is the *EntitySet* of all the *Customer* instances. The result of this query is a list of *DbDataRecord* instances, each of which describes a customer.

By now, this code is not very interesting. In fact, it is not much different than any other code to query a database using ADO.NET. Nevertheless, consider the code automatically generated from the CSDL file. It defines a .NET type (a class) for each *Entity* defined in the source CSDL file–for instance, consider the *Customer* type shown in Listing A-8.

Listing A-8   An excerpt of the *Customer* type auto-generated from the CSDL file

```
[System.Data.Objects.DataClasses.EntityTypeAttribute(
    SchemaName = "NorthwindModel", TypeName = "Customer")]
[System.Runtime.Serialization.DataContractAttribute()]
public partial class Customer: System.Data.Objects.DataClasses.Entity {

    // [...
    [System.Data.Objects.DataClasses.EntityKeyPropertyAttribute()]
    [System.Runtime.Serialization.DataMemberAttribute()]
    [System.Data.Objects.DataClasses.NullableAttribute(false)]
    public string CustomerID {
        get { return this._CustomerID; }
        set {
          this.ReportPropertyChanging("CustomerID", this._CustomerID);
          this._CustomerID =
        System.Data.Objects.DataClasses.StructuralObject.SetValidValue(
          value, false, 4000, true);
          this.ReportPropertyChanged("CustomerID", this._CustomerID);
      }
    }
    private string _CustomerID = string.Empty;

    // [...
    [System.Data.Objects.DataClasses.RelationshipPropertyAttribute(
        SchemaName = "NorthwindModel",
        RelationshipName = "FK_Orders_Customers", TargetEndName = "Order")]
    [System.Xml.Serialization.XmlIgnoreAttribute()]
    public System.Data.Objects.DataClasses.EntityCollection<Order> Orders {
        get { return FK_Orders_Customers.GetOrderEntities(this); }
    }
}
```

The *Customer* type inherits from the base class *Entity* defined in the common namespace *System.Data.Objects.DataClasses.* This base class provides all the features to manage object state, change events, validation rules, and so on. The code is decorated with .NET attributes taken from the same namespace of the *Entity* base class for the purpose of defining the behavior of each property to be compliant with the EDM definition. For instance, you can see that the *CustomerID* property is marked with an *EntityKeyPropertyAttribute* instance. This marking indicates that from a conceptual point of view the property is the unique identifier of each *Customer* instance. Moreover, these types are serializable as a *DataContract* of *System.Runtime.Serialization* version 3.0; thus, they can be used as message content in Windows Communication Foundation (WCF) services.

The code also defines a root .NET type called *NorthwindEntities*—which is also described in the CSDL file—that acts as a container for all the *EntitySet* instances. In Listing A-9, you can see an excerpt of its definition.

Listing A-9   An excerpt of the *NothwindEntities* type auto-generated from the CSDL file

```
public partial class NorthwindEntities: System.Data.Objects.ObjectContext {

    public NorthwindEntities()
        : base("name=NorthwindEntities", "NorthwindEntities") { }

    public NorthwindEntities( string connectionString )
        : base(connectionString, "NorthwindEntities") { }

    public NorthwindEntities( System.Data.Common.DbConnection connection,
        System.Data.Metadata.Edm.MetadataWorkspace workspace )
        : base(connection, workspace) { }

    public System.Data.Objects.ObjectQuery<Customer> Customers {
        get { return base.CreateQuery<Customer>("Customers"); }
    }

    public System.Data.Objects.ObjectQuery<Order> Orders {
        get { return base.CreateQuery<Order>("Orders"); }
    }
}
```

The class inherits from *System.Data.Objects.ObjectContext* and internally defines the *Customers* and *Orders* sets as instances of the generic type *ObjectQuery*. *ObjectQuery* describes a typed result of a query over a set of entities. We can use instances of *NorthwindEntities* to access and query all the typed and object-oriented entities. In Listing A-10, you can see an example of querying the list of *Customer* objects to extract all the customers.

Listing A-10   An ADO.NET Entities query to extract all the customers

```
using (NorthwindEntities db = new NorthwindEntities()) {

    var customers = db.CreateQuery<DbDataRecord>(
        "SELECT c FROM NorthwindEntities.Customers AS c");

    foreach (var c in customers) {
        Console.WriteLine( ((Customer)c[0]).Display() );
    }
}
```

We create the query over entities by invoking the *CreateQuery* generic method of the *NorthwindEntities* object. The *CreateQuery* method is defined in the base *ObjectContext* class and does not return its result immediately; instead, it defines a query tree that will be evaluated when it is enumerated. This behavior suggests a potential conjunction with LINQ queries, which we will discover later in this appendix. The result of the query is a set of *DbDataRecord* objects, each of which contains a single column row representing a single *Customer* instance. In fact, we cast the zero column of each row into a *Customer* instance and invoke a custom extension method to *Display* the result.

We are working with a typed environment, and *Customer* is not a database row, but a defined and known entity. Therefore, we can invoke the *CreateQuery* method, assigning to its generic type the *Customer* type itself, as shown in Listing A-11.

Listing A-11   An ADO.NET Entities query to extract all the typed customers

```
using (NorthwindEntities db = new NorthwindEntities()) {

    var customers = db.CreateQuery<Customer>(
        "SELECT VALUE c FROM NorthwindEntities.Customers AS c");

    foreach (var c in customers) {
        Console.WriteLine(c.Display());
    }
}
```

We used the *VALUE* keyword to ask for an already typed and fully compiled *Customer* instance—for each item in the physical data storage—as a result to the query engine.

We can also filter entities based on conditions, which are eventually mapped to parameters. Consider the sample code in Listing A-12, in which we extract all the customers located in Italy.

Listing A-12   An ADO.NET Entities query to extract all the customers located in Italy

```
using (NorthwindEntities db = new NorthwindEntities()) {

    var customers = db.CreateQuery<Customer>(
        "SELECT VALUE c FROM NorthwindEntities.Customers AS c " +
        "WHERE c.Country = 'Italy'");

    foreach (var c in customers) {
        Console.WriteLine(c.Display());
    }
}
```

We can also use parameters to feed a parametric query instead of using explicitly declared values. In Listing A-13, you can see a parametric query used to filter customers on a *Country* property basis.

Listing A-13   An ADO.NET Entities query to extract all the customers of a particular country

```
using (NorthwindEntities db = new NorthwindEntities()) {

    var customers = db.CreateQuery<Customer>(
        "SELECT VALUE c FROM NorthwindEntities.Customers AS c " +
        "WHERE c.Country = @Country");

    customers.Parameters.Add(new ObjectParameter("Country", country));
    foreach (Customer c in customers) {
        Console.WriteLine(c.Display());
    }
}
```

Under the cover, the *System.Data.EntityClient* framework parses the queries over entities and converts them to SQL queries to extract from the physical data layer the data mapped on the entities. After this, it loads the entities with the content received from the database server. In the end, this is a smart and maintainable surrogate for a custom data layer. In the following block, you can see the SQL code produced to execute the query described in Listing A-13:

```
exec sp_executesql N'SELECT
0 AS [C1],
[Extent1].[CustomerID] AS [CustomerID],
[Extent1].[CompanyName] AS [CompanyName],
[Extent1].[ContactName] AS [ContactName],
[Extent1].[Country] AS [Country]
FROM [dbo].[Customers] AS [Extent1]
WHERE [Extent1].[Country] = @Country',N'@Country
nvarchar(7)',@Country=N'Germany'
```

> **Important**   The SQL queries generated by ADO.NET Entity Framework that we illustrate in this chapter are only indicative. Microsoft reserves the right to change the SQL code that is generated, and sometimes we simplify the text. Therefore, you should not rely on it.

You can probably appreciate that the querying engine of *EntityClient* tries to optimize query plans and avoids SQL injection by using parametric queries. The EDM also defines relationships between entities. Consider the example in Listing A-14, in which we retrieve all orders filtered by customers of a specific *Country*.

Listing A-14   An ADO.NET Entities query to extract all the orders of customers of a specific country

```
using (NorthwindEntities db = new NorthwindEntities()) {

    ObjectQuery<Order> orders = db.CreateQuery<Order>(
        "SELECT VALUE o FROM NorthwindEntities.Orders AS o " +
        "WHERE o.Customer.Country = @Country");
    orders.Parameters.Add(new ObjectParameter("Country", country));

    foreach (Order o in orders) {
        Console.WriteLine(o.Display());
    }
}
```

In this last example, we traverse the object graph to filter each *Order* on a *Customer*'s property basis. There are many other opportunities for querying entities. For instance, in Listing A-15 we extract all customers who placed orders in the last two years, leveraging the *NAVIGATE* keyword to traverse an object relationship between *Customer* and *Order* instances.

Listing A-15   An ADO.NET Entities query to extract all the customers who placed orders in the last two years

```
using (NorthwindEntities db = new NorthwindEntities()) {

    var customers = db.CreateQuery<Customer>(
        "SELECT VALUE c FROM NorthwindEntities.Customers AS c " +
        "WHERE EXISTS( " +
        " SELECT VALUE o " +
        " FROM NAVIGATE(c, NorthwindModel.Relationship_Orders_Customers)" +
        " AS o " +
        " WHERE o.OrderDate > @Date)");
    customers.Parameters.Add(new ObjectParameter("Date",
        DateTime.Now.AddYears(-2)));

    foreach (var c in customers) {
        Console.WriteLine(c.Display());
    }
}
```

Querying ADO.NET Entities with LINQ

You have seen how ADO.NET Entities can be queried using text queries based on an SQL "dialect" specifically and intentionally defined for querying entities. However, entities are a typed representation of conceptual information, and it would be great to write queries using a fully typed approach. As you saw at the end of Chapter 5, "LINQ to ADO.NET," we can leverage LINQ to Entities to query ADO.NET Entities using a LINQ query approach. Listing A-16 offers a quick review of these capabilities, showing a possible way to translate the query used in Listing A-15 into LINQ to Entities.

Listing A-16   A LINQ to Entities query to extract all the customers who placed orders in the last two years

```
using (NorthwindEntities db = new NorthwindEntities()) {

    DateTime referenceDate = DateTime.Now.AddYears(-10);
    var customers = (from   o in db.Orders
                     where  o.OrderDate > referenceDate
                     select o.Customer).Distinct();

    foreach (var c in customers) {
        Console.WriteLine(c.Display());
    }
}
```

The LINQ approach enables you to write fully typed code, as you can see from the typed *DateTime* filter.

Changing and Updating ADO.NET Entities

One last matter to consider is updating entities and persisting their state back to the physical data layer. ADO.NET Entity Framework transparently monitors object state and instancing whenever we change an object's contents, leveraging the base class *Entity* from which every single entity type inherits. Let's start with Listing A-17, which provides an example of how to modify an entity instance.

Listing A-17   Entity modification and data persistence

```
using (NorthwindEntities db = new NorthwindEntities()) {

    var customer = (from   c in db.Customers
                    where  c.CustomerID == "ALFKI"
                    select c).AsEnumerable().First();

    Console.WriteLine("Customer ContactName: {0}", customer.ContactName);
    Console.WriteLine("Customer state: {0}", customer.EntityState);

    customer.ContactName = "Maria Anders - Changed";

    Console.WriteLine("Customer ContactName: {0}", customer.ContactName);
    Console.WriteLine("Customer state: {0}", customer.EntityState);

    db.SaveChanges();

    Console.WriteLine("Customer state: {0}", customer.EntityState);
}
```

The output of this code is like the following:

```
Customer ContactName: Maria Anders
Customer state: Unchanged
Customer ContactName: Maria Anders - Changed
Customer state: Modified
Customer state: Unchanged
```

You can see that as soon as we change the customer instance, we implicitly also change its *EntityState* value, which keeps track of the entity status throughout its lifetime. This property can assume the classical values of *Added*, *Deleted*, *Detached*, *Modified*, and *Unchanged*. The entity status is tracked by the *ObjectContext* engine. In fact, we are working inside a *using* block applied to a *NorthwindEntities* object, and every query is executed against the current context. Whenever a user queries for an entity instance, the *ObjectContext* base engine checks to determine whether the object has already been loaded into memory. If the object is already available, the engine returns that instance; otherwise, it retrieves the instance from the physical database and keeps track of it. Whenever a piece of code changes the object instance, the *ObjectContext* is notified and tracks the information. In Listing A-18, you can see the instancing and object concurrency policy in action.

Listing A-18   Entity status and concurrency

```
using (NorthwindEntities db = new NorthwindEntities()) {

    var customer1 = (from   c in db.Customers
                     where  c.CustomerID == "ALFKI"
                     select c).AsEnumerable().First();

    Console.WriteLine("Customer 1 ContactName: {0}", customer1.ContactName);
    Console.WriteLine("Customer 1 state: {0}", customer1.EntityState);

    customer1.ContactName = "Maria Andersa - Changed";

    Console.WriteLine("Customer 1 ContactName: {0}", customer1.ContactName);
    Console.WriteLine("Customer 1 state: {0}", customer1.EntityState);

    var customer2 = (from   c in db.Customers
                     where  c.CustomerID == "ALFKI"
                     select c).AsEnumerable().First();

    Console.WriteLine("Customer 2 ContactName: {0}", customer2.ContactName);
    Console.WriteLine("Customer 2 state: {0}", customer2.EntityState);

    db.SaveChanges();

    Console.WriteLine("Customer 1 state: {0}", customer1.EntityState);
    Console.WriteLine("Customer 2 state: {0}", customer2.EntityState);
    Console.WriteLine("Customer 1 HashCode: {0}", customer1.GetHashCode());
    Console.WriteLine("Customer 2 HashCode: {0}", customer2.GetHashCode());

    Console.WriteLine("Customer 1 Equals Customer 2? {0}",
        customer1.Equals(customer2));
}
```

The result of the previous code excerpt is the following:

```
Customer 1 ContactName: Maria Anders
Customer 1 state: Unchanged
Customer 1 ContactName: Maria Anders - Changed
Customer 1 state: Modified
Customer 2 ContactName: Maria Anders - Changed
Customer 2 state: Modified
Customer 1 state: Unchanged
Customer 2 state: Unchanged
Customer 1 HashCode: 7765704
Customer 2 HashCode: 7765704
Customer 1 Equals Customer 2? True
```

The object instances that hold *customer1* and *customer2* are exactly the same. They have the same *HashCode*, and *Equals* returns *true*. Perhaps you are wondering how *ObjectContext* identifies object instances. It uses the key of the entity; therefore, it is very important to correctly define unique keys within the CSDL.

Every time you need to change an entity, you can simply update its properties or invoke its methods. Under the cover, the ADO.NET Entity Framework engine guarantees that you do not have multiple instances of the same entity—thereby helping you to avoid concurrency issues within your own application. It does this by validating input against the EDM you defined and keeping track of every kind of change you make over entity instances. Changes are made in memory, and none of them are directly persisted to the physical storage until you invoke the *SaveChanges* method of the *ObjectContext* instance. Only when you invoke this method is the data sent to the database.

Your actions could be concurrent with those of other users or applications. *ObjectContext* prevents your code from being concurrent, but someone else could change an entity on the persistence layer that you have changed in memory. In this situation, an *OptimisticConcurrency-Exception* is thrown.

Whenever you need to perform transactional activities, you can use either a *TransactionScope* or an old-style explicit *DbTransaction* object. We suggest that you adopt the new transactional framework of .NET Framework 2.0 (*System.Transactions*), but providing a transaction management explanation is not a goal of this book. Simply consider the example in Listing A-19, in which we use *TransactionScope* to cover the result of an entity modification sentence.

Listing A-19   Entity modification using *TransactionScope*

```
using (NorthwindEntities db = new NorthwindEntities()) {
    using (TransactionScope scope = new TransactionScope()) {

        var customer = (from c in db.Customers
                        where c.CustomerID == "ALFKI"
                        select c).AsEnumerable().First();

        customer.ContactName = "Paolo Pialorsi";

        db.SaveChanges();
        scope.Complete();
    }
}
```

LINQ to SQL and ADO.NET Entity Framework

You should be aware that this beta version contains a partial overlap of LINQ to SQL and ADO.NET Entity Framework. Although they operate at different levels of an application architecture, they have similar functionalities—such as the tracking of changes made to object entities. Remember that we are talking about technologies that are still in a beta stage. We could see some changes in these areas before the final version of the product.

Summary

In this appendix, we described what ADO.NET Entity Framework is and how to use it to realize a conceptual abstraction from the physical data layer. You have seen how to define EDM schemas using the metadata files (CSDL, SSDL, and MSL) and the code automatically generated by Visual Studio Orcas in parsing these metadata files. The entities generated from the metadata can be queried with an SQL-like query language, and they can also be queried using LINQ to Entities. Finally, you have seen how to change and persist entities—including how to handle concurrency and transactions—using the *ObjectContext* infrastructure.

Index

Symbols
, (comma), 57
= (equals sign), 57
( ) parentheses, 33–34
? (question mark), 96
_ (underscore), 57
%> tag, 63–65
<%= tag, 63–65
=> token, 32, 34

A
Add method
    DataContext class, 152–153
    IEnumerable interface, 45
AddAfterSelf method (XNode), 173
AddBeforeSelf method (XNode), 173
ADO.NET
    LINQ to ADO.NET, 15–16, 123
    LINQ to Entities, 164
    Transaction property, 156
ADO.NET Entity Framework
    abstracting from physical layer, 201–203
    ADO.NET standard approach, 197–201
    entity data modeling, 204–207
    LINQ to SQL and, 216
    manipulating entities, 214–216
    querying entities, 207–213
Aggregate operator, 100–103
All operator, 105–106
ALTER TABLE statement, 158
Ancestors method, 187
AncestorsAndSelf method, 188
Annotation method, 180
annotations, 180
Annotations method, 180
anonymous methods
    C# support, 23–25, 69
    delegates and, 21
    lambda expressions, 31–36, 69
    LINQ to XML support, 168
    parameters, 24
anonymous types
    C# support, 46–48
    defined, 94
    storing query results, 49
    Visual Basic support, 58–59
Any operator, 105
APIs (application programming interfaces), 1, 167,
    169–180
ArgumentException error, 98, 119

ArgumentNullException error, 77, 99
ArgumentOutOfRangeException error, 112
AsEnumerable method, 160–162
AsEnumerable operator, 117–118
AssociateWith method (DataShape), 137–138
Association attribute
    class entities, 132
    EntityRef class, 133
    Name property, 138
    OtherKey property, 134, 138
    Unique property, 138
associative queries, 148–149
attribute axis, 67
attributes, LINQ to XML queries, 182
Average operator, 99–100
Axes functions (XPath), 187

B
BeCareful method, 53
BeginTransaction method (IDBConnection), 156
binding metadata, 157–159
break keyword, 27

C
C# language
    anonymous methods, 23–25, 69
    anonymous types, 46–48
    declarative programming, 12–13
    delegates, 21–23
    enumerators and yield, 25–28
    extension methods, 36–42
    generics, 19–21
    imported namespaces, 15
    lambda expressions, 31–36
    local type inference, 29–31
    object initialization expressions, 42–46
    query expressions, 48–49
    type checking support, 14
    yield statement, 27, 69
Cast operator, 122, 159
change notification, 138–139
change tracking service, 152
ChangeConflictException error, 155
child axis, 67
classes
    anonymous types, 47, 58
    delegates as, 21
    entity, 127–129, 153
    extending, 4
    inheriting, 36

About the Authors

Paolo Pialorsi is a consultant, trainer, and author who focuses on software development, concentrating on .NET, XML, and Web services. He is a founder of DevLeap (www.devleap.com), a group focused on producing sophisticated content for the developer community. He has written three books about XML and Web Services.

Marco Russo is a founder of DevLeap. He is a regular contributor to developer user communities and is an avid blogger on Microsoft SQL Server Business Intelligence and other Microsoft technologies. Marco provides consulting and training to professional developers on the Microsoft .NET Framework and Microsoft SQL Server and is the author of two Italian books about C# and the common language runtime.

What do you think of this book?

We want to hear from you!

Do you have a few minutes to participate in a brief online survey?

Microsoft is interested in hearing your feedback so we can continually improve our books and learning resources for you.

To participate in our survey, please visit:

www.microsoft.com/learning/booksurvey/

...and enter this book's ISBN-10 number (appears above barcode on back cover*).
As a thank-you to survey participants in the United States and Canada, each month we'll randomly select five respondents to win one of five $100 gift certificates from a leading online merchant. At the conclusion of the survey, you can enter the drawing by providing your e-mail address, which will be used for prize notification only.

Thanks in advance for your input. Your opinion counts!

* Where to find the ISBN-10 on back cover

ISBN-13: 000-0-0000-0000-0
ISBN-10: 0-0000-0000-0

0 0 0 0 0

0 000000 000000

Example only. Each book has unique ISBN.

www.microsoft.com/learning/booksurvey/